n **Man** is a historian with a special interest in Asia and nature of leadership. His books, published in over twenty uages, include bestselling biographies of Genghis Khan, lai Khan and Attila the Hun, as well as histories of the it Wall of China and the Mongol Empire. He is fast ming one of the world's most widely read historians.

AMAZONS

The Real Warrior Women
of the Ancient World

JOHN MAN

CORGI BOOKS

TRANSWORLD PUBLISHERS
61–63 Uxbridge Road, London W5 5SA
www.penguin.co.uk

Transworld is part of the Penguin Random House group of companies
whose addresses can be found at global.penguinrandomhouse.com

First published in Great Britain in 2017 by Bantam Press
an imprint of Transworld Publishers
Corgi edition published 2018

Map on pp. viii–ix by Liane Payne

A CIP catalogue record for this book
is available from the British Library.

ISBNs
9780552173285

Typeset in Sabon by Falcon Oast Graphic Art Ltd.
Printed and bound by Clays Ltd, Bungay, Suffolk.

Penguin Random House is committed to a sustainable
future for our business, our readers and our planet. This book
is made from Forest Stewardship Council® certified paper.

1 3 5 7 9 10 8 6 4 2

For T

CONTENTS

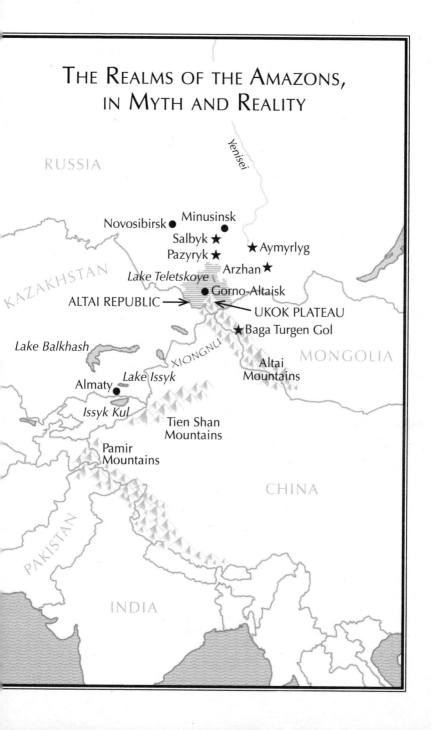

THE REALMS OF THE AMAZONS, IN MYTH AND REALITY

RUSSIA

Yenisei

Novosibirsk ●   ● Minusinsk
Salbyk ★   ●
Pazyryk ★   ★ Aymyrlyg
                  Arzhan ★
Lake Teletskoye
                  ● Gorno-Altaisk
ALTAI REPUBLIC →
                  ← UKOK PLATEAU
KAZAKHSTAN
                  ★ Baga Turgen Gol

Lake Balkhash
                  XIONGNU
                              Altai   MONGOLIA
Almaty ● Lake Issyk   Mountains
Issyk Kul
              Tien Shan
              Mountains
Pamir
Mountains
                              CHINA

PAKISTAN

INDIA

Introduction

CHANGING MYTHS, EMERGING TRUTHS

WHEN I WAS SIX, MY PARENTS TOOK ME TO SEE A STAGE version of *Peter Pan* in London. I was amazed by Peter's ability to fly, a skill he passes on to the Darling children. I asked my mother if she could teach me. She told me to ask Peter. So I wrote to him, c/o whatever theatre it was. To my intense joy, he replied. Revealing a remarkable ability to use a typewriter, he told me that the key was practice. My mother warned that it might take a while. I was up for it, and set about learning to fly by jumping off my parents' bed, many times, with my mother assuring me that I had remained aloft just a split second longer each time I jumped. It was hard work, and progress immeasurable. Soon it was time for tea. I don't recall a second flying lesson.

Growing up in an English village, I lacked a ready source of books but read comics, which were already evolving into what would become graphic novels. One of the protagonists was Dan Dare, Pilot of the Future, who was totally convincing to me. Another was Superman, who wasn't. At eight, I had grown older and wiser. I knew from personal experience that flying was impossible. For me, Superman lacked credibility. I simply did not buy into any of his abilities, super-strength, super-vision, all the rest.

I was out of step with popular culture. Superheroes, a term that includes superheroines and supervillains, have remained the mainstays of countless comics, graphic novels and films for fifty years, and show no sign of falling from grace. One website lists 699 of them in alphabetical order from A-Bomb to Zoom. Only one appeals to me: not because she's been around for over seventy years, not because she has recently starred in her own blockbuster, but because of the depth of her back-story. This is Wonder Woman, daughter of Zeus, princess of the Amazons.

In fact, Wonder Woman is even more Amazonian than the Amazons of Greek legend. About 2,750 years ago, the Greeks spun tales about their Amazons as superb women warriors in order to show how terrific men were to defeat them in battle or tumble them into bed. Wonder Woman is not about to be defeated or bedded, even by superheroes. She is equal to, even superior to, any man, super or not. The ancient fable has evolved to suit today's market for superheroes.

But there is now much more to the Amazons than myth.

Aristotle defined man as a political animal, meaning he was most at home in a *polis*, a city-state like his own Athens. Well, he was wrong in two senses – wrong morally, at least from today's perspective, because he ignored Athens's women; and also wrong in the sense of being incorrect. Long before his time, people who were no less human than Greeks had developed an entirely un-*polis*-like existence on the grasslands of inner Asia, one in which men and women shared a different way of life, without cities or states. The men were both herders and warriors. So were their women.

Thanks to archaeologists, we now know more about them than Aristotle possibly could. Wonder Woman, it turns out, had real ancestral sisters. Right across inner Asia are grave mounds, tens of thousands of them. These tombs were made by 'Scythians' – a generalized term for several related cultures – who were expert in using the grasslands that run in irregular swathes from Hungary to Mongolia. Most tombs were robbed; but some contained treasures, preserved by cold. Archaeologists have found – are finding, will go on finding – what the grave-robbers missed: deep-frozen gold, decorations, clothing, bones and bodies. Among them are women whose possessions included weapons and whose remains show signs of violent death: real Amazons, products of a different way of life and a far more sophisticated one than the Greeks dreamed of.

The myth endured, growing new branches down the centuries, influencing art and literature and popular culture, giving the name of Amazon not only to individual warrior women (and countless women fighting for countless causes) but also, more accurately, to very rare *groups* of women fighters. The myth interacted with the real world: the Amazon rainforest and amazon.com are branches of the same tree. Another branch is Wonder Woman, with her surprisingly radical agenda. In the vision of Wonder Woman's creator – not Zeus, but William Moulton Marston, in *All Star Comics* No. 8 in 1941 – Amazons were as strong and sexy as in Greek legend, but destined for domination of men not defeat by them. That (he believed) was the way to enduring peace between women and men. 'Give them an alluring woman stronger than themselves to submit to,' he said, 'and they'll be *proud* to become her willing slaves!' Aristotle would have been appalled.

1

A LEGEND AND ITS MEANING

IMAGINE YOURSELF TO BE A SUITABLY EDUCATED SCHOLAR, transported back in time to Athens 2,500 years ago. It's a fine spring day. Wishing to feel in tune with Athenian history, you find yourself climbing the Areopagus, the summit of creamy marble near the Acropolis. You know it as the Hill of Ares, named after the god of war – Mars as he would become in Roman times. You are not alone. You come upon an old man in a tunic, resting on a boulder, his head on a stick. You could do with a break. You start a conversation. He's glad of the company, and something of a historian himself. You ask: was this really the famous rock on which the early city

1

council met? Of course it was, he says. He explains that it has nothing to do with Ares. No one ever worshipped Ares here. It's actually named after *arae*, curses, because at the bottom of the hill is the cave of the Dread Ones, the Awful Goddesses, the Eumenides, the Furies, who hunted and cursed criminals. The council sat here because it was the key to the city from ancient times, long before the Acropolis. Why, this was the place that stopped the Amazons when they attacked Athens. Oh, you say, you mean the Amazons were real? You thought it was just one tale among many. Of *course* they were real, these warrior women who lived somewhere to the east, just beyond the edge of the civilized world. Tales passed down the generations – from before writing, before the Siege of Troy, before Homer – recorded how the heroes of old had actually visited them. The Amazons were as much part of Greek history as the gods.

Ah, you say, so you believe in the gods?

'Well, of course, no one has actually *seen* a god,' he explains. 'At least, not in my time.' But the evidence is there in the stories told by our forefathers and in all the shrines and the rituals and sacrifices and oracles and dreams and the way people behave. 'Do you know what men are like in battle? Have you seen the wildness of a bereaved woman? They're possessed! We are all driven by the gods. That's why we pray to them, and please them with sacrifices.' To doubt the gods would be to doubt Greek identity. 'So of course we believe the gods to be real, and the Amazons too.'

We, here and now, in the twenty-first century, have our doubts. Why should anyone take these beliefs seriously? Because they are evidence of a sort – doorways to the minds of those who lived in a long-vanished society that is still with us, rooted in our thought, government, art, drama. Perhaps in our minds as well as theirs the gods represent psychological truths about rage, love, jealousy, loyalty and betrayal. Perhaps also the legends hint at historical truths, as Homer's great epic of a legendary war points towards the real city of Troy that you can still visit today. It's worth taking a look at the legends. We may learn something about our history and about ourselves.

Stories of the Amazons arose in the dream-time before written records, centuries before the fifth century BC, the Golden Age of the Greeks. Back then, the ancestors of the Greeks dominated the eastern Mediterranean from great cities, like Tiryns, Argos and Mycenae, after which their Bronze Age culture is now named. Some time around 1250 BC, the Mycenaean Greeks fought a people across the Aegean in what is now western Turkey. They were probably Luwians, a culture related to the Hittites of central Turkey.[1] In any event, they were not Greeks. Their main city was the port of Troy, today's Hisarlik, where Troy's ruin is a tourist site. The legends blamed the start of the war on a Trojan who stole the divinely beautiful Helen from the Greeks. The storytellers gave the Trojans Greek names: Paris, Priam, Hector, Hecuba. Homer, rewriting the legends in the *Iliad*, mentions 'Tiryns with her tremendous walls'. Tiryns, like its sister-city Mycenae, was and is real. Both had tremendous walls, which are still tremendous today – vast blocks of stone, each carved to fit its neighbour, irregular and snug as newly moulded clay.

Our first story concerns Eurystheus, king of Argos, Mycenae

[1] Luwian was written in both cuneiform, a widely used script invented in what is now Iraq, and hieroglyphic, from Egypt. Both predated Greek alphabetical script by over 3,000 years.

or Tiryns, perhaps all three, for versions vary. It sounds a little bit credible, because they were and are all real places. But no one knows if Eurystheus was real, let alone when he ruled, because at that time the Greeks had no script and no records. His legendary rival was the semi-divine, ingenious and muscular hero Heracles (Hercules as he became in Roman times). Heracles needs to expiate the crime of killing his own children in a fit of madness. So he accepts the challenges laid down by Eurystheus: he must take on twelve tasks, all of which are supposedly missions impossible, but the most heroic of all Greeks accomplishes them all, as he must, for he is one of those who, after the collapse of Mycenae in 1100 BC and after 300 more dark-age years, became one of the founding fathers of what we call Ancient Greece.

Task No. 9 is given by the king's daughter, Admete, a priestess of Hera (Juno to the Romans), the goddess who is always seeking Heracles's destruction. Admete covets the power of the queen of the Amazons, Hippolyte as she is in Greek (Hippolyta in later times). Her name reveals something, because it means 'Releases the Horses' – in *Greek*, not some Amazonian tongue, so clearly we are in the realm of fable, not historical truth. On the other hand, she shares the horsey element of her name (*hippo*, as in hippopotamus, 'water horse') with many other Amazons – the Greeks knew these awesome creatures were horse-riders.

Like many a legendary and semi-divine figure, Hippolyte is defined by her attribute, a golden 'girdle', a belt of some kind, perhaps to hold a dagger or sword. The girdle is the MacGuffin in this story, a MacGuffin being defined by the film director Alfred Hitchcock as something that everyone wants and which therefore drives the plot of a film, or in this case a legend. Sometimes, the MacGuffin is merely desired for reasons no one can quite understand. Sometimes, it really is powerful, like the Ark itself in *Raiders of the Lost Ark*. In this case the girdle is more like the ring in *Lord of the Rings*. It has no power of its own, but it drives people mad with desire. Hippolyte was given it by her father, the war god Ares, and he was the son of Zeus (the Roman Jupiter), so she, as granddaughter of the top god, owns something which pretty much means she should rule the world. That's why Admete wants it for her Mycenaean people, and why it would be good for the future of Greece if Heracles can get it.

So he ventures eastwards, out of Greek territory, along the southern shores of the Black Sea. If there is a smidgen of truth in this fable, the journey would have taken Heracles and his companions close to territory claimed by the Hittites of central Turkey. On the Black Sea coast, Hittite rule was tenuous. This was no-man's-land, occupied by who knew what barbarians. The Greeks filled this blank with their worst fears, a tribe of women, for what could be more threatening to a male-dominated society than untamed women? What more of a challenge to male warriors than to tame them?

As rumours become credible when sourced to a friend of a friend, so legends gain conviction if firmly located in time and place. The Greeks attached this one to the river Thermodon, now known as the Terme, which wanders across a grassy plain. The Amazon warrior women had a capital, Themiscyra,[2] now overlain by the little town of Termes,

---

[2] Often misspelled 'Themyscira', especially online. Its etymology is *Themis* (with an *i*), 'established by custom', plus '*cyra*' (with a hard *c*, as in 'case', and a *y*), which derives from the same root as *kyros*, 'lord'. To Greeks, its name suggested it was the nation's long-established place of government.

near the river's mouth. The people of Termes are grateful for the link, according to their website, because they hold an annual festival celebrating the Amazons – 'ladies-only archery, horseback-riding, cooking contests and row-boat rides'. Archery and horses sound appropriate, cookery and rowing less so.

The Amazons have long had their reputation, recorded in the words of many later writers: a people great in war, and if ever they gave birth to children, they reared the females and killed the boys. Diodorus, writing in Sicily in the first century BC, says the Amazon queen 'made war upon people after people of neighbouring lands, and as the tide of her fortune continued favourable, she was so filled with pride that she gave herself the appellation of Daughter of Ares, but to the men she assigned the spinning of wool.' He goes on about how she trained the Amazon girls in hunting and warfare, and conquered her neighbours, and built palaces and shrines galore, and handed power to queen after queen 'who ruled with distinction and advanced the nation of the Amazons in both power and fame', until many generations later Heracles arrived.

He camps. Queen Hippolyte comes to see him. He explains about her girdle (not, it seems, troubled by linguistic differences). They get on well. Perhaps, as some versions say, they are attracted to each other. She agrees to give him her girdle, just like that, no questions asked. But inspired by Heracles's opponent, the goddess Hera, some Amazons whip up their troops with the fear that the Greeks are about to kidnap the queen. They charge, Heracles kills Hippolyte, seizes her girdle and beats a hasty retreat with it, back to Tiryns, where he places it in the temple of Hera.

That's the default version of the legend. The many other

versions before and since pile detail on detail. In one, Heracles resorts to a surprise attack on the unsuspecting Amazons. In another, Heracles and Hippolyte fight it out in a long duel. Or there is a great battle between the two armies, with many combatants being named on both sides. Heracles kills Aella, named for her speed, but now too slow, then Philippis, and Prothoe, a sevenfold victor, and Eriboea, who boasts she needs no help but finds she's wrong, and another eight of them, all named, the last being Alcippe, who had vowed to die a maiden, and does, falling to Heracles's sword. So, in Diodorus's words, 'the race of them was utterly exterminated.'

Well, not exactly, because there was a problem with the Amazons. Their Black Sea homeland, though part of legend, was also part of the real world and, as the Greeks began to explore further, they would have discovered that there was, in point of fact, no nation of Amazons. To retain credibility, they needed another homeland. Legend provided one. Herodotus, writing in the mid-fifth century BC, repeats it.

When the Greeks sail away from the River Thermodon, they take with them a bunch of Amazons. Once at sea, these battle-hardened warriors mutiny, slay their captors and seize the ship. Unable to handle it, they are blown 400 kilometres north across the Black Sea to the Sea of Azov – the shallow, marshy lake that the Greeks called Maeotis – landing them somewhere near the marshes at the mouth of the River Don. This is the land of the horse-riding Scythians. The Amazons steal some horses and set off in search of booty. The Scythians determine to resist, but, having discovered that the new arrivals are women, they set about trying to win them over by persuasion. Young Scythian men camp peacefully nearby and edge closer day by day. They see some Amazons leaving camp to relieve themselves on the steppe, the way girls do in Mongolia today. One of the lads approaches. They have sex, the difference in language being no hindrance. She makes signs: *Let's meet again – bring a friend – so will I.* The word spreads, the camps combine. The girls start to learn Scythian. 'Come back with us,' say the men. 'We'll marry you.' In Herodotus's words, the independent-minded girls demur:

> Our ways are too much at variance. We are riders, our business is with the bow and the spear, and we know nothing of women's work. But in your country no woman has anything to do with such things – your women stay at home in their wagons occupied with feminine tasks, and never go out to hunt or for any other purpose. We could not possibly agree.

Instead they tell the men to go off home, bring back their share of their family property and settle the other side of the Don. Agreed. All migrate three days east and three days north, forming a new tribe, the Sauromatians (more on them later). The women keep to their old ways, hunting on horseback, sometimes with their men, sometimes without, raiding and fighting. 'They have a marriage law which forbids a girl to marry until she has killed an enemy in battle.' Thus the Amazons can remain in Greek legends as a distant nation, though when all this is supposed to have happened is lost in the mists of time.

The next chapter in the saga of the Amazons concerns Theseus, legendary founder of Athens. Plutarch, writing in the first century AD, takes the story as seriously as possible, trying to tease history from hearsay. It's a hopeless task, because the facts, if there are any, are lost in a mass of contradictory folklore. 'Nor is it to be wondered at,' says Plutarch, commenting on his inability to write a definitive account, 'that in events of such antiquity, history should be in disorder.' He has many sources, but they all disagree. Names and events shift like phantoms, and no one has a clue when these supposedly great events happened.

One thing everyone agrees on is that the Amazons invaded Greece.

It was Theseus's fault for going to the land of the Amazons. Perhaps he went with Heracles, or perhaps later. Anyway, he is given a generous reception. A beauty named Antiope, who may or may not be the Amazon queen and is sometimes confused with Hippolyte, falls for Theseus. The plot is thickened by a young man called Solois, who falls for Antiope, is rejected and drowns himself for love. Pausing to rename a river after the boy and found a city in his honour, Theseus either captures Antiope or she follows him home. There she has a son, Hippolytus, but Theseus abandons her for a new love, Phaedra, opening another chapter in which Phaedra falls in love with her stepson. Both die nasty deaths.

Meanwhile, back in their homeland, the Amazons are furious about Heracles killing Hippolyte and about Antiope's fate. They invade Athens, forcing their way inside the city walls, right up to the Areopagus. Yes, they really did, says Plutarch. Local names, graves and sacrificial practices prove it. Certainly, many other writers believed it. Aeschylus, Herodotus's contemporary, playwright and author of the trilogy *The Oresteia*, presents an Athens that had come through war (with the Persians) thanks to benevolent gods and great leaders. Among past disasters was the Amazon invasion. For four months the two sides battled, back and forth between gates, rivers and hills, all named and known to Athenians. The Athenians gained the upper hand, the Amazons surrendered. Antiope died in action, fighting against her own people, on the side of progress and civilization.

Towards the end of *The Eumenides*, the third of the *Oresteia* plays, Athena, on the very outcrop supposedly reached by the Amazons, proclaims the dawn of a new era, overruling the Furies:

> This will be the court where judges reign.
> This is the Crag of Ares, where the Amazons
> pitched their tents when they came marching down
> on Theseus, full tilt in their fury.

In an age when legend was history and history legend, who would doubt that the Amazons were real?

The Amazons re-enter the legends again unmeasured years later, during the Siege of Troy. That brings us to the verge of written history. Assuming the siege took place, it would have been about 1250 BC, being recorded in folk-memory, passed down the generations from bard to bard, its many versions constantly revised, until the whole oral library of legend was distilled by Homer and written down about 750 BC, using a version of the alphabetical script invented 1,000 years earlier in Egypt, which had been working its way northwards ever since.

In this, the final version of the Trojan War legends, pinned like butterflies by script, the war has been going on for nine years. Homer takes us inside Troy for a flashback. The radiant Helen joins King Priam on the walls to look out over the battlefield. They see great Greek warriors below, and Priam wonders at the size of the Greek army, the Achaeans as Homer calls them (after a legendary ancestor, Achaeus). The sight takes Priam back to his youth, when he was campaigning against some unnamed enemy with Phrygians on the steppes of central Turkey. (Trojans and Phrygians were neighbours and natural allies: Priam's wife, Hecuba, was a Phrygian princess.) Camping on what is now the River Sakarya, the Phrygians had summoned help from a third force:

> And they allotted me as their ally
> My place among them when the Amazons
> Came down, those women who were a match for men;
> But that host never equalled this,
> The army of the keen-eyed men of Achaea.

Now the Amazons, Greek enemies of old, are about to re-enter Greek legend as allies of their other enemy, the Trojans.

The story is told by Quintus, a Greek poet who lived in Smyrna on the west coast of today's Turkey in the third century AD. He, like Homer, edited together many versions of legends that fill the gap in Homer's epics, between the near-end of the Trojan War – it is Quintus who tells the story of the Trojan Horse – and the adventures of Odysseus.

Quintus picks up the story from the end of the *Iliad*. Troy's hero, Hector, is dead, dragged around the city by the horses of his killer, Achilles, his body burned and buried. The war will go on. But a new force enters the fray – the Amazons led by

Hippolyte's sister, Penthesilea. It turns out, for the purposes of this version of the story, that Hippolyte was not killed by Heracles after all, but by Penthesilea, by mistake, with a spear, when she missed her intended target, a stag, and struck her sister instead. She has come with twelve companions as a sort of penance, to help the Trojans and escape 'the dreaded spirits of vengeance, who . . . were following her unseen.' She is a glory, standing out from her troops as the full moon shines through departing storm clouds. The Trojans, running to greet her, are astounded by the sight of her:

> Looking like one of the blessed immortals; in her face
> There was beauty that frightened and dazzled at once.
> Her smile was ravishing, and from beneath her brows
> Her love-enkindling eyes like sunbeams flashed.

She comes like rain on a parched land. Priam, like a blind man who miraculously sees the light of day – for Quintus, like Homer, is never short of a simile – leads her to his palace, feasts her, and learns her purpose: to kill Achilles, destroy the Greeks and toss their ships upon a fire. Fool, mutters Hector's widow, Andromache: doesn't Penthesilea know she's no match for Achilles?

But she wakes full of confidence, 'thinking she would perform a mighty deed that day.' She arms herself – golden greaves (the soldier's equivalent of shin-pads), breastplate, helmet, shield, sword in its silver-and-ivory sheath, two-edged battleaxe, and two spears. Out she rides, proud beyond all bounds, leading Trojans as a ram its flock, advancing on the Greeks like a wind-whipped bush fire. This, remember, is the daughter of the god of war and granddaughter of Zeus himself. The Greeks see her coming, and stream from their ships to fight her.

Like flesh-devouring beasts, the armies clash. Greek warriors die by the dozen, all named, and others butcher Amazons in gory detail:

Quickly Podarkes struck the beauteous Klonie.
Right through her belly passed the heavy spear, and with it
Came at once a stream of blood and all her entrails.

Penthesilea strikes back, her spear piercing Podarkes's right arm, opening an artery. Spurting blood, he pulls back, to bleed to death in a comrade's arms. Divine Bremousa, speared close to her right breast, falls like a mountain ash to the woodsman's axe, her joints undone by death. Spears and swords cut hearts and bellies and collarbones. Two of Penthesilea's twelve companions, Alkibie and Derimacheia, lose their heads to a single stroke of Diomedes's sword, and like slaughtered heifers

So these two fell by the hand of Tydeus's son
Out on the plain of Troy far away from their heads.

Countless hearts are stilled, falling fast as autumn leaves or drops of rain, many listed by name and parentage and birthplace, crushed into the blood-drenched earth like threshed grain. It's a wonder that warriors can swing their swords in such a forest of similes. The lioness, Penthesilea, pursues her prey as a wave on the deep-booming sea follows speeding ships round bellowing headlands. Her strength and courage grow, her limbs are ever light, like a calf leaping into a springtime garden, eager for its dewy grass. Trojans marvel. Surely, says one, this is no mere woman, but a goddess – fool that this Trojan is, unaware of grievous woes approaching.

But the woes are still a way off. Achilles – hero of Greek heroes, sacker of cities, vulnerable only in his heel – is mourning at the grave of his friend, Patroklos, with his cousin Ajax, both unaware of the battle raging nearby.

Now the scene shifts inside the city. Trojan women long to join in, roused as humming bees at winter's end, until reminded by the prudent housewife Theano that war should be left to the men, and

As for the Amazons, merciless warfare, horsemanship
And all the work of men have been their joy from
     childhood.

Therefore, she says, stay away from battle and 'busy yourselves with looms inside your homes'. The author being male and Greek, this is not fertile ground for feminism.

Now Ajax and Achilles hear the dismal clamour of Greeks dying at Penthesilea's spear-point like lofty trees uprooted by a howling gale. They arm themselves and rush to join the fight, killing like lions feasting on an unshepherded flock.

And there is Penthesilea. She casts a spear, which shatters on Achilles's shield. A second glances off Ajax's silver greave. Ajax leaps aside, leaving the two to fight it out.

Achilles mocks Penthesilea, reminding her that he and Ajax are the greatest warriors in the world, telling her she's doomed, like a fawn confronted by a mountain lion. He attacks, spearing her above the right breast and moving in to drag her from her horse. Despite her wound she has time to consider – draw her sword and fight, or surrender and hope for mercy? Too slow: Achilles casts his spear and impales her and her horse together. (Don't think about this too closely, because it doesn't make sense.) They fall. Pillowed by her horse, she quivers and dies like meat on a spit, or a fir snapped off by the north wind's icy blast. The Trojans see her dead and flee for the city, leaving Achilles rejoicing at his victory.

Then he removes Penthesilea's glittering helmet, to reveal a beauty that astonishes the watching Greeks and turns Achilles's jubilation to grief for killing her instead of marrying her. A warrior named Thersites, known for his insulting behaviour, says he's shocked by Achilles's reaction. Does he want to marry a wretched dead Amazon? What sort of pervert is he?

> Your accursed mind has no concern at all
> For glorious deeds of valour once you catch sight of a
>   woman . . .
> Nothing is more pernicious to mortal men
> Than pleasure in a woman's bed.

Incensed, Achilles punches Thersites on the jaw, below the ear, knocking out all his teeth. He falls face-forward in his own blood, to the delight of the other Greeks, all except Thersites's cousin, Diomedes. It takes a mass of them to hold the two apart and prevent a further fight.

A message arrives from Priam, requesting Penthesilea's body for a lavish burial. Both sides arrange a ceasefire. Feeling only pity and admiration, Achilles and Ajax hand her body over. A great funeral fire consumes her. After the flames are doused with wine, the Trojans collect her bones, drench them in perfumed oil, lay them in a casket, pack them with the fat of the best cows and bury her outside Troy, beside the walls, in the rich tomb of Priam's father, Laomedon. Her fallen companions are buried nearby, while the Greeks burn and bury their own dead. Alone amongst them, Podarkes, speared by Penthesilea when the battle opened, is given a burial mound. And then the Greeks feast through the night till the goddess Dawn's arrival.

These tales existed in many versions. They were popular for hundreds of years, from the seventh century BC onwards, with scores of writers referring back to the victory over the Amazons and the slaying of Penthesilea as essential to Greece's origins. No one made a distinction between myth and history. Everyone just 'knew' that there had been a victory over the Amazons, just as they knew that there had been a victory over the Persians (490–478 BC). The first was myth, the second was fact, but it was impossible to tell fact from fiction: both carried conviction.

And not only in words. War with Amazons was just as popular in painting, ceramics and architecture, so popular that the theme's countless manifestations have a collective name: they are amazonomachies ('Amazon battles'). They are one of three popular '–machies', each of the others being equally legendary: the wars against the Centaurs (centaur-omachies) and the giants (titanomachies). These subjects appear on hundreds of vases and in friezes and paintings held in museums around the world.

They were included in one of the most famous of Greek sculptures, the vast (12-metre) gold-and-ivory statue of Athena, patron goddess of Athens, in the Parthenon. Made by, or under the direction of, Phidias, the greatest sculptor of the ancient world, some say of all time, it stood for about 1,000 years as a statement of Greek wealth and power, until stolen by the Romans, after which it vanished. But it was portrayed on coins and in small-scale copies, providing research for a replica in Nashville, Tennessee, finished in 1990. The point for our subject is not Athena herself, but her shield, on the outside of which were thirty silver or bronze figures of Greeks fighting Amazons. Nothing could have better proclaimed the significance of the theme in Athenian eyes.

Its importance is emphasized again by a series of marble slabs that have been on show at the British Museum for 200 years. Their story is worth telling because it involves a mystery, a murder and much controversy.

It starts about 430 BC, in the Arcadian village of Skliros, surrounded by the forested hills of Messinia, some 160 kilometres south-west of Athens. In 429 BC, plague struck Athens. In remote Arcadia, it left remarkably few dead. On the flanks of Mount Kotilon (1,226 metres high), at a place called Bassai (now better known in its Latin spelling, Bassae), a platform of rock gives terrific views over mountains to the sea. In this wild spot, some extremely talented architect – perhaps even Ictinos, who co-designed the Parthenon – built a temple to Apollo in his manifestation as Apollo Epikourios, 'the Helper'. The name is the only evidence that the temple dates from the year of the plague: no one knows for sure. If it was a thank-you note, it was a very fine one, with many features similar to those of the Parthenon: thirty-eight lime-stone columns, a marble roof held up by marble beams, and much more, which we will get to shortly. 'Of all the temples in the Peloponnese,' wrote the Greek traveller and writer

Pausanias in his guide to Greece 500 years later, this ranked as No. 2 'for the beauty of its stone and the symmetry of its proportions.' (No. 1 was in Tegea, 40 kilometres to the east.)

For the next 1,500 years, that was all anyone knew of the temple. Hills, trees, malaria, remoteness and bandits combined to hide it from the world, until in November 1765 a Parisian architect, Joachim Bocher, took a break from supervising the building of villas on the island of Zakynthos and started exploring the Arcadian mountains of the Peloponnese peninsula (in the eighteenth and nineteenth centuries still often referred to by its medieval name, the Morea). Quite by chance, he stumbled on the ruined temple, recognized what it was, took some notes and planned to return to do a proper survey. He never made it. On his next trip, he vanished, without explanation. A French traveller named François Pouqueville was in the area in 1798 and heard what happened. The locals, he wrote,

> relate to all strangers a story of a traveller who was assassinated more than thirty years ago as he went to visit the ruins of Apollo Epicurius, the Saviour . . . they speak of his death as if it was a disaster fresh in their memories, and had happened within a few months, but say that all their endeavours to find out the perpetrators of so horrible a deed were unavailing. I have thought that this might very possibly be Mons[ieur] Bocher, the architect, who had travelled once successfully over the Morea, but, returning there a second time, disappeared suddenly and was never heard of more.[3]

---

[3] From the English version, *Travels in the Morea, Albania and other parts of the Ottoman Empire*, 1813. The French original was published in 1805. Pouqueville had an astonishing life as adventurer, diplomat and scholar.

So the temple remained hidden for another forty-five years, and then one year more. In 1811, a team of four antiquarians with armed guards, a tent and cooking pots arrived at Bassae, hoping for great things. They were met by a crowd of 'young Arcadians' carrying baskets of fruit and flowers. The local Turkish administrator – Greece then being under Turkish rule – was not so welcoming, accused them of lacking authorization and ordered them to leave. They returned the following year, with a larger team, 200 local workers, the right permits and a deal with the Turkish governor to share the proceeds of finds, which – he imagined – would be of silver.

Now at last, after removing several metres of rubble, the temple's real treasure came to light: the Bassae Frieze, 23 metres of marble panels, which had once run all around the temple above its limestone columns, carved not in bas (that is, low) relief but high relief, portraying Greeks fighting Centaurs and Amazons. The finds were obviously masterpieces. The Turkish governor was disappointed, and relinquished his share for £750 – just in time, for he was replaced by a new pasha who sent his men chasing after the disappearing stones. Too late: the panels reached Zakynthos,

---

Ex-priest, revolutionary and doctor, he accompanied Napoleon to Egypt in the fight against Nelson's fleet, negotiated an exchange of prisoners, met Nelson, was captured by pirates, was handed over to Ali Pasha, the Albanian ex-bandit, mass-murderer and torturer who ruled semi-independent Turkey-in-Europe, became his physician, won enough freedom to explore the area (hence his book and this quote), spent two years in prison in a plague-ridden Constantinople, kept a secret journal in code, was again granted freedom for his skills as a doctor, studied and later wrote about the plague, won fame and fortune with an autobiography, served as France's envoy to Ali Pasha, researched the archaeology of Greece, became a passionate advocate of all things Greek, wrote up his travels and researches in six meticulous volumes, and became an established figure in Parisian *salons* – and all this before his death at 68, in 1838.

where a British gunboat stood by to guard the agents of empire against Turkish officials, and also a curious French privateer. These were dangerous waters and dangerous times, for the French, under Napoleon, had only recently been driven from Egypt and were that very summer advancing on Moscow, soon to be driven back by General Winter. In the port, a British Museum rep bought the carvings for 60,000 Spanish dollars.

More troubles lay ahead. Charles Cockerell, the expedition's leader, was not there to complete his notes, so the finds were minutely recorded by a German, Carl Haller von Hallerstein, who lost almost all of his drawings in a shipwreck. He started to redraw them, but died before he finished. His papers were sent for safe-keeping to Prince Ludwig of Bavaria, who lost them; they eventually turned up in a cupboard bought at an auction almost fifty years later. Other members of the expedition and later visitors to the site made their own records, none of them definitive, all conflicting. But at least the British Museum gave the frieze its own temple-sized room, Gallery 16, where you can admire it today.

And ponder. Sixty thousand Spanish dollars was a staggering sum, something like £20,000 at the time (when a family could live comfortably on £100 per year), or around £10 million today. Where did the cash go? Not to the local Greeks, nor to their Turkish rulers. The whole episode is like a lesser version of what happened to the Elgin Marbles, taken from the Parthenon and Acropolis over the previous decade – stolen or saved, depending on your point of view. So far, the Greeks haven't asked for the Bassae Frieze back, but then the temple itself is still in the process of restoration, under wraps. Watch this space.

Meanwhile, admire. Naked Greek heroes fight Amazonian heroines in diaphanous dresses that leave little to the imagination. All of the bodies are naturalistic, seemingly carved from life, but also stylized, like athletes performing battle scenes. Like athletes, but very unlike real warriors, they are all beautiful. The panels look as if they should be telling a story, like an archaic graphic novel, but no one can agree on an order and thus determine what the storylines should be, if they ever existed. The British Museum grouped the panels into eleven centauromachies and twelve amazonomachies, but any further connection depended on details of carving (like an elbow overlapping a join that seems to fit into a blank space on the neighbouring panel) and on matching up the holes where bronze dowls had been inserted. That was persuasively done in the 1930s,[4] but there are seven *trillion* ways of arranging twenty-three panels. Ten have been seriously proposed. The controversy continues.

Still, there are a few things that can be said about the frieze's purpose.

You feel you should know who is who, and many have felt they do. But one thing we *can't* say is that all these warriors are individuals. In fact, only three are identifiable – Heracles, because he always wore a lion skin, and Apollo and his sister Artemis, goddess of the hunt (Diana to the Romans), identified by their war chariot, drawn by deer as legend decreed. The rest are enigmatic. Take the panel that may show Achilles and Penthesilea. She is defeated, facing death, dressed in a negligee; he's the rampant warrior, stark naked,

---

[4] William Bell Dinsmoor, 'The Temple of Apollo at Bassae', *Metropolitan Museum Studies*, Vol. 4, No. 2 (March 1933), pp. 204–27.

wielding sword and shield. Is it really them? She's begging for her life, and he seems to be hesitant. Is this the moment he falls in love with her, just as he must kill her? That doesn't quite fit. In the myth, he sees her face when he removes her helmet after her death. So perhaps the two are Theseus and Antiope? Or is that Theseus in another slab, helping his wounded friend Pirithous? And those Amazons on horseback – are they Amazon queens (Hippolyte, Orithia and Antiope or Menalippe) or just any Amazons? Nothing quite works if you try to pin names and incidents on the figures.

Perhaps that was never the intention. After all, the frieze was originally too high up for anyone to identify individual figures. It's the themes that matter. Anyone, even at a distance, can see there is the rough balance of forces and morality. Five Amazons beat their opponents, eight Greeks do the same, four fights seem to be in the balance, three Amazons and Greeks are wounded. There are examples of compassion on both sides. Both care for companions, one Amazon restrains another, a Greek prevents another Greek from killing an Amazon. Achilles may or may not deliver the death-blow to the Amazon who may or may not be Penthesilea raising an arm, either in a gesture of submission or a request for mercy. In one panel, two Amazons flee towards an altar, which should grant the holy right of sanctuary, but two Greeks attack them, apparently ignoring this civilizing rule. Who's going to win? It's not clear. There's a similar balance in the battle against the Centaurs.

The only clue to the outcome is the panel showing Apollo and Artemis approaching in their deer-drawn chariot. Surely, this being Apollo's temple, he will carry the Greeks to victory? This seems to be the bottom line: Greek warriors are matched in heroism and compassion by the heroism and compassion of their enemies, but Greek civilization will triumph over the forces of barbarism, because god, or rather a god, in this case Apollo, is on the Greek side.

The question raised by all these tales and dramatic poses is: why? What on earth was so appealing about the Amazons that Greeks should have been obsessed by them?

In historical terms, of course, the idea is rubbish. There was no nation of Amazons, as there were no Centaurs or Titans. That's what we say, now, in the twenty-first century, because we have a well-developed sense of what is real and what is not, don't we? Or do we? Are dreams real, in the same way that my desk is real? Obviously not: dreams are in my mind, cannot be reproduced, do not exist outside me. Yet I may be frightened by a dream, believe it to have meaning, may act upon it by talking about it, may decide I need psychiatric advice and end up paying money to seek understanding. So my dream can affect the real world. How real is the past? It exists in objects that endure, in the present consequences produced by past events, in evidence like writing and memory and the memory of others. But sometimes that evidence is as ephemeral as the snows of yesteryear. Sometimes we are deceived about the nature of 'reality'. My mother had a suspicion that fairies existed, because as a child she had seen fake photographs that seemed to prove them to be real. In a world that knew nothing of evolution or the nature of comets, unicorns and dragons seemed like certainties. If God exists, as many assert, if the gods existed, as many once asserted, then perhaps Titans did, battling in the heavens with bolts of lightning. Those who had heard of men and women riders who were at one with their horses had no good reason to doubt the existence of Centaurs and Amazons.

But still the question remains: why settle on Amazons as a major theme for legends and pseudo-histories and art?

One suggestion is that perhaps all these mythical battles symbolize the recent real battles against the Persians. Well, almost certainly not. For one thing, Greeks portrayed Amazons long before the Persian Wars. For another, the Greeks were never shy of mentioning the Persians. Herodotus wrote about them at great length. Greek artists often portrayed Persians, showing the Greeks as victorious, the Persians as inferior. No writer suggested that Amazons were really Persians. There is no need for that hypothesis.

There are three other possibilities. Here are two of them (we'll get to the third in Chapter 2).

First, fashion. The Greeks just loved their mythologies. As an artist or sculptor, you simply could not escape them. Years ago, I spent time with a tribe in the rainforests of eastern Ecuador. The Waorani had very little contact with other tribes, and decorated their bodies with red and black lines (red from the juice of achiote fruit and black from a mixture of charcoal and a hard, inedible fruit called genipa). Mostly, they made zig-zag patterns and dots on their arms. On their backs, men drew a solid black patch, the women a candlestick shape. Why? I was writing about these people. I wanted an explanation. What did the decorations mean? Did the zig-zag lines symbolize the meandering rivers? Were the dots insects? No, the patterns didn't mean anything. 'We think it's nice,' they said. 'That's how you paint bodies.' In Ancient Greece, if you wanted to sponsor or make art, you focused on mythology, not the current world. That was how to add value to buildings and objects. That's what you did if you painted or sculpted.

Second, symbolism. It's a fair assumption that Athenian art asserted Athenian values – civilization and high culture as opposed to barbarism. This was, after all, a culture in which men ruled. Athenian democracy excluded women. Women were to be kept in their place, in the home, at the loom. Female emotions were a sort of Greek unconscious, a threat to the stability of the family and the state. Given a chance, they explode and destroy, as Medea murdered her own children, or Antigone challenged the state by burying her brother Polynices against the instructions of her uncle King Creon.

The Amazons symbolize the ultimate threat to Greek masculine ideals. Take Herodotus's story of Amazons mating with Scythians. The Amazons – the women – are in control. They mate with the Scythian youths by choice. They refuse to join Scythian society. Instead, they entice the youths into forming a new tribe, the Sauromatians, who retain the old ways, with the Amazons as horse-riding, virginal man-killers. It looks as if the Scythian youths are in fact Greek youths going through their transition to adulthood, who never return to their own people but remain trapped in an endless youth, entirely dominated by their Amazon lovers. It is a cautionary tale.

To these 'facts' add in xenophobia. It always boosts the self-image of a state to show how culturally inferior foreigners are. Athenians defended themselves on foot, with swords and spears. So did their main rivals, the Persians, who were therefore, though enemies, at least half-civilized. The deeper threat came from further afield, from the dark heart of Asia, the vast steppe-lands beyond the Black Sea. No one knew much about them, except that they rode horses and fought on horseback using powerful little bows to devastating effect. To cap it all, the women were as good at horseback archery as the men, and had their own sub-group, the Sauromatians. They were the Other, the ultimate threat – not a practical threat, because they were not about to invade, but a threat to Greek values.

The elements are all in place to present the ultimate threat: women. The Amazons are sexy, demanding and beautiful, women through and through, and therefore at the mercy of dangerous emotions. They are also superb warriors, acting as an army when necessary. Both their femininity and pugnacity combine with the fact that they are aliens, barbarians – a people whose language sounds like *bar-bar-bar*. They are the very opposite of everything sophisticated Greek men stand for.

That's the point. The Greeks needed them as opponents, to be conquered whenever they appear, even if only in stories. They must be defeated; but not easily. As the Bassae Frieze shows, they are equal to the Greeks in fighting ability. It takes *real* heroes to defeat them, plus a little extra from the gods. The stronger the Amazons are, the harder they fight, the greater will seem the heroism, courage, sexual prowess, fighting ability and sheer divine *rightness* of the Greek men. In this view, the whole industry of amazonomachy was an exercise to shore up the Greek male idea of themselves and their male-dominated culture.

This was true in 500 BC. It remained true for 700 years, inherited unchanged by the Romans. They put the battling warriors on their coffins, especially after they became fashionable for the rich in the second and third centuries AD. Mostly made of marble, imported from Greece either ready for use or half-made so that they could be custom-finished in Italy, it was only natural for Roman clients to want Greek mythological themes, of which the battle of the Greeks and Amazons was among the most popular. Some scholars have read significance into the choices, but others say that the only thing that mattered was to display wealth and status in traditional terms. The Romans were as macho as the Greeks, and rich Romans were just as eager to identify with heroes who could put the almost-but-not-quite-as-heroic Amazons in their place.

2

CLOSE ENCOUNTERS OF
THE SCYTHIAN KIND

THERE'S A THIRD REASON WHY AMAZONS WERE SO IMPOR-
tant to the Greeks, fashion and symbolism apart: they really
were real, these horse-riding, bow-wielding wives, daughters
and mothers of numerous inner Asian tribes. Every now
and then, they emerged from legend and from their distant
homelands, bursting into the Greek world like aliens from
another dimension.

They were not, of course, Amazons as the Greeks believed
Amazons to be. These horsewomen were not from any nation

as such, but from many sub-groups of 'Scythians', a general term for unrecorded tribes of hardy 'pastoral nomads', as anthropologists call them, who were the products of a long-term social revolution 3,000 years before the Ancient Greeks.

As every schoolchild used to know, early civilizations rose around the continental edges and along the great rivers. The Eurasian heartland – an ocean of grass stretching from the Far East to Hungary, flowing between northern forests and deserts and vast mountain chains – was no use to anyone, except hunters who could kill grazing animals like gazelle and wild horses. But in well-watered valleys, Bronze Age peoples led settled lives, leaving great burial mounds of piled-up rocks, graves made of massive slabs of stone and pillars carved with animal images, principally deer. Anyone driving round the Mongolian countryside today – easy enough in dry weather because there are no roads or fences – comes across rock piles (*kherigsurs*) and 'deer stones' dating from the second millennium BC.

About 3500 BC, we learned how to ride, which changed everything. With nothing but a bit and reins, horse-riders could herd horses, sheep, cattle, goats, camels, reindeer and yaks. Saddles helped, but were not a necessity. Iron stirrups even less so, because a rope looped round the toe did the job – the first iron stirrups probably date from the second century AD. To stay with your herds, all you needed was a tent (which evolved into today's warm, cool, wind-shouldering domes of felt) and a wagon to put it on. Grass, when processed by animals, became food, fuel, clothing and more. This new grassland culture spread slowly, then received a boost from climate change round about 1000 BC. As the milder climate spread from east to west, pastures became richer, herds and populations grew, and clans of pastoral nomads drifted west-wards. By now, they knew how to forge iron for swords and arrowheads. Horse-riders, armed with powerful little bows, could gallop wherever there was grass and raid who-ever happened to be in the way, like other pastoral nomads and merchant caravans and – on the edges of their world – villages and cities. Settled societies had no answer to them, because they vanished like mist at dawn. For 2,000 years, Central Asia was the source of anthropological tsunamis, waves of tribes displacing and absorbing each other in unre-corded revolutions, but sometimes washing up against settled societies at their edges, whether the Great Wall in the east or the Danube in the west.

In the early first millennium BC, pastoral nomads known as Cimmerians had established themselves from the borderlands of China to the Black Sea, where they became the distant neighbours of the Greeks. By then, some pastoral–nomadic groups had settlements of their own, where they produced fine works of art, especially gold ornaments. The Assyrians recorded wars with them from 714 BC, but they themselves had no writing, so, even as Greek civilization rose in the seventh and sixth centuries BC, nothing except enigmatic burials hint at how the Cimmerians were displaced by various Scythian peoples. The Greeks knew about the Scythians only from peripheral contacts. Sometimes they came as traders or mercenaries to Athens, where Greeks made fun of them for their drunken, crude ways and appalling Greek. In Greek comedies, Scythians, in their high-pointed hats, perform the role of foreign country bumpkins, talking pidgin Greek.

Herodotus is our major source. In about 460 BC, he travelled to Olbia at the mouths of the Bug and Dnieper rivers, then a thriving Greek frontier city on today's Ukrainian coast, now a fine archaeological site. From here, trading caravans run by Scythians set out for Central Asia and vanished into who-knew-where. In Herodotus's day, somewhere unvisited by Greeks there was a Scythian king, Ariapeithes, ruler of the so-called Royal Scythians, who had agreed to place Olbia under his protection. He had a local agent called Thymnes, who became Herodotus's informant.[5]

So Herodotus knew a little about the Scythian home-land, if only from the edge. He spoke of big rivers and much pastureland. He particularly admired the Dnieper for its blue waters and fish. He probably knew the marshy, reedy lower reaches where it merges with the Bug, never travelling upriver to the rapids that made the river unnavigable until they were dammed in the 1930s. But that was a fraction of the whole, the world of the steppes, which remained a mystery to him. As he wrote, 'I have never met anyone who claims to have actually seen it.'

The daunting reality was this:

To the north, from the Carpathian Mountains eastwards, stretches what came to be called the Pontic Steppe (from *Pontos*, 'the Sea', as Greeks called the Black Sea) – 6,500 kilometres of grass, all the way to the Khingan Mountains of Manchuria. It flows irregularly. To the south lie deserts and mountains, the wastes of the present day –stans and western China, the ice-bound peaks of the Tien Shan and the Tibetan plateau. Northwards, infinities of forest. Scythians, like many other grassland cultures, needed both: the grass, of

---

[5] Olbia lasted another 500 years, in steady decline, before it was ruined by one of the Scythians' barbarian successors, the Goths.

course, but also the forests to supply wood for bows, arrows, carts and tent frames; and animal furs, especially luxurious ones like sable, ermine and mink, which conferred status and were useful as trade items.

To outsiders, the steppe was depressing, even in summer: oceans of herbs and grasses – wormwood, vetch, milkweed, sage, lavender, caraway, mint, mullein, spurge – billowing to the horizon. Chekhov described it in his short story, 'The Steppe', as it was in summer in the 1880s before the plough claimed it:

> On and on you travel, but where it all begins and where it ends you just cannot make out. First, far ahead where the sky met the earth – near some ancient burial mounds and a windmill resembling from afar a tiny man waving his arms – a broad, bright yellow band crept over the ground . . . until suddenly the whole wide prairie flung off the penumbra of dawn, smiled and sparkled with dew . . . Arctic petrels swooped over the road with happy cries, gophers called to each other in the grass, and from somewhere far to the left came the plaint of lapwings . . . Grasshoppers, cicadas, field crickets and mole crickets fiddled their squeaking monotonous tunes in the grass. But time passed, the dew evaporated, the air grew still and the disillusioned steppe assumed its jaded July aspect. The grass drooped, the life went out of everything. The sunburnt hills, brown-green and – in the distance – mauvish, with their calm pastel shades, the plain, the misty horizon, the sky arching overhead and appearing so awesomely deep and transparent here in the steppe, where there are no woods or high hills – it all seemed boundless, now, and numb with misery.

To someone without a horse, it was a nightmare, especially in winter, when the temperature plunges to –40° (Centigrade or Fahrenheit, it's the same at –40) and ice-storms cover the grass in a frozen armour; or springtime rains, which turn earth to mud; or high summer, when grasses fade and rain fails. Even on a fine summer's day, with larks twittering in a vast dome of blue, visitors seem to communicate by semaphore, because they're swatting flies. To horse-people, whose tents have dung fires to cope with winter cold and summer flies, the steppe is at least security, and at best unbounded, glorious freedom.

Here the Scythians lived, with ways that for a Greek were barbaric, literally: they couldn't speak Greek, only their own incomprehensible *bar-bar-bar*. The Greeks stereotyped them as fat, flabby and not much interested in sex, a view that does not fit with their reputation as warriors. Though some groups had taken to farming and had permanent houses, most were nomads who lived in ox-drawn wagons, carrying felt tents, divided into two or three rooms. The women lived in the wagons, while the males rode on horseback followed by their herds. They would stay in one area and moved on only when there was no more pasture.

Herodotus listed their peculiar habits. They blinded their slaves and forced them to labour at stirring milk, separating it to make the dozens of products that Mongolians use today: yoghurts, whey, curds, fermented drinks of many kinds, from the mild-but-bitter mare's-milk beer known as *kumiss* to spirits like camel's-milk brandy.[6] They sacrificed

---

[6] Herodotus mentions a spirit-wine called *aschy*, which he says is made of fruit mixed with milk. The word is similar to the modern Mongolian *arkhi*, which is distilled alcoholic drink of any sort.

animals by strangling them and boiling them over a fire made from their bones. They sacrificed men to their war god – to whom Herodotus refers by the Greek name, Ares – by slitting the victim's throat, while prisoners had their arms and legs cut off nearby. In war, they drank the blood of the first man they killed. Enemies slain in battle were brought to the king, who turned the flesh of their skulls into soft handkerchiefs. 'Sometimes they flay a whole body, and stretch the skin on a wooden frame which they carry around with them when they ride.' The skulls of their worst enemies they sliced off across the forehead to make drinking cups. 'When important visitors arrive, these skulls are passed around and the host tells the story of them . . . Which passes for a proof of courage.' To make an oath or 'solemn compact', Scythians drank a mixture of wine and blood, into which a weapon was dipped. One Scythian group, the Argippaei, 'are said to be bald from birth, women and men alike.'

Herodotus mentions eight different sub-groups (including the Sauromatians). One of these groups, the Tauri, lived on the Black Sea coast, and were particularly feared by the Greeks because 'it is the custom of the Tauri to sacrifice to the Maiden Goddess' – apparently Iphigenia, daughter of Agamemnon, though this seems odd for a non-Greek tribe – 'all shipwrecked sailors and such Greeks as they happen to capture upon their coasts; their method of sacrifice is, after the preliminary ceremonies, to hit the victim on the head with a club,' then fix the head on a stake.

When a Scythian king died, the body was embalmed, a process that Herodotus describes as if giving a recipe: 'The belly is slit open, cleaned out, and filled with various aromatic substances, crushed galingale,[7] parsley-seed and anise.' It was then sewed up, covered in wax and taken round to different tribes, who in ritual mourning cut bits off their ears, made 'circular motions with their arms' – a gesture still used in Mongolia today – gashed their foreheads and noses, and pushed arrows through their left hands. Finally, the corpse was placed in a pit, along with the bodies of strangled servants and horses, and covered with a great mound. A year later, fifty more servants and fifty more horses were throttled, gutted, stuffed with chaff and fixed upright with stakes around the grave.

When non-royal people became old, at least among one group, the Massagetae (about whom more in a moment),

> they have one way only of determining the time to die, namely this: when a man is very old, all his relatives give a party and include him in a general sacrifice of cattle, then they boil the flesh and eat it; this they consider the best form of death. Those who die of disease are not eaten but buried, and it is held a misfortune not to have lived long enough to be sacrificed.

Among other groups, the dead were taken round to relatives in a wagon for forty days, made into the centrepieces of feasts, and finally burned. Afterwards, the relatives cleansed themselves in saunas made of three tent-poles, a cloth and a dish of hemp brought to the boil with red-hot stones. 'The

---

7 'The aromatic root of certain East Indian plants of the genera *Alpinia* and *Kaempferia*, formerly much used in medicine and cookery' (Oxford English Dictionary). These are types of ginger, mostly found in south-east Asia. Hints here of extensive trading and expertise.

Scythians enjoy it so much they howl with pleasure,' says Herodotus. 'This is their substitute for an ordinary bath with water, which they never use.' The women plaster themselves in a paste made of frankincense, cypress and cedar, which leaves their skin 'clean, glossy and fragrant'.

A lot more is known about the Scythians now, not only from their remains (more on those in Chapter 4), but also from sources written in Akkadian, the cuneiform script of the people who dominated Mesopotamia during the Neo-Assyrian empire (911–612 BC).

The Scythians emerged from Central Asia in the early seventh century, chasing out their predecessors, the Cimmerians. Assyria, Lydia (in Turkey) and Egypt all recorded campaigns involving the Cimmerians, who were eventually defeated and vanished from history, leaving the steppes to the Scythians. They formed three dynasties, covering 1,000 years:

1 In the region of the Kuban River, north-east of the Black Sea (700–550 BC).
2 Between the Don and Dnieper (550–third century BC), these being the people known to Herodotus. He mentions a dozen names of rulers, and records many interactions with Greek cities and settlements.
3 In Crimea (170 BC–third century AD).

Greek contact with these people was intense, but mainly commercial. Conquest was almost impossible, as the Persian king Cyrus the Great found to his cost in 530 BC, a century before Herodotus's day. His nemesis was an Amazon in all but name.

After establishing his empire, Cyrus turned north and east, to Scythian lands. One of the tribes – probably a confederacy – was the Massagetae, whose way of life fed into the Greek belief in a nation of Amazons. Kumiss-drinkers known for their sexual equality – shocking to the male-dominated Greeks and Persians – the Massagetae fought on horseback with battleaxes and bows, men and women alike. At the time, they were ruled by a queen named Tomyris.

Herodotus relates how Cyrus, having discovered the hard way how difficult it was to defeat nomadic horse-archers, resorts to trickery. He sets out a banquet with much wine, which is unfamiliar to the milk-drinking nomads. The Persians withdraw, the nomads advance, find the banquet, eat, drink and fall into a stupor. The Persians return, kill most of them and take Tomyris's unconscious son prisoner. When he awakens, he commits suicide. Tomyris swears revenge. 'Leave my land now,' she says, 'or I will give you more blood than you can drink.' In the next battle, the nomads destroy the Persians and kill Cyrus. Tomyris finds the king's corpse, fills a skin container with blood, and cuts off his head. 'Although I am alive and gained victory over you in battle,' she says, 'you have destroyed me because you took my son by trickery. Now I shall do just as I threatened, and give you your fill of blood.' With these words, she thrusts Cyrus's head into the blood-filled container.

The Amazons as a nation made another of their rare appearances in 330 BC, two centuries after Cyrus's death. This story is about Alexander the Great. He has just conquered Persia and is on his way eastwards, mopping up minor king-doms in present-day Iran, in a region called Hyrcania, on the southern shore of the Caspian Sea. The earliest version of this story, now lost, was written by one of Alexander's aides. Many other versions followed (Plutarch says he knew of fourteen). The earliest *surviving* version of the story dates from the first century BC, 200 years after the supposed event, having acquired ever more colourful details along the way. Here is a version by the first-century AD writer Curtius, interspersed with my comments:

> There was neighbouring on Hyrcania, a race of Amazons, inhabiting the plains of Themiscyra, about the river Thermodon. They had a queen, Thalestris, who ruled all who dwelt between the Caucasus mountains and the river Phasis. She, fired with a desire to visit the king, came forth from the boundaries of her kingdom.

The Thermodon and the Phasis (today's Rioni in Georgia) marked the hypothetical original frontiers of the Amazons, so this account ignores their supposed shift to inner Asia and the formation of the Sauromatians. The region is 1,500 kilometres from Hyrcania, not exactly round the corner. It would have taken these Amazons a few weeks' hard gallop to reach Alexander, which meant they would have needed to set off before he arrived. Something's not right.

> When she was not far away she sent messengers to give notice that a queen had come who was eager to meet him and to become acquainted with him. She was at once given permission to come. Having ordered the rest of her escort to halt, she came forward attended by three hundred women, and as soon as the king was in sight, she herself leaped down from her horse, carrying two lances in her right hand.

Curtius then adds a few semi-pornographic details on a subject to which we will return in the next chapter:

> The clothing of the Amazons does not wholly cover the body; for the left side is nude as far as the breast, then the other parts of the body are veiled. However, the fold of the robe, which they gather in a knot, does not reach below the knee. One nipple is left untouched, and with it they nourish their female children; the right is seared, in order that they may more easily stretch their bows and hurl their spears. With fearless expression Thalestris gazed at the king, carefully surveying his person, which did not by any means correspond to the fame of his exploits . . .

Alexander was apparently quite small, and 'prone to drink and choleric', according to Plutarch. 'The pleasures of the body had little hold upon him, and he indulged in them with great moderation, while his ambition kept his spirit serious and lofty.' Nor was he muscular, being 'averse to the whole race of athletes', which apparently included the tough, hard-riding, single-breasted Amazon queen. Thalestris was not put off . . .

> . . . for all the barbarians feel veneration for a majestic presence, and believe that only those are capable of great deeds whom nature has deigned to adorn with extraordinary physical attractiveness.
>
> However, on being asked whether she wished to make any request, she did not hesitate to confess that she had come to share children with the king, being worthy that he should beget from her heirs to his kingdom; that she would retain

any female offspring but would return a male to his father.

Alexander asked her whether she wished to serve in war with him; but she, giving as an excuse that she had left her realm without a guard, persisted in asking that he should not suffer her to go away disappointed in her hope.

The passion of the woman, being, as she was, more keen for love than the king, compelled him to remain there for a few days. Thirteen days were spent in satisfying her desire. Then she went to her kingdom.

And no one ever heard of her again, or of any child.

What is all this about? The writer who first described the incident was Onesicritus, one of Alexander's entourage on the Asian campaign, about which he wrote a long history. So it's a contemporary – perhaps even an eyewitness – account. But how could it be, since there was no kingdom of Amazons?

Onesicritus's words suggest a resolution. He was certainly in a position to report accurately. He was go-between for Alexander when he wished to contact an Indian philosopher and also had such a reputation as a sea captain that Alexander put him in charge of the fleet that took him down the Indus back towards Persia, or so Onesicritus himself said. But he was also a self-promoter who knew how to curry favour with the powerful. He remained at court with Alexander's successor Lysimachus, but his account of the Asian campaign was derided as exaggerated by later writers. Some said he was never an admiral of the fleet, as he claimed, but only a river pilot.

Two centuries later, Plutarch told this story against him: 'Onesicritus was reading aloud to Lysimachus, who was now king, the fourth book of his history, in which was the tale of the Amazon, at which Lysimachus smiled gently and said: "And where was I at the time?"' Well, he was on the spot, with Alexander, and knew Onesicritus was over-dramatizing. But why spoil a nice story? It served everyone's purpose to interpret the Scythian princess as an Amazon queen eager to have a child with the great Alexander.

Here is a possible explanation. Alexander is met by a contingent of Scythians, among whom there are some women. They come from nearby steppes. One of the women is clearly the boss. Alexander is already a heroic conqueror, in a long tradition of Greek heroes. These heroes, men like Heracles and Theseus, had met the Amazons – that was how everyone 'knew' the Amazons were real; here's proof that they still are. Therefore it is only right and proper that Alexander, a modern Heracles, should encounter Amazons. There is a language problem. No one understands what the Amazons want. They are not hostile. They hang around for a few days. Alexander, recalling Cyrus's fate at the hands of Tomyris, is hospitable. Sometimes the Scythian 'queen' is alone with Alexander in his tent. Then they all vanish, back into the grasslands. It is a small step for Onesicritus to turn the Scythian visit into an incident that enhances Alexander's status; and his own.

3

A SHORT CHAPTER ON BREASTS

THE ONE THING EVERYONE 'KNOWS' ABOUT THE AMAZONS IS that they cut off their right breasts in order not to obstruct their bow strings. When I told people I was writing a book about the Amazons, this was what they asked about. Did they *really* do that? No, they didn't. It's rubbish, nonsense, balderdash, tosh, twaddle, and in all ways totally daft. But the idea is so widely believed, even now, that it demands explanation and refutation.

It seems to have arisen in the fifth century BC, when the

myth of the Amazons was already well known, and growing in popularity as one of the legends that told Greeks about their identity. That posed a question: why 'Amazon'? Where did the name come from? There are many theories – a queen named Amezan, numerous supposed origins in various languages – but the truth is that no one knows. Homer called them *Amazones*, with an *–es* ending which is not specifically female. But he adds the term *antianeirai*, 'a match for men'. Possibly, the Amazons were originally a tribe in which men and women were equal, perhaps in ability, perhaps in status – some long-forgotten sub-group.

For people trying to understand something that everyone 'knew' to be true, that left a hole to be filled. In other similar circumstances, a hole like that is often filled with an entirely spurious explanation – folk etymology, in which analogy and charm trump truth. The artichoke known as a Jerusalem is so-called because the English had no idea what its Italian name, *girasole* (turn-(with-the)-sun), meant and opted for the nearest English-sounding name. Some people prefer to think that 'marmalade' derives from a chef's recipe for an ailing Queen Mary that he termed '*Marie est malade*' – 'Marie is sick' – which is rather more appealing than the obvious and boring root in the Portuguese *marmelada* (quince jam). A peccadillo is 'little sin' in Spanish, but how much more interesting it would be if it derived from a rare Amazonian animal that was a cross between a *pecc*ary and an arma*dillo*, hunted to extinction by Spanish colonists, thus causing the creature's name to stand for a small crime. Somehow Greeks fixed on the idea that 'Amazon' meant 'without a breast', from *a-* 'without', as in 'amoral' or 'asexual', and *mastos*, breast, as in 'mastectomy'. Of course, it doesn't work: *a-mastos* is not *a-mazon*. Nor is it 'without' anything else, although there have been many suggestions: without breast milk, without corn. Perhaps it derived from the fact that steppe horse-women wore leather armour, which hid the female shape – but armour constrained both breasts, so that doesn't work either. In any event, there is no good explanation now, nor was there in the fifth century BC.

Still, it was 'without a breast' that caught on and evolved, apparently in order to make some practical sense out of an idea that had none. It's a horrible thought, that a girl would have a breast cut off. And if a breast was to be destroyed, surely it would be better to cauterize it when the girl was young? That was what Greeks told each other, and many writers repeated this 'fact' as if it were a truth universally acknowledged.

For example: in about 400 BC, in his *On Airs, Waters, Places*, Hippocrates, usually called the 'Father of Medicine', linked diseases to various external causes. As part of his survey, he has this to say about the Sauromatians, founded (you will remember) when the Amazons mated with the Scythians. These people are different from all other races.

> Their women ride horses and shoot arrows and hurl jav-elins from horseback and they fight in campaigns as long as they remain virgins . . . They have no right breast since their mothers heat a specially made iron [or 'copper instrument', for translations vary] and apply it to the breast while they are still children. This prevents the breast from growing, and all the strength and size of it go into the right arm and shoulder instead.

Of course Greek women were supposedly home bodies, not noted as archers or javelin-throwers, so perhaps he had no evidence from his household. But he really should have known better. A little research would have proved him wrong. Herodotus, writing at the same time from personal experience, makes no mention of the practice, although he records some fairly horrific Scythian rituals.

So the idea remained, fixed. Here, for instance, is Justinus, writing in the second century AD, repeating the accepted 'truths':

> Having thus secured peace by means of their arms, they [the Amazons] proceeded, in order that their race might not fail, to form connexions with the men of the adjacent nations. If any male children were born, they put them to death. The girls they bred up to the same mode of life with themselves, not consigning them to idleness, or working in wool, but training them to arms, the management of horses, and hunting; burning their right breasts in infancy, that their use of the bow might not be obstructed by them.

But Greek artists and sculptors never took the idea seriously, always portraying the Amazons with breasts intact. That was the point: the Amazons were heroic warriors, but also fully women, and beauties. Usually they were shown with only one breast exposed, but the other one was obviously *there*. Otherwise, their beauty would be marred.

Perhaps for this reason the idea dropped out of fashion. Artists avoided the matter. Authors seldom mentioned it. But there remained those who insisted on taking it seriously. One was a late-seventeenth-century French writer, Pierre Petit, in his *De Amazonibus dissertatio* (*A Dissertation on Amazons*). He was convinced that legends about the Amazons had to be accepted as true, simply because it defied belief that so many people had got it wrong. That being so, what, he wondered, made them special? His answers were a cold climate, diet, education and physical training. Since they existed, obviously it must also be true that they did away with their right breasts. Why would they do that? Not because it strengthened their right arms – that was ridiculous – but because it strengthened *their whole bodies*. How did they do it? Obviously not by cutting off the breast – that was ridiculous too, because it was far too dangerous. So they must have done it by using some sort of drug, which only they knew about, because otherwise everyone else would do it too. To prove his point, he collected as many apparently one-breasted images from the classical world as he could. It was beyond his comprehension that his 'evidence' was legend piled on legend, untruth upon untruth. He was a single-issue fanatic, interpreting everything by the light of his own obsession, and no one took any notice of him, except one or two who used him as additional 'evidence' to 'prove' that 2,000 years of repeating falsehoods somehow made them true.

Yet the idea is with us still, as a few mouse-clicks show. Greeka.com, which should know better, says: 'Peculiar, but perhaps justified from the Amazons' perspective, was the removal of a girl's right breast. While still a girl, the right breast would be cauterized using a searing hot bronze tool. It was thought to be a necessary evil, to mutilate and remove all possible hindrances to using a spear or drawing an arrow.' The idea is fodder for psychologists, because it is so obviously contradictory. The Amazonian body 'visibly gives and withholds itself, promises and frustrates both oral and aesthetic satisfaction, defines nurture and aggression as equal aspects of its nature; it is vulnerable in the possession of one breast while toughened by the absence of the other.'[8] A paper 'from the perspective of a plastic surgeon who has been living in this region that the Amazons inhabited', states that 'the primary purpose was to facilitate the efficient use of a bow. Another explanation would be that breast mutilation was performed for medical reasons, including the prevention of breast pain, the development of a tender lump, or cancer. There is another school of thought on this involving religious and sociological reasons that breast mutilation was a badge of honor for warrior women.' Even the old, disproven etymology gets repeated: 'While the Greek for breast is *mazos* (whence the name Amazon, or "without breast") . . .'[9]

Such nonsense. OK, girls have been and are subjected to appalling practices every bit as painful as the excision of a breast, two obvious examples being female genital mutilation in many parts of Africa, the Middle East and Indonesia, and foot-binding done in China up until 1949. But in such societies girls were and are treated as objects and possessions. The Amazons, whether in legend or reality, protected their daughters. Forget the lack of visual evidence, forget dictionary definitions – just consider the practicalities. At what age was the mutilation supposed to happen? Would Amazonian mothers really perform such major surgery? How many girls would have died? Why risk killing your own future soldiers?

[8] Gail Kern Paster, *The Body Embarrassed: Drama and the Disciplines of Shame in Early Modern England*, Cornell, 1993, p. 238.
[9] Simon Richter, *Missing the Breast: Gender, Fantasy and the Body in the German Enlightenment*, University of Washington Press, 2006, p. 35.

Anyway, the operation has no practical justification. When using a bow and arrow or throwing a javelin, women have no problems. Anyone watching the 2016 Olympics could see that women archers and javelin-throwers are not impeded by breasts, any more than female mounted archers are. If it helped to cut a breast off to improve performance, some hyper-ambitious athlete would surely have done it. It's just blindingly obvious that to cut or cauterize a breast could not conceivably strengthen an arm or shoulder, let alone the whole body.

The opposite would be the case, which is why no one ever did it, and why the idea has no grain of truth.

4

TREASURES IN BONE
AND GOLD

HERODOTUS WAS ON THE RIGHT LINES WHEN HE TALKED OF
the Sauromatians. He said these people, who lived beyond
the Scythians, had been formed by a union of Amazons and
Scythians. They then retained their 'old ways', by which he
meant Scythian ways. To get to the Amazons demands a
closer look at the Scythians, the *real* Scythians. In the fifth
century BC, no one could say much more about them than
Herodotus, because there were no good sources: no script,
no histories. Herodotus records a few tribal names and a

few gods – Tabiti, Papaeus, Api – but that's not much help. We now know rather more about the Scythians than Herodotus did, because they left behind funeral mounds covering the graves, bodies and possessions of their leaders.

How many? No one has counted. Certainly tens of thousands, perhaps hundreds of thousands. They run from north of the Black Sea, across present-day southern Russia and Kazakhstan into Mongolia and southern Siberia. Many were treasure chests of possessions, presumably to sustain the rich and powerful in the afterlife, so for centuries they were literally gold mines for grave-robbers.

In the early eighteenth century, under Peter the Great, Russia began her great expansion eastwards into Siberia and southwards into what is now Ukraine and the various –stans of Central Asia. Russian colonists and explorers could not miss the grave mounds, which became known by the Russian term *kurgan*s. It turned out that grave-robbers had not taken everything. In 1716, sixty items were given to Peter the Great, starting the ever-growing collection of Scythian gold that now dazzles tourists in the Gold Room in St Petersburg's Hermitage Museum. During the second half of the nineteenth century, archaeologists started to do serious research on the Black Sea kurgans, revealing skeletons, golden plaques and immense cauldrons by the score. Historians meanwhile were looking at Herodotus with sceptical eyes, because he had not visited the far-off places he wrote about and was so vague about his sources that they suspected him of plagiarizing. Since then, he has gained respect for his honesty and industry. As one of his biographers, Sir John Myres, wrote in 1953, 'his information is now seen to be such as an intelligent and observant man . . . might reasonably accept as true.'

Archaeologists agree. They have opened hundreds more kurgans, in ever remoter areas, recording, theorizing, arguing,
revealing what scholars call the Scythian World.

More emerges every year. Over 1,000 mounds have now
been excavated. The truth about Scythia and related places
and peoples is far richer, far more complex and altogether far
less barbaric than Herodotus could possibly have dreamed.
Their women, for instance, had a higher status than in
male-dominated Athens. Among them were real Amazons,
and others who were something much more than warrior
women.

'Scythia' was not like a nation-state, with a capital and
a centralized government, or a land-empire like Genghis
Khan's, controlled from the centre. No pony express linked
east and west. Scythia was a collection of cultures, spanning
all Central Asia from the Black Sea to Mongolia, unified
by a few main traits: funeral mounds, horses, weaponry
and a love of the so-called Animal style of art, made up of
convoluted creatures, part real, part mythological. Every
Scythian tribe and culture would have known, traded with,
intermarried with and fought with its neighbours. Ideas
spread and customs changed, though slowly, over centuries. Tribes grew, fought, migrated and mixed. Herodotus
lists several: Arimaspians, Issedonians, Massagetae, Sacae
– a name that still endures in Kazakhstan, where ancient
Scythians are known as Saka. Beyond these, in the mythical
shadows, were the 'gold-protecting griffins' and the legendary Hyperboreans, the 'Extreme Northerners'. Griffins, a
mythical cross between a lion and an eagle, were common
images in Scythian art.

A few inscriptions and mentions of words in other cultures

suggest that there were many Scythian languages. Herodotus was told that Black Sea Scythians who traded with a remote group called the Argippaei needed seven lots of interpreters along the way.[10] Scholars generally agree that the languages were part of the vast Indo-European family, specifically Iranian – actually east Iranian – with one surviving member, Ossetian, still spoken on the borders of Russia and Georgia (more on them later). Much depended on local conditions, but the transcontinental links were strong: there is no gold to be found north of the Black Sea, except in kurgans – it was all imported along trade routes from the Altai Mountains of southern Siberia and western Mongolia. Altai is connected to the Mongolian for gold, *altan*, which perhaps explains why these mountains were the traditional home of griffins. If a few Scythians from western Mongolia had magically found them-selves transported 4,000 kilometres to the Scythians north of the Black Sea, once they had found good interpreters, they would not have been entirely at a loss.

In the late nineteenth century, the fourth-century BC burial of a Scythian woman was discovered in a kurgan in the middle of Ukraine, on the left bank of the Tyasmin River, a tributary of the Dnieper. The remains of a young man of about eighteen lay at her feet, a servant perhaps. She was clearly a warrior, because near her were two iron lance-points, a wooden quiver with forty-seven three-feathered arrowheads, and two bronze knives. Another female warrior from a kurgan near the Ukrainian port of Bilhorod-Dnistrovskyi – once the

---

[10] We're getting into worlds of rumour again. Supposedly the Argippaei were all bald, lived under cherry trees, and were peaceful people 'protected by a special sort of sanctity'.

Greek colony of Tyras, then Akkerman under the Turks – was buried with a quiver of twenty arrows, four lances and a heavy fighting belt covered in strips of iron.

At first, these women were assumed to be wives, daughters and mothers, mere adjuncts to the male warriors, who had been buried with weapons for unknown reasons. But these female skeletons had wounds. The second one had a crushed skull and a bronze arrowhead buried in her knee. Her death had been violent. The women had been warriors in their own right. They had actually used their weapons in battle and suffered the consequences.

Since then it has become clear that the two women were not unusual. Women were routinely given burials matching those of men. Of the graves of women found between the Danube and the Don (112 by 1991, and more since), some 70 per cent belonged to women aged between sixteen and thirty.[11] And in some areas 37 per cent of burials are those of *armed* women. From surveys in the 1980s and 1990s, about 20 per cent of those graves with weapons belonged to women, and these were not the graves of upper-class people, but ordinary women.

The evidence for the violent lives lived by Scythian women – Amazons if you like, for that is how they seemed to the Greeks – was revealed in large burial grounds in southern Siberia. The Minusinsk Hollow is one of them, prime pasture-land some 200 kilometres across. It and its surrounding territory have some 30,000 kurgans acquired in the course of 1,500 years (1000 BC–AD 500). The biggest, the Great Salbyk Kurgan (fourth century BC), is surrounded by twenty-

[11] Valeri Guliaev. See Bibliography.

three gigantic stones, weighing up to 40 tonnes, each cut and hauled from a quarry 60 kilometres away. Another prime site is in Tuva, 200 kilometres to the south-east.

Until just over a century ago, Tuva was Chinese, when China ruled all Mongolia plus a bit more. After escaping from Chinese control, Tuva was briefly an independent mini-nation, then part of the Soviet Union, and is now a semi-autonomous part of Russia. They speak Tuvan (a Turkic language, the Turks having dominated these parts before the Mongols came), they are famous for herding and riding reindeer, they're Buddhist and (like their neighbouring Mongolians) they have terrific throat-singers. The 300,000 or so Tuvans share huge spaces of forest, mountain and grassland. This was the heartland from which the Scythians originally came before migrating west. Tuva, with its extreme temperatures (−50° or below up to +40°), is about as far from any salt water as it is possible to get,[12] and is usually described as 'remote', though not by the Tuvans, for whom their homeland is the centre of the universe. It is only right that they should have an important place in the evolution of a way of life that dominated central Eurasia for several thousand years.

The earliest evidence for Scythian ways comes from two immense kurgans, known as Arzhan 1 and 2, after the nearby village in the valley of the Uyuk River. This is a fine, gentle pasture, with not much snow in winter – a rarity in these austere regions, and a focus for Scythian nomads for many centuries as they migrated between summer pastures in the mountains and winter pastures along the Uyuk. The valley is (appropriately) an

---

[12] The Pole of Inaccessibility – the point furthest from any coastline – is actually 700 kilometres to the south-west, in China.

arrowhead of grass, 50 kilometres long and 30 wide at its base, fenced by mountains. There are some 300 burial mounds, so many that they call it the Valley of the Kings.

These Scythians, of the so-called Uyuk Culture, were not just simple nomads, surviving off their herds. As many sites reveal, they had their tents, but they ate freshwater fish, grew millet, built log cabins and made stone tombs with domed roofs. They mined for copper and iron, which demanded specialist miners, tools and good knowledge of the geology. Stone pillars carved with spirals, rosettes and circles suggest they worshipped the sun. They believed in an afterlife and made sure their leaders were well prepared for it, preserving their bodies wherever they died and bringing them back to ancestral cemeteries for burial. They worked metals into animal shapes, like curled-up snow leopards and birds of prey, perhaps admired for their strength, agility and vigilance.

Most of their mounds are not obviously royal, more like a collection of family tombs, with multiple burials. From them archaeologists have gleaned what looters left, showing that the women cared a lot about their looks, even in the after-life. Tombs contained earrings, pectorals, beads, rings, neck decorations made of bronze wire and gold, belt buckles in the shapes of animals, bronze mirrors in leather pouches hung on belts, combs of iron or wood, and pins made of iron, bronze and bone. Small cylindrical and conical cases made of horn, many well carved with animal shapes, probably contained the equivalent of make-up. And lots of horse fittings – bridles, bits, rings and badges. Some pottery, though they were not much good at it, preferring wooden dishes and cups, or an enemy's skull for special occasions.

The royal tombs were on a different level of sophistication.

They are only on the edge of our subject, because the women, being of the ruling class, were not warriors (unlike their legendary sisters), but the two Arzhans reveal the upper-class wealth of the culture that produced the real Amazons.

The Valley of the Kings: Arzhan 1 alone would justify the title. Its start date was around 750 BC, about the time Homer was writing the *Iliad* and *Odyssey*, making it the oldest known kurgan. Once, it was a huge platform, 110 metres across, with a surrounding wall and a 4-metre-high dome. Almost all kurgans are of wood and earth; this one was uniquely covered in stones, which turned it into a giant refrigerator. Over the years, looters mined it, locals used it for their July celebrations, and in the 1960s bulldozers ground across it as part of the Soviet-era campaign to turn steppes into farmland. Even so, when archaeologists arrived in 1971, they found wonders: a wheel-shaped complex of seventy interlocking wooden chambers (though some had been torn up by the bulldozers). These chambers surrounded a central space that enclosed a 4 x 4-metre larchwood tomb, with two coffins containing a chief – ruler, king, terms vary – and a woman, presumably his wife. (Or was she the dominant partner, the 'queen'? Was she or he killed to be a companion in the afterlife? We cannot tell.) Round the tomb were eight hollowed-out logs holding the bones of retainers, killed to accompany their master and mistress into the next world. Nearby lay the remains of six horses, richly decorated with gold, as the surviving unlooted items showed.

All this was right in line with Herodotus. Having been carried around and mourned in outlying areas (he says), the king is buried in a roofed pit. 'In other parts of the great square pit various members of the king's household are buried beside him . . . all of them strangled. Horses are buried too, and gold cups . . . and a selection of his other treasures.'

No expense had been spared: sables and four-colour woollen clothes for the retainers, horse-trappings of bronze and gold in the shapes of snow leopards and boars, even a golden coiled panther in the Animal style familiar from neighbouring cultures as far away as the Black Sea (and reminiscent of the deer-stone designs from 1,000 years earlier). In the surrounding chambers were another 160 horse skeletons, almost all of 12–15-year-old stallions, along with several 'grooms', plus numerous daggers, arrowheads, a torc (a semi-circular sheet of gold worn around the neck), gold earrings with turquoise inlays, and pendants. Who knows how much had been there originally, before the looters arrived. All of this was built by 1,200–1,500 people in one massive week-long operation: 6,000 mature larches, stripped and roughly joined to form the seventy chambers, with passageways to link them; thousands of rock slabs up to 50 kilograms in weight, cut, collected and placed; and the 2.5-metre wall built around the whole thing. Then, to complete the ritual, the people held a huge feast outside the wall – or perhaps it was an annual affair; anyway, they left the remains of 300 horses and uncounted numbers of cattle, sheep and goats.

Arzhan 2, made about a century after Arzhan 1, proved even more remarkable, both for its contents and for the fact that it had been largely untouched.[13] The builders had got smart, as the excavation team discovered when they dug it up in 2000–4. The two central pits were mock-graves, which

[13] The finds have been meticulously recorded in a superb 500-page book kindly sent to me by Hermann Parzinger, from Germany. See Čugunov, Parzinger and Nagler in Bibliography for details.

had fooled would-be looters. The main burial was 20 metres off-centre. Digging almost 4 metres down into the mound, Pavel Leus, a Russian heading a small team of local labourers, found a layer of larch logs.[14] Lifting one, he glimpsed in the shadows two skeletons and a glint of yellow. 'Guys,' he called up to his bosses, 'we've got a problem. We need the police.'

Yes, indeed, as the expedition leader, Konstantin Čugunov of the State Hermitage Museum in St Petersburg, confirmed when he joined Leus in the pit, followed by his partners, Hermann Parzinger and Anatoli Nagler of the German Archaeological Institute in Berlin. Over the next three weeks, well guarded, the archaeologists and their 100 workers found not only the royal couple, but also sixteen murdered attendants, and twenty-three other skeletons buried later, probably Turkic – twenty-nine graves in all, women in the western half, men to the east – and the *real* treasure: 9,300 objects, of which 5,700 were gold, weighing 20 kilograms, a record for a Siberian grave. The king, aged between fifty and fifty-five, wore a golden torc and a jacket decorated with 2,500 small panther figurines, all gold, trousers sewn with golden beads, and gold-cuffed boots. On a belt hung a gold-encrusted double-edged dagger. The woman, twenty years younger, wore a red cloak also covered with 2,500 panther figurines in gold. She had an iron dagger with a gilded hilt, a golden comb and a wooden ladle with a golden handle. Her headdress was a gold pointed cap, decorated with two gold horses, a panther and a bird of prey. The two were buried together, suggesting equal status. Was she killed to keep her man company in the afterlife? Or vice versa? Or was

[14] Details from 'Masters of Gold', *National Geographic*, June 2003.

he her father, she a daughter? Nearby were thousands of beads, 431 of them made of amber, carried as trade goods all the way across Eurasia from the Baltic.

The Arzhan tombs are for royalty. For those whom we might term Amazons, the rank-and-file women warriors, there's more information 100 kilometres to the south-west. The cemetery, Aymyrlyg, stretches for 10 kilometres along a tributary of the Yenisei. This is a landscape of rolling hills and high pastures, with mountains lining the horizon, and a foreground now under water, drowned by a reservoir created by a vast hydroelectric dam further down the Yenisei. Here, the Scythians and their descendants had made an ancestral cemetery, burying some 800 bodies mainly in the third and second centuries BC, spanning the time when the Scythians started to give way to, or assimilate with, or develop into, the so-called Hunno-Sarmatians, a mix of Sarmatians and Xiongnu (known locally as Huns, or Hunnu, though whether they were the forefathers of Attila's Huns is an open question).

Eight hundred burials in 200 years – four burials a year, on average – doesn't seem much. Perhaps the burials, typically in tombs made of logs or stone slabs, came in irregular bursts, after particularly significant battles, when bodies had to be dealt with en masse. Some tombs have as many as fifteen bodies. Buried with the bodies were weapons, Animal-style artefacts, tools, pins, combs, mirrors, belts with bronze buckles, and horse fittings, the things commonly found in Scythian tombs. Generally, bows did not survive, but the imprint of one shows they were about 1.5 metres long.

The bones, from 600 individuals collected in 1968–84 from 200 graves and taken to St Petersburg before the reservoir's waters rose, are an encyclopedia of the pains, diseases and injuries suffered by ordinary Scythians. With the fast-developing sciences of bioarchaeology and palaeopathology, scholars can read stories in the remains. Skull shapes reveal that they looked more European than Mongoloid. Furrows and pits in the teeth speak of diets. Lesions in the eye-sockets point to vitamin deficiencies (still a problem, by the way, for some steppe nomads). The chemical and sub-atomic structure of bones hints at changes in climate and plant cover. Disease and malnutrition in childhood cause the enamel to grow more thinly in developing teeth (hypoplasia). Mechanical stresses build muscles and their attachments unevenly (long-bowmen in medieval England, training from childhood, had massively distorted backs and shoulders). Causes of death are catalogued in bone: murders, domestic violence, executions, ritual sacrifices, battles, accidents. There are, for instance, signs of long-term changes in weaponry: battleaxe injuries predominate during the Scythian period and sword wounds are more common during later Hunno-Sarmatian times.

Eileen Murphy, of Queen's University, Belfast, has made an extensive study of these bones in the Kunstkammer, the Museum of Anthropology and Ethnography started by Peter the Great in St Petersburg. She has never been to Tuva, but knows more about the perils of everyday life for herders and mounted archers in ancient Scythia than anyone else on Earth, thanks to the Russian archaeologists who collected and recorded the bones in the first place.[15] She analysed over 3,000 of them, and published the results in 'one of the first

---

[15] Murphy lists the names in a meticulous 242-page monograph. Her findings are summarized in my other references.

detailed palaeopathological analyses . . . on a substantial corpus of Iron Age human skeletons from Eurasia.' They provide direct evidence that Herodotus got a lot right: a few skulls show signs of scalping, a few others of being cut open, possibly to remove the brain, 'an aggressive post-combat activity that was part of a war-ritual.' Beyond this, as Murphy says, 'The Aymyrlyg excavations enable us to gain real insight into the lives and lifestyle of the "ordinary" members of these semi-nomadic societies', many of whom displayed a range of diseases and malformations. One man, for instance, had congenital dislocation of the hip, another a 'malformed proximal femur', which would have made them walk with fearful limps. There were facial deformities, eye defects, distortions of the skull, a whole catalogue of medical catastrophes. One woman had neurofibromatosis, an extremely unpleasant condition in which tumours grow in the nervous system.

People with serious congenital defects find life difficult in any society, let alone one as harsh and reliant on herding, horses and hunting. As Herodotus says, this was not a society that took much care of its old people. You would think that they would not tolerate deformity of any kind, rather as the Spartans allowed weak children to perish. Apparently not. Perhaps because injuries and wounds were so common, there seems to have been a tolerance of deformity – perhaps even a support system – that ensured that cripples of all sorts had useful roles until they died, to be buried along with their sturdier fellows.

Murphy wonders if these dire cases could be the origin of some of the so-called myths about the more distant regions of Central Asia:

To a visitor from the Greek world, these Scythian individuals with abnormalities would probably have seemed abhorrent and incredible, particularly if such people were eliminated at birth or ostracised by Greek society. It can be argued, therefore, that the fabulous accounts of unusual individuals and peoples in Scythia . . . may have had their origins in real people with abnormal physical appearances who lived freely among the populations.

Herodotus himself mentions 'the tale (which I do not believe) that the mountains are inhabited by a goat-footed race, beyond which still further north are men who sleep for six months of the year – which to my mind is utterly incredible.' Could a hibernating bear be mistaken for a man? Could a club foot look like a hoof? Could a congenital malformation explain the 'one-eyed Arimaspians'? Or could the Cyclops, the monster that captured Odysseus, be someone with Goldenhar syndrome or cebocephaly, which (if the sufferer survives) may result in the absence of an eye, or even a single central eye? One or two individuals with such defects could have been enough to inspire exaggerated tales of monsters.

Horse-based cultures are tough for everyone. Of course, people fell off horses all the time, mostly without damage; but the healed injuries show that if you fell off you had a 1–2 per cent chance of breaking a bone, with men twice as likely as women to break something. One 35–45-year-old woman, who had fractures in her right shoulder and forearm, also had the fourth finger on her right hand so badly broken it had solidified into a claw-shape (ankylosis), all her injuries probably being caused by a very nasty fall.

Fair enough, you would think, in a horse-riding community.

But women had it worse in other ways, as their lower backs reveal. They had more than their fair share of hairline fractures in the lumbar region, a condition known as spondylolysis, as well as a type of fracture called 'clay-shoveller's fracture' because of its association with heavy physical labour in the modern world. Today, young male athletes (median age: twenty) suffer from it if they do too much of anything that is one-sided: tennis, throwing the javelin, high jump, rowing. Some 5 per cent have the condition in modern populations; Scythian women suffered over twice that. Three-quarters of the affected skeletons were female. As Murphy points out, this 'suggests that, contrary to the assertions of the historical accounts relating to the activities of female Scythians, the women did not spend all their time sitting around in wagons but that they were also engaged in heavy physical labour.'

(For some reason, the work got easier as time passed: later female skeletons show fewer signs of spondylolysis. Imagine a grandmother muttering the Scythian equivalent of: 'Kids today, don't know how lucky they are. When I was their age, I was lifting wagon wheels all day and cauldrons of kumiss all night. Then it was horseback archery and sword practice. How I had time to get pregnant I'll never know.')

Apparently, this tough life occasionally involved in-fighting: revenge killings, domestic violence, rows between argumentative teenagers ending in fatal assaults. Some skulls were bashed in with clubs. The numbers are not great, a dozen over the course of 200 years, a quarter of them women, the rest divided equally among men and 'sub-adults'. Most fractures were 'on the left side of the frontals or parietals . . . the site at which an injury would commonly be afflicted in hand-to-hand combat when faced by a right handed opponent.'

Fractures of the facial area and jaws were more common later, suggesting that in 'the Hunno-Sarmatian period individuals only employed their fists in aggressive activities' instead of clubs. Perhaps, perhaps not, because other fractures usually produced by fights – head fractures, fractures of the forearm, 'boxer's fractures' of the fingers – 'all attest to the occurrence of interpersonal and intergroup conflict in both the Scythian and Hunno-Sarmatian period populations'. In most cases, as you would expect, those affected were men, but one Scythian woman displayed multiple fractures – including a forearm break, a broken right finger-bone and a fractured rib – suggesting that she gave as good as she got.

Then there were the war injuries, notably non-fatal arrow wounds, sword wounds and holes in the skull from battle-axes. There were twenty of those, sixteen of them with no signs of healing: they were death blows. Most victims of course were men, but two were women. Children too were victims, presumably killed when their camps or wagons were attacked. 'There is, however, no justification for assuming that females and older sub-adults would not have deliberately participated in the practice of warfare.' Several of the women had damaged left arm-bones, as if they had held up that arm to ward off blows.

Five people living in later Hunno-Sarmatian times were beheaded. One, a woman of 35–45, had a wound in the thigh, and then lost her head to a single blow from an 'extremely sharp' sword. The attack came from behind, perhaps from horseback. She didn't have a chance. Nor apparently did her assailant. 'The angle of the sword chop . . . indicates that the blow had probably been struck from left to right, with the aggressor positioned posterior to the victim. The skull had been buried with the cadaver, and evidently the head had not been carried away as a trophy.' Perhaps, Murphy speculates, the head was left attached by a strand of flesh, and the attacker had no time to finish the job; or perhaps someone stepped in and dealt with the attacker. Another woman had a sword wound in the shoulder, and was then finished off with a blow just above her left ear. Perhaps she was carrying the one-year-old child killed with a sword-blow to the head. Swords had apparently been refined over the previous centuries.

The evidence is overwhelming that ordinary Scythian women fought, and were victims of fighting. 'There is no reason,' Murphy concludes, 'why the Aymyrlyg females might not have obtained their cases of weapon trauma during pitched battles, where they would have joined the men and young adults in defence of the clan and its possessions.' Like a police report from the forensics department, the cold language of science conjures the heat of battle, galloping hooves, flashing swords, screams, quick deaths.

The message of the bones is clear: Scythian women and their successors were Amazons as the Greeks imagined them, but individually, not as part of some spurious female-only nation, but as ordinary members of Scythian society.

Now come 1,500 kilometres south-west of Tuva, to the mountains east of the principal Kazakh city (not capital – that's Askana), Almaty. From the northern slopes of the Tien Shan flow rivers that have turned temperate valleys into fine pastures, which now make farmland. Kazakhstan has kurgans by the thousand, about forty of which lie in a pretty valley near a lake called Issyk (Esik in Kazakh). Despite its name it has nothing to do with the huge freshwater lake of Issyk-Kul, just over the border with Kyrgyzstan to the south.

In the summer of 1969, a farmer ploughing a field near a 6-metre-high kurgan noticed something glinting in the newly turned dark earth behind him. He got down, kicked the soil and found a small piece of patterned gold. Amazingly, he did not pocket his find, but reported it. The Kazakh Institute sent a team to investigate, led by the renowned Soviet archaeologist Kemal Akishev. He was already honoured nationally, both for his work and as a fighter in the Second World War. Among his post-war projects, he opened up Otrar, the long-buried city that was Genghis Khan's entry-point when he invaded the Islamic world in 1219. Akishev later became the much-revered father of Kazakh archaeology, and remained so until his death in 2003, aged seventy-nine. What happened when he arrived in Issyk took him from the national on to the international stage.

The kurgan near where the farmer found the plaque was one of those astonishing rarities, an unrobbed tomb. Actually it had been robbed, and spruce logs that made the 4 x 6-metre grave had fallen in, but the robbers had missed a side-grave. In it, under piles of dirt, lay a very crushed skeleton, quite a small one, which is what makes this story significant for our subject. Surrounding the bones was treasure – 4,000 small gold plaques and ornaments, almost as new.

The American archaeologist Jeannine Davis-Kimball relates what followed. First, let me introduce her. She took her time getting to inner Asia, only starting work there at the age of sixty-five. Three marriages, six children, work as a nurse, hospital administrator, English-language teacher in Bolivia and cattle rancher finally led to a BA in art history. She was cataloguing near-eastern art for the Los Angeles County Museum as part of her Masters when she became intrigued by the museum's 200 bronze plaques and animal statuettes: a deer with a net of antlers, a tiger attacking a horse. The world of the Eurasian nomads seized her: its size, its place in history as the stage for horse cultures succeeding each other for 2,000 years. An excavation in Israel gave her experience of archaeology, and a new purpose. She would focus on the role of women in nomadic societies.

That meant working in Russia, which was hard to arrange in the last days of the Cold War. A Kazakh art exhibition gave her contacts. A visit to Kazakhstan – a train journey marred by unnerving confrontations with KGB agents – inspired her to set up a research organization, now the Center for the Study of Eurasian Nomads. Very little was known outside Russia about the region and the subjects. Then, in 1991, came an invitation to excavate kurgans on what would shortly become Russia's border with Kazakhstan, and with luck modify the current Western view of nomads as 'merciless warlords with jet black hair and dark-slanted eyes, who marauded on tiny ponies . . . besieging cities and wiping out the men before carrying off the women.'

Chapter 6 looks at Davis-Kimball's first experience of the Russian kurgans. This is what happened at the newly discovered Issyk grave, as told to her by Akishev's team leader, Beken Nurapiesov, when he took her to the site thirty years later:

'The skeleton had been cleaned and all the gold plaques were in full view in the pit. Dusk was falling. What were we to do? We didn't have time to finish recording and remove the thousands of objects before dark, and we couldn't leave the skeleton and all that gold alone overnight, so we hired two local men as guards'. Beken paused, and pushed his thick white hair back from his forehead. 'Do you know what happened next, after the crew left? Well,' he said with a mirthless laugh, 'those guards weren't about to spend the night in the cold by an open grave without a little liquid courage. They went into town to buy a bottle or two of vodka, and while they were gone someone came and scooped up the gold pieces that were on the boots and even took the bones of both feet and one lower leg.' He shook his head ruefully at the memory. 'Of course the thieves would have melted down the gold. The plaques are gone, for ever.'[16]

There's something fishy about this story. Why would a thief take bones, but not more of the gold? How did the guards discover the theft, returning the worse for wear and in darkness? What did they do about it? Isn't it rather more likely that the guards themselves took advantage, and then came up with an explanation that shifted the blame on to an anonymous thief?

Whatever the truth, the loss was only a fraction of the whole. What remained was the most remarkable of all Saka finds. Other than the skeleton, the fifth-century BC burial contained: a jacket decorated with 2,400 arrow-shaped gold plaques edged with more gold plaques in the shape of stylized lions (and even more that went missing on the boots); a belt with thirteen golden deer-heads, and three of moose and deer with griffin heads; a golden torc around the neck, with

---

[16] *Warrior Women*, page 101. See Bibliography.

snow-leopard clasps; a gold-bound whip handle; a silver cup engraved with an unidentified script in an unidentified language (more on this later); a dagger and a metre-long sword, the blades embossed with gold animals and in gold-encrusted scabbards; there were earrings, beads, a gilded bronze mirror, and beaters for churning milk into kumiss; and to cap it all, literally, a towering 63-centimetre headdress made of a cone of wood covered with felt.

The headdress was a masterpiece in its own right. Towering headdresses marked high status in Saka–Scythian cultures; they were known by neighbours as 'people of the peaked cap', or 'long hood'; but there was more to this than status. It had a flap covering the ears and neck, adorned with gold plaques in the form of ibex, snow leopards, horses and birds. Attached to it were four gold-foil 'arrows' or miniature spears almost as high as the headdress itself, set in gold-foil feathers over a pair of horses with ibex horns. Akishev reconstructed it by comparing it to a Persian portrait of a Saka, one of the many peoples of the Achaemenid empire, in the great reception hall in Persepolis, designed by Darius the Great in the sixth century BC.

The skull was too damaged for the physical anthropologist, Orazak Ismagulov, to tell the sex of its owner, but the sword and dagger seemed to leave no doubt. Akishev called the find the Golden Man, fitted him with leather trousers and put him on display. He became so famous that he was adopted as the new nation's symbol when Kazakhstan emerged from the ruins of the Soviet Union in the 1990s.

A Golden *Man*: that was the assumption. Fair enough, at the time. But there were things that didn't quite fit, and they began to bother Davis-Kimball, who worked close up with Akishev's find. For one thing, those words a few pages back: 'quite a small one'. Akishev called his Golden Man a youthful chieftain. Remarkably youthful he would have been, hardly out of boyhood. The skeleton was of a person only 160 centimetres (5 foot 3 inches) tall, which is 7.5 centimetres (3 inches) shorter than the average Scythian woman. The headdress's 'arrows' (with two barbs, as opposed to the normal three) might not have been arrows or miniature spears, but some sort of flower, perhaps a fertility symbol; earrings and beads were female items, never seen in male burials; mirrors were associated with priestesses; a couple of items were shamanic symbols familiar from other sites – a ring impressed with a head emanating rays or feathers; birds on trees (a shape often called the Tree of Life) decorating the base of the headdress – but there was nothing to say they had to belong to a male shaman, especially given the figure's apparent youth; and there were kumiss-beaters, which were attributes of female shamans, symbols perhaps of the transformative powers of women.

Even while the grave was being excavated, the headdress reminded the Kazakh archaeologists of the tall hats worn by brides at local weddings. Such hats, passed down the generations as dowries, were decorated with small pieces of gold and silver.[17] Another major find – the 'Ukok Princess', whose story is told in the next chapter – had a high hat and short jacket and twisted-animal tattoos. The sword was no proof that the owner was male – plenty of females were

[17] Traditional tall hats are still worn. In Mongolia, they are known as *bocht*, and are made like the Issyk one, with felt over a wooden frame. Kublai Khan's wife Chabui was portrayed in one in the thirteenth century. They haven't changed much in 700 years.

buried with swords. Many of the artefacts were so similar to those found in other women's tombs that Davis-Kimball felt impelled to go public, and did so with an article in *Archaeology* magazine in autumn 1997.

Her conclusion: the Golden Man was not a man after all. 'This person was actually a young woman . . . a high-ranking warrior priestess.' In the reconstruction, it would be enough to replace the leather trousers with a skirt, as other Saka women wore. If Herodotus's Scythian source had seen the result, he would have had no doubts: here was an Amazon queen.

After publication, Davis-Kimball was apprehensive. Would Russian colleagues see her as an interloper? A feminist challenger to the 'male-oriented Soviet archaeological system'? But there was no backlash. For those in the know, there was nothing very controversial in her view. Rumours had been circulating about the Golden Man's sex. Even the physical anthropologist Orazak Ismagulov, who had examined the skull, told her by phone, 'The bones were very small and could have belonged to a female.'

No backlash, just a wall of official silence. By 1997, it was possible to determine sex from ancient DNA. A small sample of bone was all that was needed. She requested one. But by then the Golden Man was on display as a national symbol, and Kazakhstan's strongman, Nursultan Nazarbayev, had declared himself a big fan. It really wouldn't do to have an ancestral king suddenly turn into a queen. So guess what? When Davis-Kimball called a few days later, Ismagulov's daughter said the laboratory had been moved and 'I can't find any of the Issyk skeletal material'. Since then there has been no trace of the bones and no record of what happened to them. The figure, restored, copied and constantly reproduced in tourist posters, is a flat-chested, trousered youth, and likely to remain so.

The main problem with doing archaeology in Tuva is that it's just too pleasant. In broad valleys, 1,000 metres above sea level, the flesh on buried bodies, plant remains, materials and leather all rot away in an eye-blink, geologically speaking, leaving only things made of metals and other minerals. But travel 400 kilometres south-west, climb another 1,000 metres into the Altai Mountains and that problem goes away, because here, in the right conditions, tombs are deep-frozen, with far-reaching consequences for graves, bodies and archaeologists.

Geopolitically, this is an intriguing region. Mongolia, China, Russia and Kazakhstan very nearly meet, except for 40 kilometres of hideously inaccessible peaks dividing Russia from China. Two thousand five hundred years ago, the local Scythians had no frontiers except their own valleys. Protected by gorges and dense pine forests, they had no need to move as often as their Tuvan neighbours. They lived in tents and log cabins. Wagons were useless. They used only horses for transport, trapping, hunting and raiding. They lived, fought, died and were buried in ancestral cemeteries, where their bodies and possessions remained deep-frozen until discovered by modern archaeologists.

Where Russian colonists came in the late nineteenth century, scientists followed. First off the mark was a German-born Russian, who called himself both Wilhelm Radloff and Vasily Radlov, depending on which language he was working in. He opened the first of the frozen graves, melting the ice-bound soil by lighting fires on top of it. His most notable successor, Sergei Rudenko, arriving in 1924, came upstream from a long finger-lake, Lake Teletskoye, turned left along the Great Ulagan River and found himself in a dry valley called Pazyryk by locals. A long-gone glacier had carved it into a U-shape, which many generations of Scythians had turned into a cemetery. There were fourteen mounds, with five big ones, all deep-frozen log chambers, which presented a mystery. The surrounding soil was not permanently frozen, not permafrost. So how come the tombs had been flooded and frozen?

Rudenko, using boiling water to turn the ice to slush, found the answer when he excavated the tombs in 1947–9.[18] The stone cairns themselves made the right conditions by creating an underground microclimate. In summer, water filtered in; the stones above prevented evaporation. In winter, the water froze; the stones, colder than the surrounding earth, acted as a refrigeration unit making the ice permanent. Gradually, ice spread downwards, an effect that weakened towards the warmer edges of the circular mound. Eventually, the frozen soil formed a lens shape 4 or 5 metres deep, holding the grave and its body in an icy grip. Once through the shell of ice, the tombs could be excavated at leisure.

It took days of labour to break through the ice. Had the robbers moved in before the ice formed? Apparently not. Some bodies had been moved, some had decayed, some had been mutilated to get their gold, some hadn't. Another mystery, another solution by Rudenko:

[18] His classic book, *Frozen Tombs of Siberia*, appeared in Russian in 1953 and in English in 1970.

It is obvious that the plundering took place quite openly, proceeding at leisure, executed by small groups of perhaps two or three individuals. Clear traces of robbing, like great open pits and piles of upcast, cannot be concealed, so this could not have taken place if relatives of the deceased were close by. The plundering could only have been undertaken by newcomers when the tribe responsible for making the Pazyryk barrows had for one reason or another left the area.

The robbers had time enough on their hands. The Pazyryk mounds date from the fifth to early third centuries BC, with the most recent research placing the five main ones in a sixty-year period *c*.300–240 BC.

Here was evidence that Herodotus had been right – some of the bodies had shaved heads, and one showed clear evidence of having been scalped: 'The skin above the forehead had been cut through from ear to ear through a forelock of hair and then torn off backwards, baring the skull as far as the neck'. Herodotus said this was only done to enemies, but he also said that at least one group, the Massagetae, killed and ate their old people, so perhaps scalping was also done to their own. The men wore leather caps with earflaps, the women had headdresses up to 90 centimetres high, even higher than the golden person of Issyk.

The bodies had been embalmed, again recalling Herodotus's words about the belly being slit open and filled with herbs. Rudenko describes numerous slits on the stomach, limbs and buttocks to remove entrails and muscles, all being sewn up with sinew (for the men) and black horsehair (for the women). 'In order to preserve the natural shape at the neck and breast of the woman, horse-hair padding had been inserted.' Heads had been opened by cutting out a plate of bone with a mallet and chisel, brains removed, the cavity filled with soil, pine needles and larch cones, and 'the plate of bone put back in its former place and the skin secured with a cord of twisted black horsehair.'

Of the many remaining artefacts – horse fittings, leather cut-outs, wall hangings, carpets, saddle-blankets – the most surprising is a beautifully made carriage, which when reconstructed has four wheels, each 1.6 metres across, with thirty-four delicate spokes. It was designed for four horses, which had been buried nearby, all with animal masks, as if in the afterlife they could transform themselves into deer, ibex or griffins. In these steep-sided valleys, the carriage was entirely useless, and obviously not Scythian. One explanation, supported by a find of silk in the same grave, is that it had brought a bride from China and been buried along with her to carry her into the next world. Later, after unification by the First Emperor in 221 BC, China had a policy of sending off princesses as wives for 'barbarian' chiefs as a way of ensuring peace and spreading the benefits of Chinese civilization, but if true this would be the first evidence of the practice.

Another surprise was that some of the people buried here had been tattooed. One man, known as the tattooed chieftain, had animals and bits of animals – legs, tails and bodies of horses, birds, snakes, rams, deer, some sort of winged monster – writhing along both his arms, while a fish lay the length of his shin, flanked by four mountain rams. A lion or griffin with a huge curly tail stood by itself over his heart. These gorgeous designs were probably of soot, pricked into the skin with a needle. They had been done, Rudenko recorded, when the man was young and fit. When he died, he was old and had put on weight: 'We are dealing with a stout man, with strongly developed subcutaneous fat tissue.'

Beside him lay a woman in her forties. As infrared analysis revealed in 2003, she too had been tattooed, with a twisted stag on one shoulder and a contorted mountain sheep on the other. In another mound (No. 5), a woman aged fifty and a man of fifty-five also had tattoos. The woman's arms and hands were covered with them, intricate, well-planned designs of two tigers and a polka-dotted snow leopard attacking two deer with vast sets of antlers.

All of which provides a context for the most dramatic of Pazyryk finds, one that takes the discussion of Amazons in a wholly new direction. It turns out that warrior women, even warrior princesses, are only half the story. The subject we should be following is not one of weapons, but of tattoos.

5

THE ICE MAIDEN

SO COME 200 KILOMETRES TO THE SOUTH, TO THE HIGHER, drier and harsher Ukok Plateau, almost on the Chinese border. Now we've climbed another 500 metres, on to low waves of grass, meandering streams and scattered lakes. Sharp, snowy mountains enclose the horizon in every direction. There's not a tree in sight. It's a beautiful place, but cloud and wind and occasional blistering heat often make it miserable. In winter the conditions are brutal. This is about as far from civilization as you can get today. But 2,500 years ago, it was a popular place for semi-nomadic Scythians of the Pazyryk culture. The pasture was wonderful in summer, and good in winter as well, because the small amounts of snow were blown clear by the bitter winds.

Here in 1990 the Russian archaeologist Natalia Polosmak, from the Institute of Archaeology and Ethnography in Novosibirsk, started researching the mounds on the plateau. Administratively and politically, these were interesting times. The Soviet Union was on its way down, local nationalism on the way up, in the form of what would, three years later, become the Altai Republic, an autonomous but highly sensitive member of the new Russia (as is its neighbour, Tuva). Altai's autonomy and sensitivity are significant in what follows.

The first season was brilliantly successful. From a frozen kurgan came two bodies, a man of forty and a girl of sixteen, both warriors, with battleaxes, knives and bows. The girl was tall, strong, well-built, perhaps the man's weapon-carrier, perhaps already an Amazon in her own right. Two more seasons produced nothing so impressive. Then, in May 1993, after a late spring, their truck dumped Polosmak and her team by a mound right next to the barbed-wire fence that marked Russia's edge. Beyond were 8 kilometres of no-man's-land, then the Chinese border. It still froze overnight, but spring sunshine freed the lakes and dotted the grass with snowdrops and edelweiss. Asters, cyclamen, daisies and wild garlic would follow as summer came.

Working with a team of six, it took two weeks to remove the cap of rock and earth. A dip in the top showed it had been looted – but the looters had been content with a man's grave near the surface, a later burial. The original grave lay deeper, its larchwood lid frozen, untouched, unrobbed. Inside was a block of ice. The team hauled buckets of water from a nearby lake, heated them and poured the steaming water on the ice, slowly melting it, as Rudenko had done in Pazyryk almost fifty years before. Gradually bits and pieces appeared on the meltwater – harnesses, parts of saddles, a table on which had been placed a meal of fatty mutton, frozen after it had started to rot, which now, after 2,000 years, gave off a foul odour in the spring sunshine. Six horses emerged, with the hole of the executioner's pick clear in their foreheads. They still had their last meal in their stomachs: their deaths and burial had been in spring.

At last, the retreating ice fell away from a curved larch-wood casket, but opening it would be a special occasion, to be done in the presence of the institute's director, as well as reporters and cameramen from *National Geographic* and a Belgian TV company.

The next day came the opening. After four 15-centimetre bronze nails had been levered out, the lid came up, revealing nothing but more solid, opaque ice. That was good. Whatever was inside was untouched. Melting the ice took many days. It was July, and hot. Every morning, team members poured on buckets of hot water, filled the same buckets with meltwater and carted it away. Mosquitoes pestered. The six dead horses stank. Polosmak's impatience grew. What was in there – a skeleton, a corpse, a mummy?

Monday, 19 July: a jawbone appeared through the ice, then some sable fur. Polosmak peeled back the fur, to see not bone, but flesh, a shoulder and the 'brilliant blue tattoo of a magnificent griffin-like creature'. The body, slowly emerging from the ice, was a mummy, in excellent condition, with much of the skin intact, the brain removed, the muscles scraped away, the rest embalmed with a mix of herbs, grasses and wool. The next day revealed a headdress, one third the length of the coffin. Only then did Polosmak realize this was a woman, the one who would soon be called the Ice Maiden, or the Ukok Princess. Polosmak referred to her simply as Devochka, the Girl.[19]

The sable fur came away in bits, revealing a robe:

It was long and flowing, with a woollen skirt of horizontal white and maroon stripes and a yellow top of silk, perhaps from China . . . In the crook of the Lady's knee was a red cloth case containing a small hand mirror of polished metal with a deer carved into its wooden back. Beads wound round her wrist and more tattoos decorated her wrist and thumb. She was tall, about 5 foot 6 inches. She had doubtless been a good rider, and the horses in the grave were her own. As we worked, the fabric gradually revived around her limbs, softening the outline of her legs, the swell of her hips. And somehow in that moment, the remains became a person. She lay sideways, like a sleeping child, with her long, strong, aristocratic hands crossed in front of her.

The flurry of media interest worked miracles. Suddenly the Ice Maiden became the cause of, and focus for, nationalist fervour. Ukok was declared a protected territory by the Altai government. In 1998 it was included in the UNESCO World Heritage List. Having been flown to Novosibirsk for further

[19] Some of the details in this account come from the *National Geographic* article published soon after the discovery. It is credited to Polosmak herself. But she speaks little English, and it is clearly by *National Geographic* staff. English for a popular readership, especially in American magazines, is often sentimentalized. In the article, Polosmak's down-to-earth Devochka, the Girl, turns into something reverential, 'the Lady'.

An Enduring Legend

Right: Battling Amazons on a 4th-century BC Greek vase. The rider has reins, but no saddle or stirrups.

Below: On a 5th-century BC Greek vase, a warrior fights an Amazon.

Right: An Amazon riding bareback reaches for an arrow to shoot backwards in a 'Parthian shot', named after the people recorded in Iran in the 6th century BC, when this Etruscan bronze was made.

Below: A thousand years later than the Greek images, this 5th- or 6th-century mosaic from Urfa (ancient Edessa), Turkey, shows the Amazon queen Penthesilea drawing her bow with a thumb-ring hidden by her hand.

The 5th-century BC Temple of Apollo at Bassae, before it was enclosed for restoration in 2001.

Below: In the Bassae Frieze, a Greek warrior falls at the feet of an Amazon.

Below: On two Roman coffins, Greeks battle Amazons. The Greek legends had migrated, and survived over 700 years as fashionable themes to decorate the sarcophagi of the Roman rich. In the first, from the 2nd century AD, the Greek hero Achilles drags the Amazon queen Penthesilea from her horse. The second is from the 3rd century.

Top: A Pazyryk tomb in the Altai Republic, Russia, near the Mongolian border.

Above: Russian and German archaeologists open the giant Scythian burial mound Arzhan 2 in Tuva.

Above right: Working on the remains of a horse-burial in Arzhan 2.

Right: A portrait of the so-called 'royal couple' of Arzhan 2, complete with gold-decorated headdresses, capes, jerkins, daggers and boots. Note the woman's peaked hat, one version of a feature common to many Central Asian peoples.

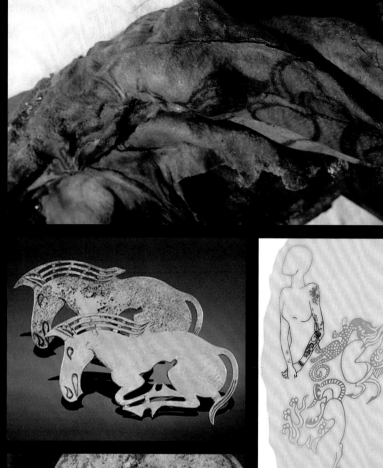

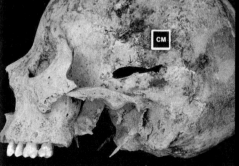

Top: Tattoos on the skin of the
Ice Maiden or Ukok Princess of
Altai.

Above right: A drawing shows
the position of the tattoos and
some of their Animal-style
motifs.

Above left: Gold-plated horses
found on a woman's headdress in
Arzhan 2.

Left: In a woman's skull found in
Aymyrlyg, a sword wound shows
the violent cause of death.

Golden Grave Goods for Scythian Royals: a Selection from Ukrainian Kurgans, 7th–4th centuries BC

Right: A comb topped by fighting Scythians.

Below right: A stag in which the antlers have been turned into a design feature running along its spine, while other animals decorate its flanks.

Bottom: Saddle decorations in the form of rams' heads.

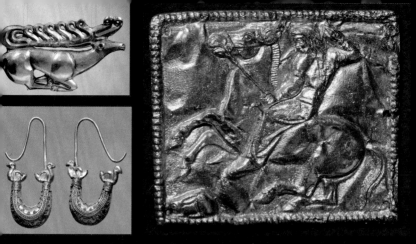

Above: A stag with distorted antlers; earrings; and a plaque showing a hunter pursuing a hare.

Below: A sword and scabbard decorated with a wolf's head and intertwined beasts.

Below: A plaque made with repeated imprints of the stag motif, similar to the one top left. Perhaps it had significance for religious rituals or as an identity marker.

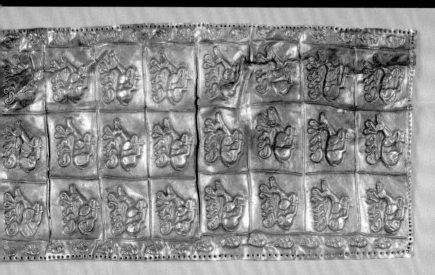

The Golden Man – or a Golden Woman?

Though seen so widely in Kazakhstan that this is virtually a symbol of the country, the Golden Man is so slight of build that he may in fact have been a woman. Towering headdresses were worn by aristocratic women across much of Central Asia.

investigation and preservation, the Ice Maiden became known worldwide. She was taken to Japan and Korea, returning to Novosibirsk. Altaians took note, and objected. Theirs was a new republic. They had a history, which needed respect. The Ice Maiden was the perfect symbol. As Rimma Erkinova, director of the Altaian Museum in the capital, Gorno Altaisk, put it: 'In the perception of the local population, the Ukok Princess embodies the image of the earliest ancestress and ancient protector of Altaian people.' She should never have been dug up. In Altai, where shamans still have influence, the dead should not be disturbed, otherwise they could try to capture the souls of the living people. 'The crudeness of her handling,' Erkinova went on, as if Polosmak had been some sort of torturer, 'and especially her forced separation from her birth land is even today perceived with sharp pain'.

What rubbish, came the reply from Reason and Science, in the form of Russian academics in Novosibirsk. There was no genetic relationship between the Ice Maiden and modern Altaians. Her people, the Scythians, of whatever clan, had moved westwards 2,000 years ago. They were no more ancestors of today's Altaians than the Manhattan Indians were ancestors of today's New Yorkers.

Altaians would have none of it. Of course she was Altaian. She was born on Altai's holy soil. Genetics and history had nothing to do with it.

In September 2003, Altai was shaken by a series of earthquakes. Locals sprang to the obvious conclusion: Altai, their homeland, was angry. There were pleas, petitions, letters from ordinary people blaming the earthquakes on the removal of the Ice Maiden ten years previously, and demanding her return. In February 2004 Auelkhan Dzhatkambaev, head of the most affected region, and eager for votes, wrote an open letter to Altai's government. Without the Ice Maiden,

> our land cannot find peace. The quakes have been getting stronger again. My fellow people think that the reason for this is the archaeological excavations carried out on the Ukok Plateau, in a place sacred to Turkic people, and above all the removal of the bodies of the princess and the prince [that would be the later burial, on top of the Ice Maiden] . . . Further retaining of the princess and the prince and, even more so, earning money through displaying their naked bodies is contrary to human values. This is not a superstition, neither is this whim – this is wisdom, which has arisen from the depth of the centuries.

Novosibirsk put forward the scientific case many times to no great effect, and finally, in August 2012, when the Gorno Altaisk museum had been given the proper facilities, they sent the Ice Maiden back to her homeland, where she now rests in air-conditioned peace.

She is likely to remain alone. Ukok has been declared out of bounds to archaeologists, despite the near-certainty of more treasures like the Ice Maiden lying in the permafrost, and despite the protests of scientists that this would deprive the world of vital knowledge.

Still, much work was done, and much more about the Girl has come to light.

She was a woman of mystery. Aged about twenty-five, she was buried alone, when most other women were buried with men. Why? Obviously because she was special. Why? Was she a priestess, goddess come to earth, a symbol of her people? How, or why, did she die? There's no clue. One thing is certain: she was no warrior. There were no weapons buried with her. Her role is all wrapped up in her flowing robe and her tattoos, and one other surprise which we'll get to later.

First, her tattoos. The 'griffin-like creature' Polosmak had seen when she first peeled back the Girl's clothing on the left shoulder was a distorted mythological animal: a deer, its rear twisted in the Scythian Animal style, with a griffin's beak and antlers sprouting either griffins' heads or flowers, a shape repeated on the animal's back. Further down her arm is a snow leopard with an extended tail and a head, if it is a head, attacking or consuming a sheep's body with legs at both ends.

The tattoos are as weird, puzzling and beautiful as several other ethnographic enigmas: the vast lines that mark the Nazca Desert, the graceful chalk trenches of the Uffington White Horse in Oxfordshire. Is this somehow a conflict between two worlds: predator and prey, linked by nature? Or just a way of stating identity and ancestry? Whatever it means, it is tattooing as an art form, which must have been refined over centuries. The images speak, in a language we cannot understand.

Polosmak speculates: 'Tattoos were used as a means of personal identification – like a passport now, if you like. The Pazyryks also believed the tattoos would be helpful in another life, making it easy for the people of the same family and culture to find each other after death.' The tattoos were used, she guesses, 'to define one's position both in society, and in the world. The more tattoos were on the body, the longer it meant the person lived, and the higher was his position' – which perhaps explains why Rudenko's aging chief was so well tattooed. 'Our young woman – the princess – has only her two arms tattooed. So they signified both age and status.'

Her looks were important to her. The bag next to her left hip held more than a mirror; it was a cosmetics bag, with a face brush made from horse hair, and a fragment of an 'eyeliner pencil' made of vivianite, a form of iron phosphate which adds a deep blue-green colour to skin. There was some vivianite powder as well, apparently to be applied to the face.

The clothing turned out to be more elaborate than it seemed. Her skirt was made of three horizontal strips, each one separately hand-coloured. The top one was crimson, the middle very slightly pinkish-yellowish, and the third of a very rich red-wine colour. The skirt had a woollen braided belt, which could change the length of the skirt by holding it either around the waist, or higher, under the breasts. There was a long, almost knee length, light shirt worn over the skirt, with a round neck, decorated with red lace and braid. The shirt is of silk, similar in style to those found in oasis burials in what is now the Chinese province of Xinjiang, though the silk itself comes from further afield, possibly Assam.

'The Pazyryk costume was made from textile which is quite unexpected for mountain people,' says Polosmak. This type of fabric was inconvenient, wore out quickly and needed to be darned often. These people put up with the inconvenience for the sake of fashion and status, because it was imported. From where? The dyes suggest answers. The crimson came from a little scaly insect that looks like a miniature armadillo, the *Kermes vermilio*, which lives only on the sap of a type of oak that grows around the Mediterranean. Another red colourant was rose madder, made with alizarin, which comes from the root of *Rubia tinctorum*, a little yellow-flowered shrub native to Europe. Recalling the silk and bronze mirrors from China, Polosmak points out that her Girl, the Ukok Princess, was an early bridge between the great, distant cultures of the ancient world.

The final surprise, which emerged only when the Ice Maiden was examined close up in Polosmak's Novosibirsk laboratory, was that her head had been completely shaved. She was bald. Her hair was not *her* hair – it was a wig, made with two layers of female hair woven under felt, with a wooden deer covered with gold foil pinned to the front. From the top of the wig rose a spike of felt, 68.5 centimetres long, with a sliver of wood as a core to keep it up. On it were fifteen birds made of leather, each smaller than the last. The device was familiar to archaeologists from Animal-style art in other Scythian graves. It was what they call the Tree of Life, the shamanic symbol of health and status, which was also present on the Golden Man/Girl of Issyk.

With every bit of new research, the Ice Maiden looks more and more like a priestess, pure and simple, with none of the Amazonian warrior about her, other than her power. We can't guess her true status, but she is the closest yet to an Amazonian queen in her own right. From all the work that went into her burial, her death must have been a tragedy for her community, a tear in the fabric of their lives, the loss of the person who embodied life itself.

By the time of the Ice Maiden's burial at one end of their world, Scythians were already pressing further westwards at the other. In 612 BC they assaulted the Assyrian empire and raided Persia. Jeremiah, the Old Testament prophet, feared the worst: 'Behold a people shall come from the north . . . they shall hold the bow and the lance; they are cruel, and will not show mercy: their voice shall roar like the sea, and they shall ride upon horses' (Jeremiah 50, 41–2). They were on the move because they were themselves under pressure from their easterly neighbours, the harder-fighting Sarmatians, an even likelier source of the original Amazons.

Discoveries keep coming. Thirteen years after the emergence of the Ice Maiden, 100 kilometres to the south-east, an eight-person team of Spanish, French and Mongolian archaeologists excavated another set of Pazyryk tombs. The two sites were part of the same world 2,500 years ago. Riders routinely roamed between them. Today they are in different worlds, Russian and Mongolian. There are no roads, and the only tracks lead in different directions, one north into Altai and Siberia, the other east, over a 112-kilometre tangle of hills, pastures, rivers and lakes to Bayan-Ölgii, the local capital, itself several hours by plane from Ulaanbaatar. The site – the first of a Scythian burial in Mongolia – is by a small river, the Little Turgen, which gives the place its name, the Little Turgen River, *Baga Turgen Gol* in Mongolian: BTG to archaeologists.

It is important for archaeology because BTG is part of a much larger burial area, as the Spanish archaeologist Xavier Jordana and the team discovered in the summer of 2007. It was a tough assignment, driving in for half a day in a truck and one of the high-riding, go-anywhere Ukrainian UAZ 4 x 4s that are the workhorses of the Mongolian countryside. They pitched their tents and a yurt (*ger* in Mongolian) beside a cemetery: fourteen burial mounds, rock circles, roughly carved little statues and slabs of stone standing like broken teeth. The bitter-cold Turgen would be spring, loo and bath. Round them, scattered firs gave way to hills of scrubby grass or grey scree, still patched with snow. These were circumstances in which you would hope not to get ill. But they were not alone: local Kazakhs, with weather-burnished faces and round caps, rode by to share kumiss and boiled mutton, and watch.

From BTG and three other burial sites Jordana and the rest retrieved the remains of nineteen skeletons – sixteen adults and three children. An analysis of their DNA revealed a surprise. This tangle of mountains, the Altai, had for centuries acted as a natural border between the two sets of people, Scythians in the west and Turco-Mongolians in the east. Then, roughly around the fifth century BC, that changed. These people no longer shared the same ancestry: they were a mixture of east and west, with the easterners steadily supplanting the westerners by the second century BC.

But we should focus on the BTG site itself. After two months, rocks had been stripped, revealing four tombs and thirteen skeletons: two children and eleven adults, of which two were women – Amazons in all but name, given that they were good with horses and bows – seven were men and the other two indeterminate. One horse per adult, a few small bits of gold, arrowheads, battleaxes, daggers.

Something extremely nasty happened here. The team's paper in the *Journal of Archaeological Science* records the clinical details:

a male, 35–45, pointed object entered skull tangentially, multiple short cut-marks consistent with scalping; male, 40–50, bone defect in the skull the shape of [the transverse section of the Scythian arrowhead]; female, 25–30, two V-shaped cut marks in the right rib-cage compatible with shape of Scythian dagger; child aged 8–9, 15mm oblique sharp-force puncture on left lateral anterior side of the first sacral vertebra; pelvic injuries on two other individuals suggestive of fatal hypervolemic shock, compatible with Scythian dagger. In all, much acute trauma: 12 injuries to 6 individuals most likely caused suddenly and with extreme violence . . . Randomly distributed injury pattern [which suggests] conflicts related to the defence of communal property or ambush or surprise attacks.

Perhaps these people died years apart, but the injuries, the 'sub-adults', a young woman – there's enough here to suggest a single incident. Perhaps a family or small clan brought their sheep and horses here, to good summer pastures. They are well able to look after themselves, even the woman and her nine-year-old boy. They don't expect trouble. They have relatives not far away. But they have enemies, envious perhaps of their animals; or perhaps the woman's teenage daughter had rejected the advances of some suitor. Horses emerge from the valley below. There's no time to mount. The whole group is caught in the open. An arrow takes out one, swords and war-axes strike heads, the boy is stabbed in the back, the teenage girl grabbed and tossed up behind her rejected suitor. In minutes, the attackers are off with the herds, leaving a scattering of bodies and weapons.

Days later, the rest of the clan find the dead. They gather the remains, dig a shallow grave, add a few precious possessions to the bodies, pile earth over them and seal the tombs with a dome of loose rocks where, 2,500 years later, Xavier and his team dig them up and reveal their story.

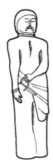

6

SARMATIANS: THE ROOTS OF THE LEGEND

TO FIND THE AMAZONS DESCRIBED BY HERODOTUS WE must look beyond the Scythians. His Scythian informant said they had mated with Scythians to form a new tribe, the Sauromatians. He had a name for them in Scythian: Oeoropata, which he said was Scythian for 'man-killers'. Perhaps: there is no way to check, since no Scythian language was recorded.

Anyway, the Scythians had reason to fear the Sauromatians, because they were a new threat from the east. There is a little confusion about their name. Later, in the first century AD, writers referred to Sarmatians. Once, Russian archaeologists argued about whether they were different from Sauromatians or not. Now, the consensus is that they were one and the same. Some classical writers suggested that 'Sauromatian' derived from *sauros*, meaning lizard, as in 'dinosaur' ('thunder lizard'), because they wore scaly armour made of horn and hooves, but most scholars dismiss this as folk etymology. Today, archaeologists use both terms: Sauromatians for earlier times (sixth–fifth century BC), Sarmatians for later ones (up to the second century AD). It's easier to ignore the academic technicalities and just call them Sarmatians from now on.

Originally, around 700 BC, they were an insignificant group living east of the Caspian, in the sparse grasslands running across to the Amu Darya.[20] Now in Kazakhstan, it is a place of weird land-forms and semi-desert. Back then the conditions were kinder, but not kind enough to keep the Sarmatians in place. Two hundred years later, they were on the grasslands between the Don and the Volga, neighbours of the Scythians. The Amazons, being mythical, could not have mated with the Scythians, but the Sarmatians could have done so. They were not yet seen as dangerous – the opposite, as Herodotus describes in one of his usual colourful passages.

In the days when Darius was leading the expansion of the Persian empire into Scythia in the late sixth century BC, the Scythian king, Idanthyrsus, asked the Sarmatians and others to help fight the Persians. 'We beg you not to remain neutral in this struggle,' the envoys said. 'This invasion

[20] Disputed, but in his *History of Central Asia*, Vol. 1, Christoph Baumer has a picture of a statue wearing a Sarmatian-style *akinates* (sword-shield) on the Mangyshlak Peninsula, which juts into the Caspian.

is aimed at you just as much as at us, and, once we have gone under, the Persians will never be content to leave you unmolested.' The others refused, telling the Scythians it was their fault for being aggressive in the first place. But the Sarmatians, together with two other tribes, came on side.

Under the command of a Scythian called Scopasis, the Scythians and Sarmatians played cat and mouse with Darius, sending the herds of cattle and wagonloads of women and children away in advance, then retreating along the same route one day's march ahead of the advancing Persians, scorching the earth as they went, drawing the Persian army ever deeper into barren territory. The allies crossed the Don – the Scythians' eastern border – the Persians followed, on through Sarmatian territory, turning north-east across the vast Eurasian steppes, into the forested territory of the Budini, finally coming to the Volga. Darius, apparently anticipating contact at last, started to build eight large forts. At this point the Scythians and Sarmatians galloped off into the void, circling back towards their own lands, hotly pursued by the Persians.

All this had taken many weeks. It was too much for Darius. He sent a message to Idanthyrsus: 'Why on earth, strange man, do you keep on running away? . . . You should rather send earth and water to your master, as the sign of your submission, and come to a conference.'

'Persian,' replied the Scythian king:

I have never yet run from any man . . . There is for me nothing unusual in what I have been doing: it is precisely the sort of life I always lead, even in times of peace. If you want to know why I will not fight, I will tell you: in our country there are no towns or cultivated land; fear of losing which, or seeing it ravaged, might indeed provoke us to hasty battle . . . And your claim to be my master is easily answered – be damned to you!

Now the Scythians and Sarmatians turned to guerrilla tactics, harrying the Persian flanks, luring them into traps with small herds of cattle. The final straw came as the two armies seemed about to engage, when a hare ran between them. Scythian horsemen were after it in a trice, obviously unimpressed by the Persian army. Darius was astonished and dismayed. 'These fellows have a hearty contempt for us,' he said. 'It is time to think of the best way of getting out of this country.' Which he did, escaping with his army intact, but no victory.

By then the Sarmatians had diversified into a loose federation of two dozen tribes, much as the Scythians had done. The Greeks knew about them at second hand. We know about them from the evidence they left behind.

Jeannine Davis-Kimball knows a lot about that evidence. From 1992 to 1996, just after the collapse of the Soviet Union, she was co-leader of a fifteen-person team excavating Sarmatian kurgans outside the dusty, one-unpaved-street village of Pokrovka, three days and 1,000 bone-crunching kilometres from Moscow, right on the Kazakhstan border. Her colleague was Leonid Yablonsky, an eminent archaeologist from the Russian Academy of Sciences. Her account of the work is a vivid portrait of the appalling heat, dust, rain, unrelenting labour and finicky expertise that went into the discovery of 'a cache of bones and artifacts that would help change established notions of a woman's place in ancient nomadic societies.' These, the *Warrior Women* of her book's title, would have been recognized by the Ancient Greeks as Amazons, if they had met them. In fact, there is a remote possibility, though no shred of evidence, that they could have done, because Pokrovka is only some 300 kilometres north of the furthest point reached by Alexander the Great in the 320s BC and so within reach of the Greek colony he left behind, which lasted another two centuries.

There were hints from Russian archaeologists that Sarmatian society was rather more complex than the traditional view of pastoral nomads as nothing more than brutal raiders, and that the women had played significant roles. The discoveries gave Davis-Kimball and Yablonsky, with their mix of American and Russian volunteers, a chance to find out the truth. Yablonsky, thick-set with a dense salt-and-pepper beard, was just the man for Davis-Kimball to have as a colleague – he had spent years digging, dusting, lifting and cataloguing in remote areas and harsh conditions.

Over four years of the excavations, Pokrovka's mounds – all sandy soil, much eroded and ploughed over – were opened by a mechanical scraper. Then volunteers dug out the pits to reveal skeletons, which were carefully cleaned with scoops, knives and brushes. This was not a valley where permafrost protected the flesh, but bones last well in the alkaline soil. They were well-built people, the men averaging almost 178 centimetres (5 foot 10 inches) and the women 165 centimetres (5 foot 6 inches).

The soil had no effect on the gold, and very little on the silver and bronze items. Earrings made of bronze wire covered with gold foil were almost as new. Iron arrowheads, daggers, swords and armour plates were badly corroded, but other precious items had survived well: fossilized seashells, jewels, coral, amber, all symbols of status. Stone and clay dishes – Davis-Kimball calls them altars – could have been used by priestesses to grind coloured ores to make body paint, as useful in the next life as the weapons, clothing and jewellery. Other finds included 300 small gold discs, a belt covered with gold foil and Animal-style plaques.

In all this women were as important as men – perhaps more important: 72 per cent of the high-status central pit burials were of women. The men were almost all warriors, as their arrowheads, swords and daggers showed, but the women had a wider range of items, domestic, artistic and cosmetic, as well as military. The men, it seems, were the specialists; the women multitasking generalists.

They loved beads, tiny seed-like discs with a hole in them, which were sewn on to fabrics. Though the clothes had long since vanished, the beads remained, evidence that their world reached out far and wide. The beads were not home-made. They were of glass, carnelian and turquoise, from China or Iran or even further west: amber beads, made from fossilized tree sap, came from the Baltic. Bead-makers at both ends of Eurasia were specialists who ground little cylinders of rock or glass, sliced them into discs and drilled holes in them with minute bronze drills.

Some had spindle whorls, small stones with holes in them which are threaded on to strands of wool. (Once set spinning, it regulates how threads twist to make yarn. Almost all cultures that spun materials into yarn invented spindle whorls independently.) Clearly, spindle whorls represented the female skills of spinning and weaving, which were vital for making clothes that in winter keep everyone alive. At –40°, bare flesh gets frostbitten in minutes. The women, in their own way, had as much power over life and death as the men.

Oddly, some of the women had 'pseudo spindle whorls' made of chalk, which means they were too delicate actually to use. They are a puzzle. Here's a possible solution: they recall the stone armour made for the spirit warriors of the First Emperor's Terracotta Army near Xian – too heavy and too delicate to be used, but useful in the spirit world as symbolic protection.[21] Perhaps a pseudo spindle whorl was a symbol of spiritual power, the equivalent of a Communion cup in the hands of a Christian priest.

One oppressively hot July day in 1994, Davis-Kimball was watching a Russian colleague cleaning a skeleton. It lay in a catacomb, beneath a roof less than a metre high. It was small and there was something green on the chest, with an iron dagger by the right leg, and clusters of green, indicating bronze arrowheads, by the left leg. 'Looks like this might be a female skeleton,' she said to an American colleague. After more cleaning, Yablonsky lifted the skull and took a close look at the pelvis. 'It's a young female,' he said. 'Probably between thirteen and fourteen years old.'

A girl of consequence, as it turned out. Round her neck

---

[21] A note on the stone armour, 100,000 limestone flakes, in dozens of suits. In a fight, it would be as much use as porcelain. So what was it for? The First Emperor wanted the best for his spirit army. After their battles in the spirit world, they would need replacement armour. Leather wouldn't last. Limestone would be eternal. The quarrying, transporting and carving of limestone armour must have spread the idea that stone could provide protection in the next world. (See my *Terracotta Army*, Chapter 13.)

was an amulet, the cause of the green colour, from a single bronze arrowhead. Another forty lay nearby, along with a quiver. At her feet lay another amulet, a massive boar's tusk, which had probably hung from her waist as a symbol of her skill as a hunter. Nearby were two oyster shells and a pink cup-like stone that had some sort of dried paste in it, possibly paint for her body or clothing. If so, the shells, stone and paste could have been part of some religious ritual in this life and the next. It seemed she was both a warrior and a priestess, or at least in training to be both when she died, around 300 BC.

Other female skeletons had similar objects near them. Of forty graves with weapons, seven belonged to women, with quivers, bronze arrowheads, daggers and swords. One had a metre-long sword. A few were buried with legs bent, as if they were riding a horse into the afterlife. They were almost all young, suggesting they trained and fought as warriors as teenagers, but then were taken off military duties when they married and bore children. Though the wooden arrows and bows had long vanished, the arrowheads seemed proof that these girls had become expert in mounted archery, at which they would have been a match for their men. (More on that in the next chapter.) Normally, men, being stronger, were the swordsmen, but perhaps the girl with the sword had shown rare ability and strength. All would have been useful in pro-tecting flocks and families from wolves and human predators. There was no telling how these teenagers had died: their skulls and limbs were unbroken by blows from swords or clubs.

From the evidence, it seems that Sarmatian religion, like that of the Saka and other Scythian-style cultures, involved the worship of several gods, ancestors and nature. Perhaps they, like the Scythians, honoured the female deity Tabiti as their top god, reflecting the significance of women in Sarmatian society. In any event, it was mostly women who played the main religious roles. Ancient Greeks would have called them Amazonian priestesses. Seven per cent of the Pokrovka women were priestesses, buried with altars, fossilized seashells, bone spoons, Animal-style amulets and mirrors. Several of the bodies were middle-aged and elderly. Theirs was a job for life, not just until they got married. It was they who scorched the shoulder bones of sheep until they cracked and then read meaning into the patterns, advising on war, alliances and new pastures. It was they who performed sacrifices and offered gifts of meat, curd and kumiss on their little altars.

What happened to the Sarmatians? They migrated, they evolved, they integrated. Their migration, like that of the Turks later, took centuries. By about 300 BC they were dominating southern Russia, making life hard for the Scythians. Locally, in Tuva, they gave way to the Xiongnu (second century BC– second century AD), whom the Mongolians and Chinese refer to as Hunnu.

In one transformation in their move westward, the Sarmatians became Alans. A wide-ranging sub-federation, they were known as As to the Persians. (It is from their name, by the way, that 'Aryan' is derived, *l* shifting to *r* in some Iranian languages; thus the tribe so admired by Hitler turns out not to be Germanic at all.) Roman authors mention them in the first century AD. Martial, a sharp-tongued master of epigrams, skewered a certain Caelia and her promiscuous sexual habits by asking plaintively how a Roman girl could give herself to almost anyone, including 'the circumcised members of the Jewish race' and 'the Alan with his Sarmatian mount', yet cannot 'find pleasure in members of the Roman race' – like himself.

The Alans raided south into north-eastern Turkey, where the Greek historian and general Arrian fought them in the second century, noting the Alan cavalry's favourite tactic of the feigned retreat (all nomads, from Scythians to Mongols over 2,000 years, did that, almost always to good effect). He made them generous offers and many joined his cavalry. Many didn't, remaining to nibble at the flanks of the Roman empire. They appear as conquered subjects on the column erected by the Emperor Trajan in AD 113, and a later emperor, Marcus Aurelius, termed himself Sarmaticus after defeating them again. They were forced to provide him with 8,000 troops, 5,500 of whom were posted to Britain, so that descendants of a tribe whose roots were in Mongolian lands ended up keeping watch on Hadrian's Wall.

The Alans would eventually form fragments of the explosion of peoples, which usually goes by its German name, the *Völkerwanderung*, the Migration of the Tribes, that undid the Roman empire. They had a talent for retaining their own identity. In the slurry of wandering peoples, the Alans were like grit, widely mixed, never absorbed, always abrasive. Their remnants in the Caucasus would transmute into the Ossetians of southern Russia and Georgia: the first two syllables of this name recall their Persian appellation, *As-*, with a Mongol-style plural *-ut* (so the current name of the little Russian enclave known as North Ossetia–Alania doubly emphasizes their roots).

At the other end of the empire, they became universal

mercenaries, joining the Romans, the Goths on their march into Spain – some derive the name Catalonia from a combination of Goth and Alan – and the Vandals, who swept them up on their flight to North Africa in about 420, and the Huns. So the Sarmatians, aka the Alans, whose women would have been seen as Amazons by the Ancient Greeks and who had started off in the depths of Central Asia, helped to defend and attack the Roman empire, eventually dissipating in the kaleidoscopic mix of tribes that would, in centuries to come, form Europe's nation-states.

7

THE RETURN OF THE MOUNTED ARCHER

SINCE BOWS HAVE BEEN FOUND IN THE GRAVES OF YOUNG Scythian women, they must have trained to use them as children, learning how to string and shoot them at the gallop, getting used to riding long distances, as Mongolian children do today (children are the jockeys in the annual *naadam* races, which are run over about 25 kilometres; using children, who are lighter than adults, allows the horses to run better).

The bow and arrow was the key to their performance as

warriors. Swords and lances are better used by men, because they demand as much muscle power as possible. But horse-back archery is all about skill. Of course, if you shot for distance in what is now called flight archery, male arms and shoulders were crucial. The little recurve bows, made of bone and wood, could pack a tremendous punch. The first written source in Mongolian is a stone recording a shot made by Genghis Khan's nephew Yisungge in 1225. His arrow carried 450 metres and hit some sort of unnamed target. But such a feat was not much use when shooting a wolf or closing on an enemy on a galloping horse. In those circumstances, the skill of the female archers matched that of the men, for 2,000 years.

But from the fourteenth century onwards, gunpowder blew the horse-archer from history. Within a very short time, the skills that had defined nomadic warriors from Manchuria to the Russian steppes had fallen from use and almost from memory. Mounted archers themselves left no manuals. No one after they vanished from Europe and Central Asia had a clue about how to slide arrows from quivers, load them and shoot them, time after time, while sitting on a galloping horse. No one tried it.[22]

Until now. Mounted archery is back, as a sport, bringing a new understanding of how these warriors gained their supremacy. In this sport, women are as good as men, as they were as warriors.

The revival is almost entirely due to one man: Lajos Kassai, who was, I suspected, the first true mounted archer in Europe

---

[22] Japanese mounted archery – *yabusame* – endured, but as a ritual; it was not used in warfare.

since the departure of the Mongols in 1242. The Mongols left from Hungary, so it is fitting that Kassai is a Hungarian.

I heard of Kassai because anyone who knows anything about mounted archery mentions him. I met him while researching the Huns, but it might just as well have been the Scythians, Sarmatians or Mongols.

I and my interpreter, Andrea Szegedi, found him in Budapest, about to perform at a fair on Margaret Island in the Danube. He was dressed in a simple wrap-around costume, nomad-style, with three assistants selling his own brands of bow. Could we have a word? A nod, that was all, not even a smile. In a refreshment tent, he fixed me with intense, steady blue eyes in a face blank of expression. It was unsettling, and became more so when I tried for some soundbite responses.

Where, for instance, did his interest in mounted archery come from?

'Something inside me,' he replied in halting English, nailing me with a fierce gaze. I rephrased the question. He switched his gaze to Andi and went on in Hungarian, just as abruptly. 'It was from the inside. I have to do it. That's all.'

'I understand interest from others is growing?'

'They come from everywhere, from the US, from Canada, to learn.'

'Why do people love it?'

'If I can't tell you why I do it, I can't tell you why they love it.'

He had no patience with me. I was an outsider, the questions were dumb, and he was fiercely concentrated, not on me, but on what he was about to do, on its brutal physical and emotional demands. It was, I guessed, like cornering Andy Murray just before a Wimbledon final and trying to get deep answers about the inner game of tennis. Besides, there was much more going on, which I was too busy with camera and tape-recorder to notice. Andi was a medical student: short-cropped hair, good on a horse, tall, lithe as a thoroughbred herself, and thoroughly professional, fortunately, because it was only later that she confessed the impression he made.

'Yes, he could look scary. But his mood changed in a second. He has this nice smile. Then he was really funny. He swore. Like something was "bitchily good", as we say. Then sometimes the way he looked . . .' She was driving us along a flat, straight road over the *puszta*, but her mind was not on grasslands. 'We have an expression, that when someone looks at you like that they can see your bones. That was how it felt. He could see my bones. He was looking into my eyes, and he was amazing.' She paused. 'He really was. Honestly.'

It took me another meeting on his home ground, more talk, and respectful observation to understand. Mounted archery is his life's work, which he explains in his book, *Horseback Archery*. But even that tells only half the story. The other half emerges in action, in teaching, in the commitment that others give him.

He is a man whose life perfectly matches what he feels is his destiny. Kassai, like a monk, heard the call, followed, and arrived at his goal. But, unlike a monk, he did not find the way and the goal through a teaching, or an organization, or a Master. He has all that, but they are all him. He invented the lot. It took him over twenty years.

Kassai grew up in a world of collective farmers and city-dwellers and factory-workers. As a child, he escaped the drabness of communism into his imagination, inspired by a novel about the Huns, *The Invisible Man*, by Géza Gárdonyi.

It is the story of a Thracian slave, Zeta, who travels to Attila's court and fights for him. It's a good, quick, vivid read for children, and never out of print since its publication in 1902. 'Yes, our ancestors the Huns were the greatest horseback archers of the world,' says Kassai. 'I imagined the wild gallops, the horses foaming at the mouth, the drawn bows. What a sensation! I wanted to be like them, a terrifying, fearless warrior.'

The first step was to become an archer. As a child and then as a young man, living near Kaposvár, 40 kilometres south of Lake Balaton, he made bows by the dozen, experimenting with wood and horn and tendons – tendons on the back of the bow resist stretching, horn on the belly resists compression – arrows for weight and rigidity, arrowheads for their penetration. He became a good shot. Muscles and sinews turned to iron. The three fingers of his right hand became raw from the bow string, then calloused (though he protects them with tape).

He still had not ridden. There was no one from whom he could learn to ride like a nomad. He had to teach himself. This he did in his twenties with the aid of a spirited creature called Prankish, who baptized him with fire, sweeping him off by galloping under low branches, dragging him by the stirrup and falling on him in mud.

One day, a wild gallop took him into a dead-end valley. Prankish stopped. In unexpected stillness, Kassai looked around. He suddenly felt as if he had found his place in the world, a place where 'accepting the sweet solitude of a voluntary exile, I could retreat from this noisy century and develop mounted archery to perfection.'

The valley – densely forested, its open spaces overgrown

with weeds, its lowest area a mess of mud and reeds – belonged to a state farm. He rented 15 hectares and set about adapting it for horseback archery. This was a long, slow process. A valley like that, where nature ruled, deserved respect. He studied the winds, the waters, the plants, the movements of animals and people, the smell of the pastures in the changing seasons, and the feel of each hilltop and every marshy area. It took him four years.

Then, at last, came the horseback archery. Everything about this ancient, forgotten skill had to be rediscovered from scratch. The landscape gave him a natural 90-metre course, along which he placed targets. He acquired a second horse, Bella, a poor sickly creature that he made sleek, gentle and sensitive with months of care. Bella learned to gallop evenly, without reins, then got used to the twang of the bow, the zip of the arrow and the feel of a rider indicating a turn or a change of pace with small movements of the legs and shifts of bodyweight.

His first target was a bale of hay, but even from 2 or 3 metres away he could fire only one arrow every pass, and hardly ever hit the mark. He found it almost impossible to perform the most famous action of the mounted archer, the over-the-shoulder 'Parthian shot', named after the Parthians and then distorted in English into the 'parting shot'. He practised for weeks, doing fifteen to twenty gallops a day. He made no progress at all. There seemed to be no way to overcome the combination of speed, bounce, the shock of hooves, and his flailing arms. The idea of reloading was a dream.

There was something he was not getting, something that every mounted archer from time immemorial must have learned in childhood. To get beyond the obscuring clouds of effort and frustration, he turned to Zen archery, which relies on internal harmony, on the 'relaxed concentration' by which an athlete produces a seemingly effortless record.

He returned to the basics: horse and rider. He abandoned his saddle to ride bareback, to feel the horse's muscle, sweat and breath. Pain became a way of life. He fell constantly. His urine had blood in it for weeks from the battering. He learned that pain and suffering are not the same. This was not suffering, because he had chosen this route as monks once chose hair shirts and flagellation, and in this painful service he found freedom.

And at last progress. He learned to separate upper from lower body, until, holding a glass of water, he could keep his hand steady while riding bareback at a trot. He acquired more horses and practised on them all. He practised in the worst conditions – rain, mud, snow, frozen ground. He turned himself into a Centaur, half horse, half man.

He perfected the technique of shooting one arrow after another, at speed. This is not something that an average unmounted archer ever does, so once again he started from scratch. An arrow has a nock in its end which slots on to the bow string, but, as I know from doing archery as a teenager, as any amateur knows, it takes many seconds and many actions to load an arrow: you lower the bow, turn it flat, reach for the quiver, extract an arrow, turn the arrow to the correct orientation with the 'lead feather' pointing away from the string, fiddle the slot on to the string, get the tips of three fingers hooked round the string, grip the arrow between first and second fingers to keep it in position against the bow, raise the bow, pull the string, refocus your attention on the distant target, aim and at last release. The whole thing takes perhaps half a minute, which is about the time it takes to read the foregoing instructions.

It took Kassai months of experimenting to work out how to shoot quickly. For a start, forget the quiver. That's only to store arrows; it is not for the arrows you are about to shoot, because it is hopelessly slow to reload by reaching down to your waist or over your shoulder to pull an arrow from your quiver.

This is how it's best done: hold a bunch of arrows in the left hand against the bow, making sure they are spread like an array of cards, with the feather ends accessible; reach between string and bow; grip an arrow with two fingers bent double so that they form firm supports either side; place the thumb just so; pull the arrow back so that the string slides along the thumb straight into the nock in the arrow; and pull, while raising the bow, all in one smooth set of actions.

After a year –

– *he could fire three arrows in six seconds.*

Say that out loud, three times, fast: that's how long it takes him to load and shoot the three arrows.

Now it was time to apply his new skills. He began loading and drawing at the gallop, aiming in all three directions consecutively, to the front, to the side, to the back. Then, at last, it became reality: a gallop past his bale, firing three arrows – failure after failure, as usual, until one day all three arrows ended up in the bale.

That was just the beginning. New discoveries lay ahead. Standing archers draw the bow to the cheekbone or chin, often kissing the string and sighting along the arrow. But for horseback archery it was hopeless. All that tension, with the bow drawn and the whole body wracked by motion – how could the rider choose the right moment to release?

The answer was first to draw the bow, not to the chin but back to the chest, to the heart, to the seat of the emotions; and second to let the unconscious choose the right moment of release. For there is a right moment. It comes when the horse's four feet are all off the ground at once, a split second in which to find peace: 'during the moment we float through the air before the horse's hoof connects with the ground again'. But the brain has no time to bring this moment into conscious awareness. It lasts a fraction of a second. There can be no thinking, no analysis. There is only action.

How do you aim? You don't, you can't, because there's no time. You leave your mind behind, and you respond by pure feeling. Like a medieval mystic wrestling with the long, dark night of the soul, he came through, into a sort of paradise:

At dawn I rode my horse at a gallop on the crystal carpet laid by drops of dew and shot arrows damp with the morning mist at my target. The water thrown off the damp arrow almost drew a line through the air. Then I suddenly noticed the fiery rays of the sun burning my face red, everything around me was crackling with dry heat, and the yellow slope of the hill was reverberating with the noontime bells of the neighbouring village.

I was awake in my dreams, dreaming awake. Time melted like sweet honey in morning tea. How much I had searched for that feeling! I had chased it like a little boy who wants to catch a butterfly in a flowery meadow. The wonderful insect zigzags in flight like a sheet of paper blown by the wind, then lands on a fragrant flower. The child catches up with it, panting with the effort and reaches towards it with a clumsy move to hold it between finger and thumb, but the butterfly flits away, and the boy is running, stumbling after it again.

I had the butterfly in my hand. I enclosed it between my palms, careful not to hurt its fragile wings.

The next challenge was to fund his obsession by turning it into a business, which meant inventing a new sport and all the rules to go with it. His valley gave him the dimensions. A 90-metre course, with three targets, each 90 centimetres across, to be shot at three times each – forward, sideways and backward – from a gallop that must take no more than sixteen seconds, with expert riders taking eight or nine seconds. To establish his new sport, he needed to make a name for himself, using his own expertise to show what could be done.

In going public, his big idea was to ride his horses – he now had eleven – in relay, along the course he had set himself, firing continuously for twelve hours. He closed the valley, shut out the curious, 'the unfaithful companions, tenacious enemies, two-faced lovers' – hints here of how difficult it must have been for others to deal with this demanding zealot – and trained for six months. 'There was not a single day I did not imagine myself to be in a battlefield. Despite being alone, I was not lonely for a minute. My imagination peopled the valley with comrades in arms and deadly enemies.'

Then it was time to let the world know of the rebirth of mounted archery. The *Guinness Book of Records*, TV and newspapers were informed, helpers and friends called back to hold horses and collect arrows. One June day, at five in the morning, he started, first using the slow horses, firing five arrows in the ten or twelve seconds it took them to gallop the course; then, as the heat built and the hours passed, he switched to the faster horses, which covered the course in less than seven seconds, firing three arrows in each pass. By five in the afternoon, catatonic with fatigue, he had galloped 286 laps and fired something over 1,000 arrows.

Fifteen years on, Kassai has honed his performance to something approaching perfection. The sport, using his scoring system, is well established and growing. Since the early 1990s several hundred men and women, more every year, have been practising this gruelling skill, first in Hungary and now also in Germany, Austria and the United States. Some of these adepts want the sport to be included in the Olympics.

But to Kassai's disciples, this is more than a sport. To Todd Delle, from Arizona, it is a fusion of body and mind, the two reflecting each other, a foundation for dealing with the successes and failures of life itself, 'for you cannot fully understand success without first understanding failure'. It's also about the group, with everyone encouraging everyone else – a collaborative spirit rare in competitive sport. There are others who claim to teach horseback archery, but – as Delle explains – 'What makes Kassai different is that what he teaches is not simply the mechanics of how to shoot an arrow from the back of a galloping horse. *What he teaches is the heart and soul of a warrior.*'

Kassai's valley is now the centre not simply of a sport but of a cult, of a way of life, and of a self-sustaining business.

The sweeping curve of the valley holds Kassai's house – simple, circular, wooden, with furniture carved from tree-trunks; a barn, sweet with the smell of hay, for the two dozen horses; a covered riding school and an arena; two training runs for mounted archery and two butts for standing archery; and, up on a hillside, a Kazakh yurt, where local children come for lessons in living history. The marsh has become a lake. In the nearby town, workshops make bows, arrows and saddles. The whole estate is underpinned by trainees – several hundred of them, mainly Hungarian, but also German and Austrian, with a scattering of English and American – and their need for equipment.

You can see him at work on the first Saturday of each month. When I was there, the thirty-five students – eleven of them women – ranged from near-masters down to a six-year-old boy. Kassai controls his world like a sensei teaching a martial art. With a crowd of 100 watching from the arena's banked sides, the day starts with rigorous drill-work, to the tap of a shaman's drum. It ends with Kassai's demonstration of his astonishing skills. Three men stand along the arena, each holding a pole on which is a circular target 90 centimetres across. Kassai gallops the length of the arena. As he passes, the man starts to run, holding his target aloft a metre or so above his head. Kassai takes six seconds to pass the first running man, during which time he shoots three arrows. Then on past the next – three shots – and the next – another three shots. Eighteen seconds, nine arrows, each released with a 'Ha!', and all strike true. And then, as an encore, the same gallop, the same men, except this time the men each have two unattached targets. As they run and Kassai gallops past, they throw the targets over their shoulders. Six flying targets, six shots, all within a metre of the runners, and not a single miss. The final runner falls on his knees, as if thanking the gods for his survival, and all line up for a round of applause.

*

The sport has now escaped its roots in Kassai's work. In Germany, Austria, Russia, the United Kingdom and the United States, hundreds of men and women are members of half a dozen clubs, performing as equals. Possibly, the women outnumber the men. The Amazon spirit is alive and well, and becoming stronger by the year.

It is, for instance, very much alive in Pettra Engeländer, Kassai's top woman graduate, who now runs her own mounted archery school, the Independent European Horse Archery School (she favours the English version of the name),[23] in glorious open countryside 100 kilometres northeast of Frankfurt. She loved riding as a teenager and also loved archery. It was natural to put the two together, 'to live like the horse-people of old, in harmony with nature.' Yes, she knows that sounds romantic, but she also knows that life on the steppes was not exactly comfortable, because she lived in a yurt for three years and spent a couple of weeks with a family in the Mongolian countryside. She saw for herself the freedom and strength that this way of life gave, especially to the women. Strength and freedom: the words keep coming up in her conversation.

Then there grew in her another ambition: to spread the word, to teach others the benefits she had discovered with Kassai, and do so in ways that took the skills beyond high-performance sport. 'I felt something was lacking to make horseback archery truly authentic. After all, the bow is a weapon that operates at a distance. It was followed by direct contact. I didn't feel at ease with something that defined itself purely in terms of competition.' So she began to treat it as a

[23] http://www.horsebackarchery.de

martial art. She performs as a latter-day Amazon in a horse show, *Apassionata*, which tours Germany and neighbouring countries with a sound-and-light pageant of different breeds and skills. She teaches men and women together as equals, but the women have pride of place, because they are so changed by the experience of horseback archery. The core experience remains that of the rider in tune with her horse, galloping without reins, releasing arrow after arrow, in complete control of herself, her horse and her weapon.

Zana Cousins-Greenwood runs the Centre of Horseback Combat in Hemel Hempstead, near London. She is a fine example of how the sport can act like a virus. It seized her, drove her into action, and then into the business of teaching, organizing and generally infecting as many others as possible.

She was always a rider, from childhood, and was organizing shows from the home where she lived with her husband, Karl, in Somerset. Having seen historical re-enactments, she thought it might be fun to try horseback archery, but had no idea that it was already a sport. One day, on the local radio, she heard mention of a guy who did horseback archery in his back yard. A friend said, 'Yeah, that's Neil Payne. Lives two miles away.' She found him and dropped him a letter, saying, 'Hi. I'd really like to do some horseback archery. Give me a call.' He did, and she had her first lesson. It was more than a lesson. That was when the virus seized her. 'I thought: This is brilliant! I need to do this! It's the most exciting thing I've ever done. Shooting a bow, on horseback . . .' She had been ambushed by passion, and she laughed with joy, struggling to capture the memory. 'It was – it was just – so *exotic*! Then to discover that it was a sport, it was like, "I can actually *do* this? It's *real*?"'

She could do it, but not like this, in a back yard. It had to be done properly. After two false starts (south of London and Wales), she and Karl answered an advertisement in *Horse & Hound* placed by a family living in a beautiful but somewhat under-used eighteenth-century estate, Gaddesden Place in Hertfordshire. The family needed someone to do something with the stables. Horseback archery had not exactly been in the forefront of their minds, but they took a leap of faith. Zana and Karl arrived in February 2012 with ten horses, boot-deep in snow, taking over a house and stables untouched (it seemed) since Jane Austen's day, with three weeks until opening. Zana drove herself, Karl and helpers with Amazonian intensity. They opened as planned.

Four years and 1,500 clients later, that was where I talked to her, in the eighteenth-century pack room, now the HQ for a successful business of eighteen horses, the old stables (which once accommodated the carriages for the big house), several acres of field, twenty bows, arrows enough for a Scythian army, and a horse-archery track.

She reckons they get more women than men. Why should this be so? 'It's all so male, isn't it, this weapon stuff? But women love weapons too. They really do. They don't want to be left out. Here, they're not. In horseback archery men and women are absolutely equal. There is no difference.' Actually, there is a difference: the men are not so good at listening. They get the arrow on the bow any old how, and it's 'Let me shoot! Let me shoot!' They get frustrated easily, they don't want to take time to learn the right technique. You have to calm down, relax, be a little spiritual about it. Women are better at that.

In February 2016, Zana and Karl were the UK delegates to

Moscow, where they had been invited by Russia's Dzhigitovka Federation, the organization that promotes military riding skills, like Cossack-style trick riding, and displays with lances and swords. The Russians wanted to include horseback archery and needed advice on Russia's first steps towards international competition. There were demonstrations. Their horseback archery was nothing – just one target, to be hit by a single arrow, and only men riders. Where were the women? Well, they did some trick riding, but only four stunts where the men did six. And in mounted archery? Oh no, she was told, girls don't do that. Zana was shocked. 'We said, hold on a minute. If you're opening this up internationally, the women are not going to have that. There's no way you can have an international sport in 2016 and say the girls can't do that. You won't get away with it.' So they changed the rules. In July that year, she competed on equal terms with men in *dzhigitovka*, the catch-all name for trick riding, which, thanks to her, is now not just for men. Zana won the silver in horseback archery.

The whole field is opening up, some in the tradition of Kassai, some in others. There's an International Horseback Archery Alliance, linking nineteen countries, though not yet Mongolia, which in this field has only recently started to recover the rather effective skills it possessed under Genghis Khan, lost under the softening effects of Buddhism and Chinese rule. In the US, the Mounted Archery Association of the Americas (MA3 for short) has seven affiliates, in Oregon, Nevada, Utah, Arizona, Texas and two in Washington state. In Arlington, WA, Katie Stearns, running the Flying Duchess Ranch just north of Seattle, says that she has seen women 'transform into warrior goddesses' over the weekend, because 'mounted archery is an equalizer and it gives women the power to be just as strong and capable as their male counterparts.' There are different forms of horseback archery in Korea, Turkey and Japan, and much controversy about styles and techniques and equipment. Do you have to hold the arrows on the bow, as Kassai teaches? Some people say it's more authentic to draw arrows from a quiver. Should arrows have three fletches for stability or two for authenticity? Should you use the three-fingered Mediterranean draw, or the thumb draw, or use a thumb ring? Should you gallop fast, like the Koreans, or more sedately, like Kassai? What about the behind-the-head shot, useful for hitting a target on the ground, or lying along the horse's neck to shoot directly up at a target on top of an 8-metre pole? It's going to go on getting better, if your measure is the number of people involved; worse, if you count the rivalry and the conflicting rules.

This is the world that today's Amazons, seeking to replicate the physical abilities and independence of spirit of their legendary sisters, must take on, as they move into a sport that may one day figure in the Olympics, if only anyone can decide whose rules to follow.

8

AMAZONIA: FROM DREAMS TO A NEW REALITY

WHAT DO THE AMAZONS HAVE TO DO WITH AMAZON.COM?
There is a link. To find it, we must enter a maze of causes and
effects, following the image of Penthesilea and her warrior
sisters into Europe's medieval mind, and out again, across
the Atlantic to a mythical California; then south and east
to the world's greatest rainforest; and finally forwards
in time and northwards to the real California of the late
twentieth century. The journey takes 800 years, with many
twists. That's what it takes to see how the myth of the
Amazons affects the world today, and almost all of us.

*

From the thirteenth century on, in the slow revival of interest in classical literature and art that became the Renaissance, the Amazons were as popular as ever. Warrior women were intriguing and contradictory creatures: virgins (good) but independent of men (bad) and often violent (very bad). To the fourteenth-century poet Giovanni Boccaccio, they were all three.

Boccaccio's *Teseida delle nozze di Emilia* (*Theseid of the Nuptials of Emilia*) is an epic of war and courtly love. The central plot is Theseus's conquest of Thebes. The love story tells of two princes competing for the love of Emilia (hence the title). The tale has a third layer: it is dedicated to 'Fiammetta', the object of Boccaccio's affections, but actually a fiction that justifies his writing in Italian, not Latin, since most women were not educated enough to read Latin – and, he says, not very bright. Courtly lovers tended to be patronizing, offering admiration in exchange for compliance. Boccaccio says Fiammetta is more intelligent than most women. Initially spurned by her, he sets out to win her over with his verses, which also tell her how to behave by presenting the fate of the Amazons as a dreadful lesson.

Under their queen, Hippolyta, these 'wild and ruthless' women kill their menfolk, govern themselves, expel all male interlopers and tax Greek ships. To avenge these 'crimes', Theseus raises an army and attacks. He underestimates the Amazons' skill and spirit. His troops retreat. He re-inspires them: 'Better for you now to have suffered the pangs of death with honour than to retreat shamefully and allow girls to advance.' Now the 'girls' retreat behind their city walls. Hippolyta tries emotional blackmail, sending a message saying that to make war on women brings shame, not glory. Theseus is adamant: 'We intend to humble your pride.' Hippolyta suddenly sees the light: better to surrender, she says, because 'it is not disgrace for us to be conquered by such an excellent man.' They meet and marry, as do many on both sides, promising 'never to return to their folly.'

It works: Fiammetta is so impressed by Boccaccio's verses and their message that she falls for him. It was successful in other ways as well. There are another eleven books to the *Teseida*, but it was Book 1, the Amazons' story, that had the greatest appeal. 'Appeal' is a little hard to measure, bearing in mind that this was a century before Gutenberg invented printing with moveable type. Popularity depended on hand-copies and loans. Even so, it was popular enough to become a common subject for paintings on the sides of the marriage chests that rich Florentine families made for their daughters. These *cassoni*, the equivalents of a Harrods wedding list, were filled with gifts and carried from the bride's home to her husband's. So Theseus and the Amazons was a tale inherited by many generations of Florentines. Brides would have heard their parents and husbands saying in effect: look, young lady, this is how to behave, and how not to.

The story also became well known in England, because Chaucer travelled to Italy, perhaps actually met Boccaccio and used the *Teseida* as the basis for 'The Knight's Tale', the first of the *Canterbury Tales*, in which we hear the story of Theseus and Hippolyta, Queen of Scythia, being spared the details of the battle between Athenians and Amazons, because (says Chaucer) it would take too long.

But I am getting ahead of myself. There were others who kept Amazonian mythology alive, most of them as tedious as their creations. Christine de Pizan[24] (*c*.1363–*c*.1431) was exactly the opposite of tedious, one of the most remarkable women of her age, some would say *the* most remarkable. If she had ever chosen to pick up a sword, she would have made a terrific Amazon. As it was, her pen was mightier than any sword: she used it to fight her corner in society, sustain her family and rescue the Amazons from tedium.

Born in Venice, she was taken to France when her father became astrologer-physician to Charles V, known as 'the Wise' from his intellectual interests and passion for good government. Given access to his vast library – the Louvre, newly expanded, with 1,200 volumes – she read voraciously, absorbing the spirit of the early Renaissance through new translations of Aristotle and other classics. At fifteen she married the king's secretary, Etienne de Castel, had three children and seemed set for a conventional life at court when her husband died suddenly. There were problems with his estate. She was twenty-five and had a mother, a niece and two surviving children to support. She drew on her major assets: her intelligence, education, connections and iron will.

She started with love poems, which led to commissions from rich patrons. She moved on into a debate about the merits of the popular verse allegory *The Romance of the Rose*, the Rose in question being both a name and a symbol of female sexuality. A satire on courtly love and a portrait of women as mere seducers, it is all about sex. In the book a young man avoids various evils – Hatred, Violence, Greed, Avarice and others – and is guided through a small door

[24] Alternatively, Pisan in French. Pizan in Italian, because the family came from Pizzano, near Bologna.

into the Garden of Love by Ease, wherein he discovers many delights and challenges as he attempts to gain access to the Rose. It is transparently symbolic and, with a little imagination, semi-pornographic. It was very popular, and Christine objected. The language was vulgar, she said. It denigrated both sexuality and women. She spent a good deal of her life defending both against male assaults.

She went on to write a history of women, a book of advice to women, a biography of Charles V, a biography of Joan of Arc, and a history of the Trojan War, all of which emphasize and promote female strengths. Indeed, in her semi-autobiographical *Le Livre de la mutacion de fortune* she says that becoming a widow changed her into a man. Not literally of course; but it drove her to emulate her mother, whom she called 'strong and free and more worthy than Penthesilea'.

She adored Amazons. In three different books, she retells the stories of Cyrus, Heracles, Theseus and Hippolyta, occasionally mixing and matching to suit her aim of showing the Amazons as powerful, beautiful, sexy, demanding, virtuous and in all ways deserving of respect, at a time when they were generally considered fodder for male warriors or totally lacking in sexuality. After all (she writes, uncritically improvising on ancient myths), did not their nation, the land of Amazoine, survive for 800 years, making it one of the longest-lasting civilizations of all time? In one of her tales, Hector, the epitome of manhood, is loved by Penthesilea, the most splendid of earthly women. He dies. She vows revenge. She fights Pyrrhus and wounds him. He, humiliated, sets his men on her and then dashes out her brains. Men, Christine de Pizan implies, could beat Amazons only with brute force and unchivalric trickery.

Almost a century later, a series of chivalric romances ensured the enduring literary popularity of the Amazons. They are credited to a Spaniard named Garci de Montalvo, writing on either side of 1500. In fact, strictly speaking, his books were rewrites of stories that had been around for decades, possibly centuries, in French and/or Portuguese, but it was Montalvo who made them famous. The series, *Amadís de Gaula* (not Gaul or Wales, but some fairytale country), follows Amadís in his knight-errant adventures fighting evil knights, sorcerers and dragons.

In the fifth book, *The Exploits of Esplandian* (Amadís's son), published in 1510, Montalvo dreams up a race of warrior women who live under their queen, Califia (probably derived from *caliph*, Spain having recently escaped Islamic rule), in her realm, California.[25] It is an island state, somewhere close to the new Spanish possessions in the New World. At the time of its writing, probably about 1500, Columbus was still insisting that he had reached the Far East, which is why he called these lands the Indies and why he thought he was on the verge of finding Eden, or the Earthly Paradise. He thought he had nearly circled the globe. For a time, confusingly, West was East. So Montalvo's Amazonian island veers from somewhere near Constantinople to the New World. It also owes much to the Spanish obsession with gold, which inspired their imperial drive. This is a translation of the original Spanish:

[25] The name was not his invention. It had been around for over 300 years. *The Song of Roland*, completed in the early twelfth century, has Emperor Charles mourning Roland (Section 209), listing possible rebels, including 'those of Califerne' – presumably the land of the caliph, i.e. Spain.

Know that on the right hand from [or 'of'] the Indies exists an island called *California*, very close to a side of the Earthly Paradise; and it was populated by black women, without any man existing there, because they lived in the way of the Amazons. They had beautiful and robust bodies, and were brave and very strong. Their island was the strongest of the World, with its cliffs and rocky shores. Their weapons were golden and so were the harnesses of the wild beasts that they were accustomed to taming so that they could be ridden, because there was no other metal in the island than gold.

Queen Califia (or Calafia, spellings vary) is a medieval version of Daenerys Targaryen in *Game of Thrones*, the Mother of Dragons. She has 500 ravenous griffins raised on human flesh, which she releases when attacking Constantinople.

Actually, *Game of Thrones* is not a bad comparison. Montalvo's books, especially the fifth, were bestsellers, now that Gutenberg's printing press had spread across Europe. *Esplandian* was reprinted frequently in Spanish, and was just one of many sequels or 'continuations' by different authors in Spanish (12 titles), Italian (28), German (21), French and English. This was mass-market publishing before its time, ensuring that readers across the continent knew of the Amazons. The fad paved the way for rather higher-quality novels, notably Cervantes's *Don Quixote*, which is a pastiche of Montalvo's vainglorious knight-errantry.

The *Amadís* novels used to be rarities in a few national libraries. Now you can find digital reprints online. I have a French edition of *Esplandian*, published in 1550. The cover says it's a translation, but in fact it's an adaptation for French readers. By that time many people knew about California, and knew that there was no Land of Amazons there. So the translator, Nicolas de Herberay, eviscerated and rewrote. The original 184 chapters come down to 56. There is no mention of the Indies (probably because there were no French there, only Spanish). Now the Amazons do not live on an island, but in a 'country', which is within reach of Constantinople, because that is the scene of a battle between Christian knights and Turks.

Just to show how enduring the success of *Amadís* was, you may at the click of a mouse pick up an English version, dated 1664, of the French adaptation published a century earlier. By the late seventeenth century, *Amadís* was really beyond its sell-by date. The translation is accurate, with a couple of significant changes. By then, no one would take Calafia or her land of California seriously, so the names have been adapted to Calafre and Califorine,[26] which is

a most fertile and pleasant country . . . This country whereof I speak was sometimes [i.e. at one time] peopled with good Knights and men of all quarters, but the women upon malice devised a means to kill them all, establishing a law among themselves, that from that time forwards they would acknowledge for Lady and Queen one of their own country women, governing themselves as the Amazons used to do. Whereby it was not lawful for any of them to use the company of men above once or twice a year, upon the days and times by them appointed . . . the maiden children were kept alive, burning

[26] In my 1664 edition, reproduced by the Early English Books Online Text Creation Partnership, these names and many others are in a modern typeface, not the original Gothic, which suggests the 1664 text had been modified from some unspecified earlier edition.

their right paps, but not the men children, for as soon as they were born they put them to death.

In these versions, Queen Califia/Calafia/Califre has only fifty griffins, but that seems to be enough for the French translator who interpolated, in the words of the English edition of 1664: 'Alas, what pity was it to see soldiers, citizens, knights and others, yea women and little children, and all whatsoever they could get into their claws, taken up into the air, and sometimes having taken them up, they let them fall upon the stones, whereby they had a strange and cruel death.'

The Christians, of course, have to win in the end. Calafia converts and gives up her kingdom. And so, once again, the Amazons fall to the forces of Civilization, in this case Christianity.

These tales did not stay in Europe. They were part of the baggage carried by the Spanish and Portuguese explorers as they opened the world to European domination. Columbus's son, Diego, had a copy of *Esplandian* (now in the Biblioteca Colombina, Valladolid). One of Mexico's conquistadores, Bernal Díaz del Castillo, recalling the sights of Aztec cities, wrote, 'We were amazed and said it was like the enchantments they tell of in the legend of *Amadís*.'

The rivalry between Spain and Portugal wrote the agenda of exploration and empire. In the late fifteenth century no one knew what lay across the Atlantic. The two were racing to find out. No other Europeans were serious contenders. The prize was the wealth of the Far East: the spice islands of south-east Asia, and China. While the Portuguese, first off the mark as an outward-looking coastal nation, focused on the route south and east via the southern tip of Africa and India, Spain looked west, thanks to Columbus and his suggestion that it was possible to take a short-cut round the world by sailing the other way, across the Atlantic all the way to China. America, entirely unknown to Europeans, just happened to be in the way, much to Columbus's surprise when he reached land in 1492. He was convinced that he had reached the East, perhaps 'the Indies'. Luckily for Spain, the inhabitants were not Chinese, but 'Indians' whose lands could be seized without fear of opposition.

For a heady few years, Spain and Portugal thought they could divide the world between them. In 1494, in the little town of Tordesillas, they signed a treaty agreeing a border between their spheres of influence. The border line ran north–south halfway between Portugal's most westerly possession, the Cape Verde islands, and the territory claimed for Spain by Columbus. Spain could have everything to the west, Portugal everything to the east, which at the time meant the route to Asia via Africa. Spain, heading west in Columbus's wake, quickly sent out other explorers, who found the freshwater mouth of a great river. In 1500, one of them, Vicente Yáñez Pinzón, sailed up it for about 150 kilometres. He called it Mar Dulce (Sweet – meaning 'Fresh Water' – Sea).

A few years later, the Treaty of Tordesillas had unexpected consequences. Amerigo Vespucci, an Italian working for the Portuguese, sailed south along the Brazilian coast. On his return in 1502, Vespucci announced that Columbus's 'China' was actually a new world (for Europe, anyway). So significant was this realization that the first man to include it on a map called the new world America, a version of Amerigo's name, feminized because land (*terra*) is grammatically feminine.

The land Amerigo had explored jutted eastwards over the dividing line agreed in Tordesillas, which made it Portuguese. That's why Brazilians speak Portuguese.

But the freshwater sea discovered by Pinzón turned out to be just a little to the west of the line drawn in the Treaty of Tordesillas. So it fell into the Spanish sphere, and was theirs for the taking, except that the tricky coastal currents and fierce local tribesmen kept other Spanish explorers at bay.

Besides, the Spanish were busy on the other side of the continent, driven by an obsession with gold and Amazons. Mexico fuelled their passions. In 1524, Hernán Cortés, having hanged, burned and shot his way to the overlordship of all Mexico, wrote to his king, Charles V of Spain, with promises of yet more wealth. He had, he said, heard of an island inhabited only by women, who were visited at pre-arranged times by men from the mainland. When they give birth, 'they keep the female children . . . but the males they throw away.' The island is, of course, 'very rich in pearls and gold.'

But where might it be? Hernán Cortés told his brother Francisco to look on Mexico's west coast, and then northwards, where perhaps the Amazons referred to in 'ancient histories' were to be found. It seems he, like many others, actually believed the *Amadís* story to be true. Somewhere just over the horizon there really was 'an island called *California*', where 'women lived in the way of the Amazons'. So when in 1542 Juan Rodríguez Cabrillo, rich from the gold mines of Guatemala and Honduras, sailed up the west coast, he referred to the land as California, and so it has remained. Moreover, there was indeed an 'island', or so the first Spanish explorers thought. It was in fact the peninsula of Baja California. The assumption that this must surely be the home of the Amazons sustained the idea that the peninsula was an island for another thirty years.

To the south, with Amazons and gold always over the next river or mountain range, the conquistadores approached the Inca empire, ruling present-day Ecuador, Peru and Chile. On the way they heard rumours of El Dorado, the Golden Man, a ruler who once every year was covered in gold and immersed in a lake. It was true, in a small way: the chief of the Muisca people of Colombia had gold dust blown on to him, then washed it off in Lake Guatavita. This small reality seemed to confirm the legend that somewhere there was a gold-rich empire, waiting to be ravaged. The Spanish were also eager to find cinnamon, the bark of trees that supposedly grew on the eastern slopes of the Andes. If true, the find would make Spain independent of traders bringing this expensive spice from the Far East.

To find these mythical regions, in February 1541 Gonzalo Pizarro led 4,000 manacled Indian porters, 5,000 pigs and 340 horse-riding Spaniards armed with guns and crossbows out of Ecuador's high and temperate capital, Quito, over the eastern cordillera of the Andes and down into sweltering rain-forests. Today, you can fly down in a few minutes or drive in a couple of hair-raising hours, skirting cliffs, with rivers raging below you and huge snow-capped volcanoes looming over the forests. Back then, weeks of clambering down single-track paths, hacking through forests and undergrowth and building bridges over ravines led only to disease, starvation, exhaustion and death. Every day it rained. There was no cinnamon, just scattered trees[27] with buds that Pizarro called

---

[27] *Nectandra cinamomoides.*

cinnamon when he wrote up his journey. Of El Dorado there was no sign. By the end of the year, the pigs were eaten, the horses were mostly dead, and almost all of the porters too.

Camping on the banks of the Coca River, Pizarro decided to build a good-sized boat to explore downriver, into the 500-metre-wide Napo and beyond, 'until I should come out in the Northern Sea [the Atlantic]', thus asserting Spain's claim to all the unknown lands in between. His men forged nails for the boat-building from the shoes of the dead horses. Two days and 250 kilometres further on, with the surviving horses being led along the bank, across tributaries and bogs, they had found no villages, no willing traders, no food.

Actually there was a lot of food. You just had to be extremely skilful and experienced to get it, as I discovered when I lived with a tribe of Indians who used to hunt over these forests. Once known as Aucas ('savages' in the language of the nearby Quechuas), they call themselves Waorani (in English orthography) or Huaorani (in Spanish, because Spanish has no *w*). They may not have been there when the Spaniards passed by, because over the next two centuries the European invasions from east and west would set off chain reactions of migrations all across the Amazon basin, but for those with the right skills, the rainforest was always a resource to be exploited, in the form of monkeys, birds, tapirs, pigs, fish, fruit (in season) and occasional glorious gobs of honey, if you can stand a few bee-nips (yes, they nip; if there are bees that sting, I didn't encounter them). To live at all, let alone well, you need astonishing expertise. The rainforest is rich – but the wealth lies mainly in the canopy. It is hard to find food on the jungle floor. The traditional homeland of the Waorani is the size of Wales, for a semi-nomadic population of only

600, who defended their territory by spearing any outsiders they came across. The hardware needed includes palm-fibre hammocks, fire-sticks, spears, fish-poison, blow-guns and darts (or bows and arrows, depending on the culture), and poison for dart- and arrow-tips (either the boiled-down juice of curare vines or the toxic secretion from various species of frog). To develop the techniques took centuries of inherited, evolving skills. To know the materials, gather them and use them demands years of experience. The Spaniards and their highland slaves lacked all this know-how, let alone a knowledge of local languages and the tribal attitudes towards outsiders. Some tribes traded, others were implacably hostile. For example: pre-contact in the late 1950s, the Waorani were the most murderous tribe ever recorded. All outsiders were fair game, and 40 per cent of male Waorani deaths were the result of revenge spearings. Given what they faced, Pizarro's army of highlanders had no chance.

In the belief that salvation would be found downriver, Pizarro's No. 2, Francisco de Orellana, volunteered to sail ahead with fifty-seven armed men and return with food. Pizarro agreed.

So began an epic voyage, starting in the province now named after him. Orellana never returned. Pizarro and his small band, abandoned and apparently betrayed, made a slow and dismal retreat, wracked by scurvy, their clothes in rags. By the time he reached Quito, he had lost all but eighty men. He had achieved precisely nothing, excusing himself in his official report by blaming Orellana for treachery and 'the greatest cruelty'.

In fact, both parties were victims of their inexperience. The Napo, fed by tributaries, flows broad and fast away from the

Andean foothills. Return by sail or oar was impossible. And still they saw no villages. Orellana's men starved, boiling up the soles of their shoes to eat, occasionally tearing up roots that proved poisonous. Seven died before, at last, the rest came across a tribe willing to trade food for knick-knacks.

After several weeks and 800 kilometres, they floated out into a vast and sluggish mainstream that would, they were sure, carry them to the huge river mouth known both as the Mar Dulce and the Marañon, and so at last to the Atlantic. Other Indian groups provided food, and also materials that allowed them to build another, better boat. Then, in mid-1542, they came up against the aggressive Machiparo, a virtual nation of warriors dominating the river for hundreds of kilometres, and providing evidence of the size and complexity of some pre-Columbian flood-plain communities. The Spaniards were allowed to meet the chief, who was so amazed by their beards and awed by their weapons that he granted them living space. But they blew the opportunity by pillaging their hosts, who drove them out, killing sixteen of them.

Downstream was another tribal nation, the Omaguas.[28] 'Numerous large settlements, very pretty country,' recalled the voyage's historian, Gaspar de Carvajal, with roads, decorated and glazed pottery 'in the style of that made in China', fine houses and stocks of food. One town stretched for 10 kilometres. Here, and further on, past the junction with the Rio

---

[28] Because large-scale tribal 'nations' do not exist today, Carvajal's reports have been dismissed as fantasy. But this sounds like eyewitness evidence, and should at least be taken seriously. Recently, in southern Amazonia, aerial surveys have revealed hundreds of 'geoglyphs' – remains of huge rectangular and circular earthworks, evidence of long-vanished and large-scale communities. Perhaps similar states existed on the Amazon itself.

Negro, where translucent 'black' waters run alongside the sediment-rich 'white' waters of the main river, the Spaniards raided village after village, shooting tribesmen and, as word of their vicious ways preceded them, fighting off flotillas of defiant warriors, paddling across a water-world swollen into an inland ocean by tributaries each larger than any European river.

Now we approach the point of this story. An unnamed tribe had villages marked by totems on a huge tree-trunk:

> ten feet in girth, there being represented and carved in relief (thereon) a walled city with its inclosure and with a gate. At this gate were two towers, very tall and having windows, and each tower had a door, the two facing each other, and at each door were two columns, and this entire structure that I am telling about rested upon two very fierce lions, which turned their glances backwards as though suspicious of each other, holding between their forepaws and claws the entire structure, in the middle of which was a round open space: in the centre of this space there was a hole through which they offered and poured out chicha for the Sun . . . the one they worship and consider as their god.

From a captured tribesman, Orellana understood that the altars were symbols of this community's allegiance to a tribe of female warriors. Huts full of feathers and feather cloaks were apparently tributes for these women.

The next villages were more threatening, and landings became rare. At one village, where Orellana agreed that his men could celebrate the festival of Corpus Christi (7 June), they found only women, until nightfall, when the men returned from the jungle and attacked. In the morning, the Spaniards retreated, taking with them prisoners, who were hanged 'in order that the Indians from here on might become afraid of us and not attack us.' It accomplished exactly the opposite. Attacks came almost daily. The crew kept their two ships well clear of the banks when possible, and killed when they ventured on land.

At some point, somewhere in the 500 kilometres of river between today's Manaus and Santarém, they saw villages, 'very large ones, which shone white'. Subsequent events convinced Orellana that these villages were the homes of the fighting women they had heard about upriver. In Carvajal's words, 'we came suddenly upon the excellent land and dominion of the Amazons.'

The Spaniards' approach attracted armadas of canoes. 'They mocked us and came up close and told us to keep going, for farther downriver they were waiting for us and would seize us there and take us to the Amazons.' Crossbows and arquebuses took a heavy toll, but the tribesmen ignored their losses and kept raining down arrows on the two Spanish ships. As the Spaniards forced their way ashore, Carvajal himself was struck by an arrow that penetrated 'as far as the hollow region' – presumably his stomach. 'Had it not been for my clothes that would have been the end of me.'

How to explain such suicidal ferocity? Carvajal thought he could see the answer, in the form of club-wielding women warriors who seemed to be of a different tribe than the men.

There came as many as ten or twelve, for we ourselves saw these women, fighting there in front of all the Indian men as women captains. They fought so courageously that the

Indian men did not dare turn their backs, and anyone who did turn his back they killed with clubs, right there in front of us, and this is the reason why the Indians kept up their defence for so long. These women are very white and tall, and have their hair very long and braided and wound about their heads. They are very robust and go naked with their privy parts covered, with their bows and arrows in their hands, doing as much fighting as ten Indian men, and indeed there was one woman among them who shot an arrow a span deep into one of the brigantines, and others less deep, so that our brigantines looked like porcupines.

The Spaniards killed seven or eight of the 'Amazons' – 'these we actually saw,' writes Carvajal, as if foreseeing doubt – before reaching their boats and drifting away on the current, too exhausted to row.

A little further on, they approached another village to get food, because it seemed deserted. In fact, the inhabitants were lying in ambush with their bows. The Spaniards protected themselves with shields, all except Carvajal himself: 'they hit no one but me, for they planted an arrow shot right in one of my eyes, in such a way that the arrow went through to the other side, from which wound I have lost the eye and (even now) I am not without suffering.'

They took with them a prisoner,[29] who in the course of the

[29] He was a 'trumpeter', says Carvajal, for his people had many 'trumpets, drums and pipes'. I'm interested because I played the trumpet, long ago, when I thought I was musical. What on earth did he mean by 'trumpets'? The only trumpets in Europe at the time were valveless open trumpets, like double-length bugles. Valves came much later (the instrument in Haydn's Trumpet Concerto used clappers and holes to play harmonics). Wooden clarinos with recorder-like holes also had trumpet mouthpieces. Rainforest tribes had no

journey onwards downriver became the source of some fascinating 'information', which he was able to divulge because Orellana had made a 'list of words'. First Orellana asked about the man's origins. He was from the village where he was captured, came the reply, and his overlord was called Couynco or Quenyue (the two written versions of Carvajal's history vary). And the women? They lived inland, a seven-day journey away. Orellana's prisoner said he had been there often, bearing tribute from his lord. The 'Amazons' ruled over seventy villages, in which the houses were built 'out of stone and with regular doors, and from one village to another went roads closed off on one side and on the other and with guards stationed at intervals along them so that no one might enter without paying duties'.

Did the Amazons bear children, asked Orellana. Yes, indeed. But how?

He said that these Indian women consorted with Indian men at times, and when that desire came to them, they assembled a great horde of warriors and went off to make war on a very great overlord whose residence is not far from the land of these women, and by force brought them to their own country and kept them with them for the time that suited their caprice, and after they found themselves pregnant they sent them back to their country without doing them any harm.

The male children they killed, the girls they raised 'with great solemnity and instructed them in the arts of war.'

---

metal. Perhaps these Indians had wooden instruments, with a bore-hole, or used deer horns. It's a mystery.

All this was done under the control of a queen, 'one ruling mistress who subjected and held under her hand and jurisdiction all the rest, which mistress went by the name of Coñori.'

They possessed 'a very great wealth of gold and silver', and high-ranking women ate with gold and silver utensils, whereas those of lower rank used wood or pottery. Five large buildings in the capital were temples dedicated to the Sun:

> In these buildings they had many gold and silver idols in the form of women, and many vessels of gold and of silver for the service of the Sun; and these women were dressed in clothing of very fine wool, because in this land there are many sheep of the same sort as those of Peru [not sheep, of course, but llamas]; their dress consisted of blankets girded about them from the breasts down, [in some cases merely] thrown over [the shoulders] and in others clasped together in front, like a cloak, by means of a pair of cords; they wore their hair reaching down to the ground at their feet, and upon their heads were placed crowns of gold, as wide as two fingers . . . As we understand him, there were camels that carried them on their back . . . which were as big as horses.

Their source went on: 'They had a rule to the effect that when the sun went down no male Indian was to remain in all these cities.' Neighbouring states were made to pay tribute, and with others they were at war, including the one they had just seen, whose men were carried home 'to have relations with them'. The women were 'of very great stature and white and numerous', as he knew for certain, because he went back and forth daily.

All this apparently confirmed a tale the Spaniards had heard not far from Quito. To see the women, men journeyed downriver 1,400 leagues (some 3,000 miles), so 'anyone who should take it into his head to go down to the country of these women was destined to go a boy and return an old man.' The country of the Amazons was cold, said the prisoner, without much firewood.

Orellana and Carvajal made a willing audience, eager to believe that not far away was a land ripe for colonization. By the time Carvajal came to write his history, the dreams had hardened into an imperialist agenda:

Inland from the river, at a distance of two leagues, more or less, there could be seen some very large cities that glistened in white, and besides this the land is good, as fertile, and as normal in appearance as our Spain . . . It is a temperate land, where much wheat may be harvested, and all kinds of fruit trees may be grown.

Grasslands that called out for livestock, woods of 'evergreen oaks, plantations of cork trees bearing acorns', rolling savannas, game galore – why, the place was an Eden fit for seizure by king, country and Christ.

What are we to make of this? Orellana gets into a fight with a previously unknown tribe and sees a dozen strapping women fighting with the men. They look different, and seem to exercise authority. There could obviously be no interpreter, because the Spaniards were the first European arrivals. Yet on the basis of a 'word list' Orellana builds a context: tribal hierarchies, a tribute system, seventy villages, stone houses, an economy.

Take the language issue first. Orellana was, no doubt, as brilliant a linguist as Carvajal claimed. He was 'next to God, the deciding factor by virtue of which we did not perish.' But no one can be *that* brilliant. Once upon a time, it was not uncommon for anthropologists working in the field to claim to learn a new language in a couple of weeks. A century ago, they were safe to do so. Few worked with indigenous groups living traditional lives. The scholar was the only source. No one could check. After the Second World War, anthropology moved on. Language turned out to be rather more compli-cated than anyone had thought. You can't pick up a language in a few weeks. The anthropologist and Waorani expert on whom I relied, Jim Yost, said it took him a year to feel comfortable in the language – and he had the immeasurable advantage that Waorani had already been analyzed by the missionary group he was working with. Waorani is a linguistic 'isolate', with no living relatives. It had taken years to crack. In a couple of months with the Waorani, thanks to a written grammar, I learned enough to ask a few simple ques-tions, but certainly not enough to understand the answers.

Yet here is Carvajal claiming that from a single 'informant' speaking an unknown language Orellana could, with nothing but a word list, elicit detailed information about an unknown culture in a few days. It's simply not possible.

So the result is rubbish. Stone houses and roads in a mud-floored tropical rainforest that was somehow short of firewood? Fields and oak trees? Take the mention of numbers: a seven-day journey, seventy villages. The numbers assume the existence of a counting system. But, it's almost safe to say, most Amazonian tribes do not count. Well, they can, but they didn't then, at least not in European terms. Both the Yanomamö and the Pirahã (more on them in the next paragraph) count 'One, two, more than two'. Waorani is a bit more sophisticated: one to five is 'One, two, two-and-one, two-and-two, a full hand.' You can go up to ten ('two full hands'), after which the system is too cumbersome to be of much use. It's nothing to do with a lack of intelligence. The Waorani can learn to count in Spanish perfectly well. Once they have that intellectual tool, they can joke about how they count: 'If we wanted to say twenty-two in our language, we would have to say "Two hands, two hands and two."' It seems that, traditionally, these cultures could do just fine without counting much beyond five. Why this was so is an open question, but it's our problem, not theirs.

How to explain what Orellana 'discovered' from his informant, at least as reported by Carvajal? The answer is: projection, explaining the alien and the far-off in terms of one's own experiences and prejudices. It's reassuring to think that our beliefs are universal. But they're not. There's a story of a teacher deconstructing *Hamlet* to Zulus, eager to present the evil deed that underpins the play: Hamlet's uncle has murdered his own brother to seize the throne. Nods of approval all round. Everyone agrees: 'He did well.' So much for Shakespeare's universal appeal. When Dan Everett, a missionary working with the Pirahã on the Madeira River, proudly read his translation of St Mark's Gospel, he was convinced that he was offering a message of salvation for all mankind. He had reckoned without the Pirahã belief in a world of dreams and spirits that was as real to them as our physical world. The morning after listening to St Mark, one of the men 'startled me by suddenly saying, "The women are afraid of Jesus. We do not want him."

' "Why not?" I asked.

' "Because last night he came to our village and tried to have sex with our women. He chased them round the village, trying to stick his large penis into them." '

Other tribesmen confirmed it. Game, set and match to the Pirahã. They were not, in Everett's words, 'in the market for a new world view.' He lost his faith soon afterwards.

Carvajal intended to be trustworthy, and was widely trusted. 'He should be believed,' wrote his friend Fernández de Oviedo, 'by virtue of those two arrow shots, one of which tore out or destroyed one of his eyes; and with that single eye, not to mention his personal prestige and qualities . . . I would believe him more than I would those who, with two eyes . . . staying at home in Europe, are continually babbling.' But he was led astray by his expectations. He was a well-educated man, familiar with the classics. He knew what Old World historians said about the Amazons, and had no reason to doubt that they were a historical reality. He came from a world of stone houses and roads and royalty, and a culture obsessed with gold, and with the idea that a gold-rich kingdom existed somewhere in the rainforest. It was this familiarity that led him to accept what Orellana said and enhance it with exaggeration and wishful thinking. Somehow, a few words exchanged with the prisoner served as a verbal Rorschach test, on to which the Spaniards imposed their culture, their dreams and their recent past. As with UFOs, ghosts, gods and the Loch Ness Monster, scanty 'evidence' inspires a spurious explanation, which inspires more 'evidence', producing a belief that seems to be a rock-solid truth.

Another major source seems to have been the Peruvian

Virgins of the Sun, about whom both men knew because they had been present during the conquest of the Incas less than ten years before. In the words of the nineteenth-century historian of the conquest, William Prescott, the Virgins of the Sun 'were young maidens, dedicated to the service of the deity, who were taken from their homes and introduced into convents . . . [which] consisted of low ranges of stone buildings, covering a large extent of ground, surrounded by high walls.'

A trustworthy character is no guarantee of a trustworthy report. There never was a tribe of Amazons in the rainforest, any more than there was a gold-rich kingdom there.

But Carvajal's hopes and dreams had tremendous impact. After more adventures – attacks and counterattacks, food stolen or traded – the expedition reached the mouth of the great freshwater river, sailed north for another 2,000 kilometres and landed in Spanish settlements on the island of Cubagua, off the coast of Venezuela, in early September 1542. While Orellana went back to Spain, Carvajal returned to Lima, wrote up his account of the journey downriver (in two versions) and spent the next forty years in the service of the church, until his death in 1584.

His account sounds like a good explanation of why the river and its forests became the region of '*las Amazonas*', at first in the plural. But it's not quite as straightforward as it looks. For a few years the river was also known as the Orellana, after its discoverer. Secondly, Carvajal's account[30]

---

[30] The two versions differ in style, but not much in content, perhaps because they were dictated separately.

is a prime source today, but it only recently became so. After he wrote it, it vanished into the Peruvian archives and was rediscovered in the late nineteenth century. So at the time his story spread by word of mouth. Orellana's trip was so extraordinary and became so well known – especially after Pizarro accused him of treachery – that the story of the warrior women came to define the whole adventure. That's why the river and its forest became the region of the Amazons.

First for Spanish speakers, then for the rest of Europe and the world. In 1555, a French author, André Thevet, published an account of mainly French exploration in the New World, based on his own journey there and other accounts. The strange title of his book, *Singularities of the French Antarctic*, takes its name from a shortlived French colony around what became Rio de Janeiro, but it covers all America.[31] It sounds like a proposal for expanding the French empire from Brazil to all points north. In fact, it is the first stab at an ethnography of the whole New World: people, animals, plants. He includes the Amazons as fact. How had they got there? No problem. After the Siege of Troy, they scattered to form an Amazon diaspora, wandering the world until they reached the Americas.

These people live in little huts and caves among the rocks, they eat fish and various wild plants, roots and fruits grown in this region. They kill their male children, immediately after having put them into the earth, or give them into the hands of those they think responsible for them. If it is a girl, they

---

[31] *Les Singularitez de la France antarctique, autrement nommée Amérique.* See Bibliography.

keep them, as did the first Amazons. They usually make war against various other nations, and treat those whom they capture very inhumanely.

Fifty years after Orellana's journey, in 1597, a Flemish map-printer named Cornelius Wytfliet published a map of the world with all the latest discoveries. The Americas are there, very roughly. South America looks like a reject potato, with just seven names: Castilia del Oro (Golden Castile), Peru, Brezilia, Parana, Chili, Chica – and, marking a transcontinental river network, Amazones, the Amazons, the first mention of the name on a map. Eventually it lost its plural form and became the singular Amazon.

By then, English explorers were laying the foundations of empire on behalf of their own warrior queen, Elizabeth, but found that Amazons were no longer taken seriously by those in authority.

Sir Walter Raleigh, passing on what he had been told by a native chief, claimed they were a reality. After all, he wrote (with the spelling updated),

in many histories, they are verified to have been . . . but they which are not far from Guiana do accompany with men but once in a year, and for the time of one month, which I gather by their relation to be in April; and that time all kings of the borders assemble, and queens of the Amazons, and after the queens have chosen, the rest cast lots for their valentines. This one month they feast, dance, and drink of their wines in abundance; and the moon being done they all depart to their own provinces. They are said to be very cruel and bloodthirsty, especially to such as offer to invade their territories. These Amazons have likewise a great store of these plates of gold.

A likely story. What language was this conducted in, and how come the local rulers all act like European royalty at play? Was his queen also expected to believe in the headless Ewaiponoma, who had eyes and mouths in their chests? It was all intended to gain royal backing for yet another expedition. But the queen died, and Raleigh was implicated in a plot against her successor, James I, and ended up like the Ewaiponoma, headless.

And anyway, by now there were doubts. Wasn't it a little odd that the Amazons' domain always moved further off as knowledge advanced? That information about them was always indirect? Samuel Purchas, in his account of the new worlds opened by exploration, dismissed these 'solitary uni-mammians' as fantasies. As a fantasy, the Amazon remained a popular character in plays and poems, as easily recognizable by her attributes – battleaxe, buskins, exposed breast – as the fairy godmother or pantomime dame is today. But now they're tamed and domesticated, no longer real warriors. As Edmund Spenser wrote in *The Faerie Queene*, his verse *homage* to Queen Elizabeth –

Vertuous women wisely understand
That they were borne to base humilitie,
Unless the heavens them lift to lawful sovereaintie,

– the queen being the exception that proves the rule. Hippolyta in *A Midsummer Night's Dream* talks of hunting, not war. They were picturesque ornaments for pageants – famously tall and valiant – but, if taken seriously, would be dangerous examples of unwomanly conduct. Elizabeth was happy to be addressed as Gloriana, but if anyone had called her an Amazon he would have risked losing his head.

Yet the Amazon myth survived, sanctioned by the name of the river, because surely such a vast entity with so many stories behind it had to contain some elements of truth?

It was kept alive, for instance, by Cristóbal de Acuña, Jesuit bishop who went with the Portuguese explorer Pedro de Teixeira from the Andes down the Napo and Amazon, and published his account of the journey in 1641. He didn't claim to see any Amazons, but had no doubts about accepting them. 'The proofs of the existence of the province of the Amazons on this river are so numerous and so strong, that it would be want of common faith not to give them credit.' The proofs? His investigation of the natives, or rather one native, of the Tupinambá tribe. This man confirmed everything that everyone 'knew': women of valour, no men, annual mating, boys killed, girls raised as warriors etc., etc. 'There is no saying more common than that these women inhabit a province on the river, and it is not credible that a lie could have spread throughout so many languages, and so many nations, without such an appearance of the truth.' Well, yes, it is perfectly credible, given that the Tupinambá lived, and still live, in Maranhão, which is on Brazil's north-east coast a good 400 kilometres from the mouth of the Amazon, let alone the regions where Carvajal said that Orellana said a local Indian whose language he didn't speak said the Amazons were.

So the Amazons of Amazonia lived on. Though a number of the sceptical philosophers and scientists of the eighteenth century denied their existence, some did not. One was the French Jesuit missionary and anthropologist Joseph-François Lafitau, who spent five years (1712–17) with the Iroquois Indians in Canada, and also learned a good deal about the Hurons. His anthropology was so good that he has been called the 'precursor of scientific anthropology'. He worked to an agenda that took a couple of centuries to fall out of fashion. His aim was to prove that all cultures evolved from others, back to the first – a comparative approach that works for languages and for the evolution of species, but not, in the end, for cultures. He couldn't have known that, which is what makes his book – *Moeurs des sauvages amériquains* (*Customs of the American Savages*) – a worthy starting point for a new science. By recording cultures and comparing them, he hoped to derive the universal laws behind the evolution of culture. He believed that primitive cultures today in the Americas not only resembled primitive cultures in the ancient world – they actually both *descended* from pre-existing ones: 'The largest number of the American peoples came originally from those barbarians who occupied the continent and islands of Greece.' His evidence was Orellana's report. The bearers of Greek culture were the Amazons. We might regard them as a myth, he said,

if we had not been assured that, in our day, there are still found on the banks of the Marañón or Amazon River, some of those warrior women who glory in the works of Mars, live apart from men, practice continually drawing the bow, keep only the girls with them, either killing the boys or returning them to their fathers at stated times when they seek their company.

He accepts the whole package, minus only the excised or cauterized breast. The second chapter of the second volume (it is an immense work of over 1,000 pages),[32] 'Women's Occupations', begins: 'The women of the Savages, just like the Amazons, the women of the Thracians, the Scythians, the Spaniards, and other barbarous peoples of Antiquity, work the fields,' just as was done then, before the 'transmigration'. Iroquois women recall the Lycians, mentioned by Herodotus. Like them, their houses are chosen by the mothers, they trace descent through the women, they have a power structure dominated by women. The unfortunate fact that Iroquois chiefs were male is explained by the fortunate fact that they were chosen by women. Like the Lycians and the Amazons, Iroquois society was a 'gynococracy' – the word now is 'gynarchy' or 'gynocracy' – rule by women. In Herodotus's words, 'Ask a Lycian who he is and he will tell you his own name and his mother's, then his grandmother's and great-grandmother's and so on.' The parallels – and Lafitau's book has a mass of classical references in its margins – seemed to provide strong evidence that the Iroquois' ways may 'have come from the Amazons, whose empire was so vast in extent.' How they got to Canada was a big question. Obviously not across the Atlantic, so they must have travelled all the way across Asia and over the Bering Strait, a suggestion backed up by the discovery that made him famous: ginseng, a plant long used as a drug by the Iroquois and which was identical to the ginseng used in China. So who brought the ginseng to Canada? Since no one yet knew the true age of the Earth, it did not occur to him that ginseng could have spread very

[32] The original is available on http://gallica.bnf.fr/

well on its own. So he concluded that it must surely have been brought to the Americas by the Amazons and the Lycians.

Another explorer who returned from the New World bearing news of Amazons was Charles Marie de la Condamine, who went to Ecuador to measure the exact length of a degree of latitude at the Equator. He travelled down the Amazon in 1743 and questioned many Indians, which he could do because there were now interpreters. No one had actually *seen* any Amazons. On the other hand, 'they had all told us they had been informed of the same by their parents.' Apparently, two centuries of questioning by Europeans had planted an idea of what Europeans wanted to hear, which had grown into a tangle of pseudo-information. La Condamine was assured by a seventy-year-old that his grandfather had actually spoken to four Amazons. More Indians, of the otherwise unrecorded Topaya tribe, told him their fathers had been given green stones by 'women without husbands' who lived above waterfalls and beyond high mountains. To la Condamine it seemed that the Amazons lived, or had once lived, in Guiana, where Europeans had not yet gone. Once again, the Amazons were to be found where no one could actually find them, just over the horizon. Of course, he wrote,[33] you can't trust natives, who are 'liars, credulous and fond of anything surprising'; and of course it was ludicrous to think that the tribe of Amazons had migrated from the Old World. How they had developed was a mystery to be solved – perhaps they had escaped violent and brutal lives and set up on their own. Anyway, even la Condamine, scientist and rationalist,

[33] *Relation abrégée* . . . See Bibliography.

concluded that 'there had been, in this continent, a common-wealth of females, who lived by themselves, without having any males amongst them.'

So the name of this distant branch of the family of Amazons lived on, to affect the real world in ways now familiar to us all.

In the twentieth century, after an extended controversy, the Amazon turned out to be the world's second-longest river (6,516 kilometres) after the Nile (6,695 kilometres). But length is not a true measure of its scale. To understand its nature you have to understand its origin. It is the remnant of an inland sea. About 150 million years ago, South America and Africa were joined, both being part of the supercontinent of Pangaea ('Earth Everywhere'). A great river, the future Amazon, flowed from the interior of what would become West Africa across what would become South America, spreading into a huge delta draining into the proto-Pacific. Torn by the slow flow of molten rock deep in the earth, the two split, moving apart by the thickness of a fingernail every year to form today's jigsaw-like slabs. South America was a raft with a bow-wave of rock that pushed up a crumple zone we now call the Andes, raising the whole leading edge of the South American plate. The great river, which had once flowed east to west, tilted until the waters, now tumbling from the new mountains, began to flow the other way. Today's Amazon is a delta in reverse, draining into the Atlantic, the ocean dividing South America from its former twin. That's why the Amazon basin looks the way it does, and why its size is measured less by its length than the bulk of its waters. It delivers into the Atlantic over 200,000 tonnes of water per second, 12 million per minute, 17 billion per day. That's five times the flow of the next biggest, the Congo. Its drainage area is twice the size of India. In world rankings of river size, No. 5 and No. 7 are tributaries of the Amazon: the Madeira and the Negro.

Its scale has nothing to do with its name, but both together matter to internet users. In 1994 a young entrepreneur working out of a garage in Seattle, Washington state, had just set up a company to sell almost anything to almost anyone almost anywhere. Books would come first. He wanted to build the greatest book operation on earth. To evoke the magic of buying things online, he called the company not Abracadabra but just Cadabra. But not enough people knew what it meant, and when spoken it sounded too much like 'Cadaver'. He needed a new name. Since he loved *Star Trek*, he suggested the catchphrase made famous by *Enterprise*'s captain, Jean-Luc Picard: 'Make it so.' He registered MakeItSo.com as a domain name, among others. None seemed right. Besides, it would be better if the name started with one of the first letters of the alphabet, to make sure it came up quickly on internet browsers. Aard.com, Awake.com, Browse.com, Bookmall.com? Still not right.

We're speaking, of course, of Jeff Bezos. In late October, he was leafing through the A section of a dictionary and stumbled on the word 'Amazon'. Yes! The world's largest river by far – it seemed the perfect name for what he had in mind. He walked into the garage next morning, told his colleagues of the company's new name, registered the new URL on 1 November and started trading in July the following year.

Amazon's rise was meteoric. With no press promotion, it

was selling books across the United States and in forty-five foreign countries within thirty days. In two months, sales reached $20,000 a week. It went public in 1997, expanded to trade almost anything, and escaped from its concept entirely. Twenty years later, Amazon sales topped $100 billion. To make amazon.com match the Amazon, you'd have to tilt South America until the river foams white all the way to the Atlantic.

9

A PAINTING, TWO PLAYS AND A SUICIDE

IN 1600, THE AMAZONS WERE FIRMLY LODGED IN EUROPE'S consciousness, placed there by Greek history, confirmed by exploration in the New World, cemented in place by novels. Everyone just knew they had once been real, and probably still were, somewhere over some distant horizon. So it was natural for writers to mention them and artists to paint them. There are good reasons why most contributions are forgotten. They're boring or insignificant, just re-stating well-worn themes. But every now and then, over the next three centuries, somebody produced something worth a closer look. This chapter is about three of these instances, in which the Amazons were made to carry meanings very different from anything in the ancient world.

Prague is a beautiful city, but it has a rather ugly tradition: they throw people out of windows. That is a bit of an exaggeration. There have been three defenestrations in Prague, each separated by centuries, so you could hardly call it a tradition. The first was in 1419, when a mob supporting the ideas of the executed heretic Jan Huss slung a dozen eminent officials to the waiting crowd below, and the third was in 1948, when Communist thugs tossed the anti-Communist foreign minister Jan Masaryk to his death. Let's focus on the middle one. In 1618 Protestant leaders defenestrated three visiting Catholic hardliners, who, rather surprisingly, survived. Later, some claimed they had been saved by divine intervention, others that they had fallen into a dung heap. The point of this story is the religions. The incident started the Thirty Years' War, which turned the Reformation begun by Luther a century before into the most brutal and destructive outpouring of barbarity until 1914.

In fast-forward, the years 1618–48 made mainland Europe into a cloud chamber of rag-tag armies fighting for changing faiths, dying dynasties and rising nation-states: German Protestants, German Catholics, German warlords – for there was no Germany yet, only a kaleidoscope of states and cities – the Emperor, the Pope, the Habsburgs (with possessions across all Europe and beyond to India, Africa and the Americas), the Wittelsbachs, France, Spain, Holland, Bohemia, Denmark, Sweden and various Italian states – for there was no Italy yet either – all combining and opposing, acting and reacting, with mercenaries changing sides at the sight of a ducat. Firearms, disease and famine turned much of the continent to a wasteland. Millions died: perhaps 3 million, perhaps over 10 million. In Germany, the heart of it all, probably more than 20 per cent of the population perished, possibly up to 40 per cent. In the most extreme case, in Magdeburg in 1631, virtually the whole population of 20,000 were murdered or burned to death in their homes. Across the continent, no one counted the atrocities, let alone the dead.

But someone recorded a little of the suffering. He was a German, Hans von Grimmelshausen, and the suffering he saw and heard about when kidnapped by Hessian troops at the age of ten in 1631 formed the basis of a novel usually referred to as *Simplicissimus*, short for its very long title. It was the most popular German novel of its day. Before we get to the point of all this, here in the words of the simple-minded hero is a hint of the suffering imposed on ordinary people: pillage, rape, wanton destruction, and torture, including the seventeenth-century equivalent of water-boarding:

The first thing these troopers did was, that they stabled their horses: thereafter each fell to his appointed task: which task was neither more nor less than ruin and destruction. For though some began to slaughter and to boil and to roast so that it looked as if there should be a merry banquet forward, yet others there were who did but storm through the house above and below stairs . . . Bedsteads, tables, chairs, and benches they burned, though there lay many cords of dry wood in the yard. Pots and pipkins must all go to pieces, either because they would eat none but roast flesh, or because their purpose was to make there but a single meal. Our maid was so handled in the stable that she could not come out; which is a shame to tell of. Our man they laid bound upon the ground, thrust a gag into his mouth, and poured a pailful of filthy water into his body: and by this, which they called a Swedish draught, they forced him to lead a party of them to another place where they captured men and beasts, and brought them back to our farm, in which company were my dad, my mother, and our Ursula.

And now they began: first to take the flints out of their pistols and in place of them to jam the peasants' thumbs in and so to torture the poor rogues as if they had been about the burning of witches: for one of them they had taken they thrust into the baking oven and there lit a fire under him, although he had as yet confessed no crime: as for another, they put a cord round his head and so twisted it tight with a piece of wood that the blood gushed from his mouth and nose and ears. In a word each had his own device to torture the peasant . . . Yet in the midst of all this miserable ruin I helped to turn the spit, and in the afternoon to give the horses drink, in which employ I encountered our maid in the stable, who seemed to me wondrously tumbled, so that I knew her not, but with a weak voice she called to me, 'O lad, run away, or the troopers will have thee away with them. Look to it well that thou get hence: thou seest in what plight . . .' And more she could not say.

That was in Germany. For Holland, the Thirty Years' War was part of something much longer lasting – an Eighty Years' War of independence from Spain (1568–1648). Holland was divided: Protestants, known as Calvinists, in the northern United Provinces, Catholics in the south (roughly modern Belgium). In the southern capital, Antwerp, Archduke Albert and Archduchess Isabella, joint rulers from 1599, built up a court that was the centre of a Catholic renaissance. They continued to try to subdue the Dutch rebels through military force, until the signing of the Twelve Years' Truce in 1609, which effectively recognized the independence of the northern provinces.

Commercially, Antwerp was giving way to Amsterdam, but Albert and Isabella provided an intellectual and artistic haven in which artists thrived. There were damaged churches to be restored, new ones built, altarpieces made, stained-glass windows put in, mansions to be filled with fine paintings. It was a great time to be an artist in Antwerp. Two of them were among the most famous of their day: Jan Brueghel and Peter Paul Rubens. Brueghel – brilliant son of the brilliant Pieter Bruegel the Elder (who omitted the *h* in his name, though his children kept it) and younger brother of the equally brilliant Pieter Brueghel the Younger – was the better established, being nine years older than Rubens. Both had their own studios, both their own special talents. Brueghel, known as 'Velvet' for his delicate touch, was expert in landscapes and multi-figure scenes; Rubens, though hardly out of his teens, loved historical subjects. They started a collaboration, like many others, artistic collaboration being a well-established practice, not only in Antwerp. A master would often paint the essence, with assistants adding the details. Art historians spend a great deal of time trying to work out who did what. In the case of Brueghel and Rubens, collaboration turned into a close friendship, in a tight-knit community of artists who were in and out of each other's studios and houses, and often intermarried. In 1598, when Rubens was twenty-one and Brueghel thirty, they produced their first work together, *The Battle of the Amazons*.

Why the Amazons? It was not a particularly popular subject with Renaissance artists. Both, though, were drawn to the themes of classical mythology and the turmoil of battle. Brueghel, newly back from Italy, did the landscape, the top half; Rubens, already well educated in the classics and soon to go to Italy, did the figures which fill the bottom half. On a wide plain, with a wooded hill to the left, the Greek army charges in, pushing the Amazons towards a river and towards us. In the foreground Hercules[34] subdues two Amazons, one of whom is wearing an incongruous plumed cap. Perhaps the Amazon in red with a gold banner, the one holding a head, is Hippolyte. A muscular figure, Theseus perhaps, holds a limp Antiope. All around warriors surge, trampling and being trampled. There are many wild expressions and much violence.

But it's all rather academic. There are as many naked bodies as figures in diaphanous costumes. A spotlit woman lying in the foreground is obviously dead, except that there is no blood and she has somehow died while preserving her modesty with a well-placed hand. In fact, there's not really much blood anywhere, given the mayhem. Even the head being held by Hippolyte, if it is she, is rather insignificant. Hercules and his two opponents recall the famous marble statue of Laocoön and his sons wrestling snakes, every

---

[34] Given that the sources were Roman (both classical and recent), writers then and now favour the Roman version of his name.

muscle tense. The design also refers to a fresco by Raphael in Rome, *The Battle of Constantine Against Maxentius*, done 100 years earlier, which Brueghel would have seen in Rome and Rubens knew from engravings. Rubens was, it seems, more eager to solve the problems of composing all the bodies than engaging with the brutality of war.

But the Amazons now had him in their grasp and would not let him go. It was as if his unconscious was telling him: 'You can do better, Peter. You can give the Amazons real meaning.' He even explored the subject in a drawing, perhaps gathering material for another version in the future. One image he kept was that of an Amazon, Hippolyte perhaps, waving a severed head. That was in 1602–4, after which the subject went on a backburner, as if he were giving peace a chance.

In 1621, three years after the outbreak of the Thirty Years' War, he was doubling as an undercover diplomat. Holland was still divided, the rebellious Protestant north against the still-Spanish Catholic south. For twelve years, from 1609, the two sides had held back. Rubens, now aged forty-four, was an established master, collector and connoisseur with an international reputation, having trained in Italy and toured Spain. Most of Europe's top art collectors had pieces by him and his studio of helpers – great hunting scenes, portraits, tapestry designs, altarpieces. As court painter to the Archduke Albert and his wife Isabella, he was the jewel in Antwerp's crown. Success gave him high-level contacts, which was why Archduchess Isabella, an equal to her husband, employed him as an unofficial envoy. His task, as the Twelve Years' Truce approached its end, was to try to broker a lasting peace between divided Holland and Spain. He failed. War broke out again. He ran his studio to the occasional sound of cannon fire and when he travelled – as he did to Paris in 1622 to plan twenty-one portraits for France's Queen Mother, Marie, a Medici from Florence – he did so across a war-ravaged land.

So he knew from the inside the disaster that faced all Europe when, in some unspecified year about this time, he painted his own *The Battle of the Amazons*, which he gave to the great collector Cornelis van der Geest. It is very different from the previous picture done with Brueghel. In a chaos of horses and two dozen half-naked bodies, Greeks and Amazons struggle on top of a small, low-arched bridge, with corpses tumbling down on either side into a shallow river. In size, imagine a school blackboard – not exactly palatial, but just right for the wall of a spice merchant and art collector. It is at first glance an appropriate piece of mythology, exactly the sort of thing a seventeenth-century aristocrat would want.

But a closer look reveals a most unlikely agenda. In ancient times, the battle would have been designed to show the fine qualities of both winners and losers. There were models to be followed in similar works by Titian and Leonardo da Vinci, both glorifying particular victories. Here, though, Rubens has made the subject his own. The figures, fighting against smoke surging from a blazing city, swirl around a Greek seizing the Amazon standard – a traditional theme in military subjects, because the flag, being colourful and visible, was the point round which troops were supposed to rally. Here there is no rallying and no glory. The Amazon standard-bearer, already collapsing and unarmed, is having the flag dragged away from her by a Greek wielding a bloody dagger, while another raises his sword to finish her off. The Amazon queen, Hippolyte, is no leader now, riding off in the background. There is no hint of heart-stopping beauty or any power-giving girdle, only barbarity. She is holding up a Greek head, leaving its owner's decapitated torso on top of the bridge, dead centre, bleeding into the river below. It is a scene of extreme and shocking brutality. Bodies are distorted in death. A female corpse almost blocks the river. In antiquity Greeks liked to see virtue in their own side for achieving victory over respected adversaries, but here there is no respect for either side. The Greeks are slaughtering defeated women, and being slaughtered in their turn.

In the bottom left corner is a woman on her back, lying dead on the steep riverbank. A Greek is hauling her cloak from under her, his foot on the inside of her naked thigh, an act that combines the implication of necrophilia – the rape of a corpse – with the theft of an item that is entirely useless in military terms. Plundering the dead was never described in Greek and Roman texts. Seventeenth-century viewers would not have expected to see it in a mythological scene, which this seems to be. But the picture is not really mythological. It is a reflection of current warfare, in which plundering corpses was punishable by death if done without orders, but commonplace.

In all this, there is no dignity or heroism, no right or wrong. Both Greeks and Amazons are victims and perpetrators. The subject is the war and its horrors, and to show them Rubens has stripped away every positive element he might have inherited from the past.

Rubens was eager to spread his universal message as widely as possible. The way to achieve this was by making an engraving of the picture and having it published. This was another monumental achievement, another display of virtuosity. He had it made two-thirds the size of the original

(85 x 120 centimetres), which meant dividing the plates into six sheets – the largest engraving made in Holland up to that time. Moreover, Rubens made his message even more explicit by dedicating the print to a woman – Alethea Howard, Countess of Arundel (her name is pronounced Al-*ee*-thea, from the Greek for 'truth'). Her husband, Thomas Howard, Earl of Arundel, was Earl Marshal of England, a famous art collector and Rubens's future patron, but it was she who was of special interest to Rubens because he had painted her (along with her jester, dwarf and dog) when she came through Antwerp and she was now part of his message – as a force in her own right, in effect an Amazon. She (he implied) was politically engaged, and could, perhaps, exert influence that would end the dire consequences of violence shown in the engraving done for her and the picture from which it was taken.

The PR worked, for art and perhaps a little in politics. The picture was given pride of place in a composite of portraits and well-known paintings in *The Gallery of Cornelis van der Geest*, done by the gallery's curator, Willem van Haecht. And the print, when reduced to normal size, became extremely popular. It still is.

And peace came at last. The Treaty of Westphalia that brought to a close the Thirty Years' War marked the end of the wars of religion in Europe, the end of Spanish military control, the start of France's rise. It settled peoples and dynasties within national frontiers. Wars were now between nations, and not continent-wide, peace ensured by a balance of powers, until Napoleon unbalanced them 150 years later, recalling some of the horrors of the Thirty Years' War and Rubens's dystopian view.

*

Move forward now to a quieter time, the mid-eighteenth century. We are in the age of the Enlightenment, a label used by self-satisfied intellectuals who liked to think that the scientific method and reasoned thought was setting aside the authority of the Church, whatever that was in a Christianity divided between Catholics and Protestants and their countless rival sects.

Nature and Nature's Laws lay hid in Night:
God said, 'Let Newton be!' and all was light.

Alexander Pope's epitaph on the man who more than any other led the scientific revolution overstated a little, because Newton himself was half-hid in night, believing that his work on the Bible was as flawless as his laws of motion. Newton died in 1727. Soon, John Locke would argue that the only true foundations for knowledge were the impressions made by the real world on the senses. The only authority, the only truth, the only way to unlock nature's secrets was to make sense of sense-impressions with mathematics and experiment and reason. Emerging from the dark and pessimistic depths of what seemed universal and enduring war, mankind was at last climbing towards sunny and optimistic uplands. If all was not yet light, it soon would be.

Moreover, it was possible for almost anyone to know almost everything if they put their mind to it. In France, Voltaire was a playwright and a poet, but he also wrote history and explained Newton's physics to the French. Adam Smith's *Wealth of Nations* founded modern economics, but he was also a moral philosopher.

There was little room in the scientific, rationalist view for

God, certainly for the God of the established churches. Of course, the revolution would take time. God and his churches remained part of thought and society, and out-and-out atheism was unusual. But religious influence would surely wane as knowledge grew. If there were still mysteries – natural catastrophes, for instance, like the earthquake that devastated Lisbon in 1756 – they should be addressed by Science. That was the way to fulfil humanity's destiny: to seek happiness, avoid misery, make Progress.

In France, intellectuals believed the way forward was to acquire knowledge step by step, not just about science but about the world and other societies. Their big idea, spearheaded by Denis Diderot and Jean d'Alembert, was a vast compilation of information, an encyclopaedia, thirty-five volumes of which were published between 1751 and 1772. This was the 'war machine' (as one of its 150 authors, known as the Encyclopédistes, put it) that would inform and change minds, spreading ideas that were believed to be universal. Thus ignorance and intolerance would vanish, the laws of nature and society would stand revealed, and mankind would advance in the interests of all. So the new priesthood of intellectuals, the *philosophes*, believed, along with their co-'philosophers' in England, Scotland, Italy and Germany.

Why France? The main answer is Louis XIV. When he died in 1715, he had ruled for seventy-two years and pursued the nation's interest and his own ruthlessly and brilliantly. The rays of the Sun King glowed over all Europe, as well as burning a lot of it. Power and prestige meant that all Europe spoke French. But he was a despot, as his heirs Louis XV and XVI also wished to be, rather less successfully. Power also constrained. If the king ruled by divine right, if God was on his side, how could he permit the toleration for which the *philosophes* wished? He couldn't. Intellectuals and artists faced many barriers. Their ideas would have to await another sort of revolution, the violent one of 1789, before they could be taken further.

For sceptics like Voltaire and the Encyclopédistes, Amazons were not considered a serious subject, at least not by many. A cleric, Claude Guyon, in his two-volume history of the Amazons,[35] insisted that 'there is no nation more celebrated, more remarkable or better attested'; the scientist and explorer Charles Marie de la Condamine was sure they were to be found in South America; Joseph Lafitau, the one who had actually worked with Iroquois Indians, insisted that all native Americans were descended from ancient races, including the Amazons. Voltaire said it was all rubbish: 'The Kingdom of the Amazons, on the banks of the Thermodon, is nothing more than a poetic fiction.' Across the Channel, Edmund Gibbon was more discreet in his monumental *Decline and Fall of the Roman Empire*. Commenting on the AD 274 victory parade of the Roman emperor Aurelian with its long train of captives, he writes that 'the title of Amazons was bestowed on ten martial heroines of the Gothic nation', to which he adds a careful footnote: 'It is *almost* impossible that a society of Amazons should ever have existed.'

But still they were there, lodged in the European consciousness, appealing to the poetic imagination, and finding an outlet through the pen of a woman, one of those remarkable eighteenth-century women who were widely responsible for the spread of Enlightenment ideas.

---

[35] *Histoire des Amazones anciennes et modernes*, Paris, 1740.

Just as important as books, letters and lectures were the Parisian drawing rooms of the rich and influential. In these *salons*, the dominant personalities were the women. The *salons* had a century of tradition behind them, looking back to Catherine de Vivonne, Marquise de Rambouillet, in the early seventeenth century. She set up a sort of counter-court, free of courtly constraints, emphasizing the arts of conversation – politeness, tact, culture, intimacy. She and later hostesses – *salonnières* – invited guests who, above all, had to be interesting. Neither wealth nor social standing was enough. The idea was to discuss and spread what was new in literature, science, art, politics, thought and society, exploring themes like friendship, marriage, love and independence. They chaired, encouraged, entertained, facilitated and educated themselves, becoming people of influence on behalf of culture. They taught the 'womanly virtues' by example, aiming to 'purge men of the boorish Academy legacy which weighed on them, in which the purpose was to crush others with the weight of one's learning.'[36] Thanks to these intelligent, ambitious women, clever members of both sexes intermingled, and all found they were the better for doing so.

The name of the *salonnière* in question is Madame du Boccage. Born Anne-Marie le Page in Rouen, she moved to Paris at twenty-three with her tax-collector husband, who liked books and ideas. She was obviously and notoriously brilliant, intellectually and socially. She knew Latin, Greek and several modern languages. She set up a salon, achieving no great fame until in 1746, at the age of thirty-six, she wrote

[36] Obituary of Anne-Marie du Boccage, *Monthly Magazine and British Register*, 1 October 1804.

a poem that won her first prize from the Academy – the good-and-great of the local intellectuals – in her home town of Rouen. She sent the poem to Voltaire, who liked it so much he wrote back addressing her as the 'Sappho of Normandy', referring to her poetic abilities, but perhaps implying more, for reasons we will get to later. A fellow Norman recommended her to the philosopher Fontenelle, still feisty at the age of ninety, who introduced her to the playwright Pierre de Marivaux. The boost to her salon seems to have injected ambition and released talent.

Two years later, she finished a French version of the first half of Milton's *Paradise Lost*. That's some 5,000 lines from very demanding English, not bad going for anyone, and for a woman in such male-dominated times quite extraordinary. The next person to try it, 100 years later, was the diplomat, historian and Romantic writer Châteaubriand. It was a task 'I would never have imposed on myself,' he wrote afterwards, 'if I had known what was involved.' He spoke perfect English, having lived there for eight years, and his translation was in prose. Hers, though an 'imitation', as she called it, rather than a translation, was in twelve-syllable rhyming Alexandrines, the form sanctioned by two centuries of use. It was not great; but it was an achievement, and admired enough for her to continue writing.

Her medium now became the stage, her subject the Amazons. As few took them seriously, since her friend Voltaire said they had never existed, we have to ask: why? One answer, almost certainly, is that she took them seriously because la Condamine, just back from travelling the length of the Amazon, was a friend. It was he, remember, who said he had almost seen Amazons, was convinced that they had once existed, and guessed they might still exist beyond a horizon yet to be explored. That was good enough for Madame du Boccage. Of course, she was not going to write about an unrecorded tribe of Indians in Amazonia. She picked up the old stories from classical Greece and changed things to suit herself and to explore contemporary themes: the nature of the state, the importance of law, the dangers of emotion.

Les Amazones, written in a year, tells the story of how Queen Orithya, who has captured Theseus – that's her invention: these Greeks are losers not victors – falls in love with him and commits suicide because she has infringed the laws of the state. The theme is mainstream Enlightenment. But du Boccage's other purpose was to advance the cause of women by providing an example of female creativity. She says as much in a rhyming dedication 'To Women', urging them to focus not on looks and subservience, but on 'character and language':

> Consider that the seductive charms
> Of your character and language
> Enslave more hearts
> Than were ever subjugated
> By the brave heroines of the ancient world.

The play itself is again in rhyming Alexandrines, and in the traditional five acts – a constraint which, like the sonnet, served to distil creativity into occasional works of genius. This isn't one of them, but it's pretty damn good. The themes are basic: love, death, shame, duty, glory. A main one is the importance of the state, which many *philosophes* said should be underpinned by the implied contract between individuals and their government. Jean-Jacques Rousseau, future author of *Du contrat social* (*The Social Contract*), was a leading *philosophe*. Even as she was writing, *De l'esprit des lois* (*The Spirit of the Laws*) by the lawyer and *philosophe* Baron de Montesquieu appeared, arguing that democratic republics depend on a readiness to put the community before the individual.

Not that du Boccage's Amazons are democrats. No one disagrees about the importance of the state. Actually, in their unanimity they seem to reflect and foreshadow something rather ominous, the militarism of Sparta, or of Nazi Germany. The play's sub-heroine, Menalippe, explains the austere Amazon code to Theseus in what is, in effect, a feminist manifesto.

Our unanimous aim, she says, is to redress the balance upset by the unjust seizure of power by arrogant males. The only way to do this is by force:

> From earliest childhood, we were destined for fighting,
> Our eyes – fierce, hard, devoid of tears –
> Know nothing of flattery, which is meant to charm;
> We inspire terror, not a desire to love;
> Our hands, neglecting finery to adorn us,
> Are busy with iron to forge our armour.

And force means rejecting traditional love. Cupid's arrows have no effect on Amazons.

> If we submit ourselves to the laws of Nature,
> It is only to control the future of our race,
> And repopulate these fields with women whose limbs

Are free, noble, and terrible in battle.
May they always be faithful to our virtues,
And see our tyrants destroyed and our laws immortalised!

It's all for liberty, 'the sovereign good', and peace, achieved by virtue, and frugality. The state is the basis of society, governed by unanimous consent, without kings, who are (says Menalippe) a prey to female charms, yet who cast aside young beauties when they age. With us, she concludes, a wrinkled brow is a mark of power. It's all well argued, very rational, in the tradition of the *philosophes*.

Meanwhile, Queen Orithya has a problem. She has Theseus in her power. She's supposed to kill him. But she's in love with him. This is wrong twice over, because (a) it's not rational and (b) it's against the laws of the Amazons. It is a forbidden love, which she tries to keep hidden. After an inner struggle, she confesses to her heir and confidante, Antiope. For anyone versed in French classics, as du Boccage's audience was, this was familiar territory. It looks back seventy years to an eminent precedent – Racine's *Phèdre*, in which Phaedra, the (later) wife of Theseus, has fallen in love with her stepson, Hippolytus. Like Racine's Phaedra, Orithya blames the goddess of love, Venus, who is using Theseus to punish her for past sins. She must keep her passion hidden, but cannot, and with its revelation the plot unfolds.

In brief: Theseus fancies Antiope, confesses, and is rejected. Orithya agonizes: should she court the hatred of her people by saving her hero? Or kill him, and condemn herself to a living death? And all for a love that is not requited. She is appalled at her own behaviour.

What! I offend our gods, my duty and my good name,
I bury the memory of my glorious deeds,
Reveal a passion that I ought to hide,
And degrade myself in the eyes of one I cannot touch.

An ambassador comes from the Scythians to ask for an alliance, to be secured by Antiope's marriage to his lord and master. Orithya begs Theseus to take her away. That's impossible. In a jealous rage, she accuses Antiope of treason. True, Antiope now loves Theseus for his fine qualities. The Greek army arrives and wins a great victory. Antiope agrees to go with Theseus to Greece. Orithya, having broken her own law, kills herself, leaving the empire to Menalippe, who will lead an Amazon nation that remains as strong as ever.

The play was put on by the Comédie Française, the national theatre then and now, in July and August 1749. It ran for eleven performances, not a complete disaster, but certainly no hit. An English traveller who saw it commented that 'It was a very poor performance, and barely suffered, not applauded, a French audience being too polite to affront a lady by condemning her production.' Word of mouth was pretty damning. Rumour had it that the theatre wanted to take it off after eight performances and only du Boccage's influence got it extended to eleven. Perhaps, muttered others, she wasn't the real author, being a woman.

That cheap jibe suggests there was more to the lukewarm reception than meets the eye. Du Boccage herself didn't see it as a failure. Voltaire, noted for his scathing opinions, loved it. Fontenelle, both a friend and the official censor, praised it as a 'play in which one sees with much pleasure Amazon warrioresses so well represented by another illustrious Amazon.'

One problem, perhaps, was the strength of its message. In political terms, it's a powerful feminist demand for equality. In other circumstances, women would cheer. But, in theatrical and social terms, strength can be a weakness. Du Boccage was a fierce voice in a polite society. People, especially men, don't generally like a hectoring tone. In plays, as in films, the message is best carried by the story and the characters, otherwise the audience loses interest.

My guess is that an English obituary[37] of du Boccage got it right – the play 'obtained its author the applause of one half of the spectators, the jealousy of the other, and soon afterwards the honour of a translation [into Italian].' The real problem was that she was a woman in a man's world. Playwrights were *men*, right? There were no women playwrights. She was an oddity, an outlier. As a *salonnière*, she was acceptable. But to be accepted as a playwright? That would have taken a work of genius, not just a highly competent one-off by a society lady with intellectual ambitions.

Undaunted, du Boccage turned to poetry, writing an epic about the discovery of America. Once again, la Condamine, her friend and New World explorer, was her inspiration. Her ambitions were all her own, as epic as the poem. *La Colombiade* is named after Columbus, founder of the New World, as Virgil named *The Aeneid* after Aeneas, Rome's founder. Being a social as well as an intellectual powerhouse, du Boccage subtitled her epic *Faith Transported to the New World* and dedicated it to the Pope, Benedict XIV, in humble, indeed grovelling terms. In these 184 pages of Alexandrines, there is also an Amazon – the Indian queen, who, spurned

[37] *Monthly Magazine and British Register*, 1 October 1804.

by Columbus, gathers an army, described with classical references: 'Penthesilea offered fewer fighters to the Trojans than there were Indians seen in the Chief's camp.'

As with her play, the context of the poem is more interesting than the work itself. Take the dedication to the Pope: she was no Catholic extremist, but she had good reason to ask for his blessing. Benedict was much admired by Enlightenment figures as the 'scholars' Pope'. He was eager to reconcile science and religion, backed the Enlightenment agenda, and – most astonishing of all – gave his support to women, most notably scientists, who are worth a diversion. One of them was Jane Squire, an Englishwoman deeply involved with the measurement of longitude, a problem eventually solved later in the century by John Harrison with his seagoing chronometer. Jane Squire's ideas, based on astronomical observations, were highly complex and too impractical to get any of the £20,000 offered by the Board of Longitude for a solution. Hardly anyone understood her, but many admired her expertise and determination to be recognized in a male domain. Other scientists received by the Pope were Laura Bassi, the first woman to be given a professorship in science (Bologna, 1732, in anatomy, at the age – would you believe – of twenty-one), and Maria Gaetana Agnesi, mathematician, whose 1748 book laid out the principles of infinitesimal calculus. I will never have any idea what that is, but to mathematicians she is a heroine. Benedict acknowledged the genius of these women, and of du Boccage when he received her in the Vatican in 1755. All three were made members of the Bologna Academy, along with another Frenchwoman, Émilie du Châtelet, physicist and friend of Voltaire, who translated and wrote a commentary on Newton's *Principia*

Mathematica, the bible of the scientific revolution. It was a tribute to du Boccage's intellect, achievements (and also possibly her networking skills) to be included in such company.

The *Colombiade* has one final claim to attention: a possible link to the gay community, a significant and long-established aspect of *salon* life. True to her feminist agenda, du Boccage asked a close but unnamed female friend, Madame D***, to illustrate the poem with engravings. Her verse of thanks suggests hidden depths. In a rough, literal translation it runs: 'Oh thou, who, by divine gift, hast received a share of the Graces, a Muse whose wise graving-tool here paints the image of Loves. What! Friendship guides your hand, your talents embellish my work. May it have your happy destiny! It would be an advantage in giving pleasure.' A message may lurk behind her words. 'The image of Loves' – why 'Loves', *des Amours*, plural? It usually means 'love-affairs'. It is a little odd, especially as 'loves' have little to do with the poem's narrative. Remember that Voltaire called du Boccage the Sappho of Normandy, and that Sappho was both poet and a Lesbian in both senses – an inhabitant of Lesbos and (supposedly) a woman with female lovers. Perhaps, in the intense social world of the *salons*, Madame D*** was more than a friend.

Du Boccage went on to travel a great deal, write letters about her travels, publish them, have them translated into English, and receive praise for them from Voltaire. She lived on into old age, widely admired. Benjamin Franklin – scientist, inventor, philosopher, the most eminent American intellectual of his day – made a point of visiting her when he came to Paris in 1767. She died in 1802, aged ninety-two, a remarkable lady who still awaits a modern biographer.

*

By the time du Boccage died, France was a different place, changed by revolution. In German-speaking lands, still a mass of states and city-states, writers and artists were going through a revolution of their own, rather less bloody. They had been in the grip of an obsession with ideals derived from Greek and Roman art, all 'noble simplicity and calm grandeur', in a popular phrase coined by the father of neoclassicism, Johann Winckelmann. While art and architecture mostly clung to classical rules, German writers didn't. Who wanted to see a play about normal people discussing polite subjects in measured tones, in rhyming couplets, always in five acts? Action and emotion were what mattered. The mood was set by, among others, Johann Wolfgang von Goethe, whose *Die Leiden des jungen Werthers* (*The Sorrows of Young Werther*, 1774) made him a literary sensation in Germany at the age of twenty-four, in all Europe a year later. Werther kills himself for unrequited love. So successful was the book that it became the first example of product placement. All over Germany, passionate young men dressed as Werther – yellow trousers, blue jacket – and bought Werther prints. So many of them (so it is said, though facts are sparse) committed copycat suicide that governments took fright; the novel was banned in Leipzig, Denmark and Italy.[38] The swing away from the formality of traditional French writing became a movement known as *Sturm und Drang* (Storm and Stress). This was youth having its day. It didn't last long. Other authors won approval for their down-to-earth sensitivity and 'natural' language, notably Shakespeare, who became an honorary

---

[38] The phenomenon of copycat suicides is now termed the 'Werther Effect'. Copycat suicides are a reality. How real the original Werther Effect was is unknown. It may all have been rumour.

German thanks to the brilliant translation by the Schlegel brothers. The adoration of all things classical – Hellenism, as it was known – continued unabated. Goethe settled in little, thatched Weimar, which, with its palace and court theatre, was the village-sized capital of a mini-state, the Duchy of Saxe-Weimar-Eisenach. There, as the greatest polymath of his day – novelist, playwright, poet, scientist, critic, theatrical director, man of letters (12,000 of which have survived) – he became the centre point of a cultural Golden Age.[39]

In 1802, Goethe was visited by a young man whose life seemed to be one long crisis. At twenty-five, Heinrich von Kleist was a restless and troubled writer. The oldest son of a Prussian officer, he had served in the Prussian army, and hated it; started on a university education, and stopped; got engaged, and un-engaged in order (he said) to seek Knowledge, Virtue and Happiness; and worked as a junior official in the Finance Ministry in Berlin, but left to travel. Later, after his Weimar visit, he came to think that acquiring knowledge was impossible. Life was nothing but absurdity and blind chance. Enduring pessimism seized him, a 'broken-hearted fascination with the depth and unilluminable darkness of the human soul'.[40] Unfortunately for his career, this was the force that drove him to write. Fortunately for posterity, he wrote like a dream.

---

[39] Here is George Steiner summarizing Goethe's genius in a review of the second volume of Nicholas Boyle's masterly biography: 'Often Goethe dictated in a week what would constitute very nearly the collected writings of lesser spirits. He did so while travelling, while helping to govern a duchy, while directing its theatre and opera, investigating its agricultural and mineral resources, accompanying its ruler to war, begetting a family and entering on erotic relationships almost each of which generated poetry of a classic force.'

[40] Joel Agee in the introduction to his translation of *Penthesilea*, from which the quotes in this chapter are taken.

In 1808, Goethe received a strange, apparently deferential letter from Kleist. 'Honourable Sir! Esteemed Privy Councillor!' He enclosed the first issue of his new journal, *Phöbus*, in which was printed a fragment of his new play, *Penthesilea*. 'It is on "the knees of my heart" that I thus appear before you.' It is the sort of letter that makes a director's heart sink. It was a fragment, Kleist continued, not yet edited, not yet ready for the stage, but still he hoped for it to be put on, even if no stage would take him seriously and he would have to 'look toward the future'.

Beside all that, the play might have been designed to antagonize the great man. His own play, *Iphigenia on Tauris*, was an expression of classic Hellenism: love, truth, modesty and beauty intertwined. Penthesilea is a figure of demonic lust and rage, a *Sturm und Drang* figure taken to an extreme of passion. Her enemy, Achilles, is the focus of that passion, and she of his. They are both amok with bloodlust and desire.

It's an extreme taken to further extremities. Penthesilea, in traditional terms, lacks a breast. Kleist turns the mutilation into a metaphor that runs through the whole play, remoulding the myth to suit his own purposes. In the climax, Penthesilea kills Achilles, not the other way around. She loves him, but must prove herself superior. She shoots him, then in a fit of passion gores him to death alongside her dogs. The scene is relayed by a priestess in classical mode, not shown on stage for obvious reasons:

> Into his ivory breast she sinks her teeth
> She and her savage dogs in competition
> Oxus and Sphinx chewing into his right breast,
> And she into his left.

Kleist invented the idea of the 'invulnerable' Achilles becoming a victim, but he did not invent this horrific form of death. It derives from a supposed Ancient Greek ritual in which the followers of the wine god Dionysus (Bacchus to the Romans) go wild in an orgy of drink and bloodlust, and tear apart an animal and/or a human being in a ritual known as *sparagmos* ('tearing apart'). And there was a recent precedent in the way women acted during the French Revolution, portrayed by Friedrich von Schiller – a frequent visitor in Weimar, friend of Goethe, acquaintance of Kleist – as part of a long poem, 'Das Lied von der Glocke' ('The Song of the Bell'), written in 1798 and already hugely popular: 'Then women become hyenas, and make a plaything out of terror – with panther's teeth they tear out the enemy's still-twitching heart.'

The next scene has Penthesilea a catatonic blank, all memory of her act repressed. As consciousness returns, she thinks she has defeated Achilles and is happy. Achilles's body is on stage under a red carpet. When, in exchanges with her appalled priestesses, she realizes it's him, she wants to see him, thinking he lives, and will stand and submit after his defeat. Nothing happens. Doubt seizes her. 'Speak, women, did I strike too close?' She lifts the carpet, sees the mutilated corpse and demands in horror to know who did this. Her women tell her. She begins to remember, coming out with a line widely reviled for being ludicrous, tasteless or just plain weird. 'Did I kiss him to death?' she asks. 'No? Didn't kiss him? Really tore him apart?'

Then comes her explanation. Biting and kissing are easily confused:

> A kiss, a bite,
> The two should rhyme, for one who truly loves
> With all her heart can easily mistake them.[41]

When Goethe read it, he was appalled. This was the opposite of everything that was meant by the word 'feminine' in the Enlightenment. By nature restrained and polite, his reply to Kleist was about as rude as he ever got. 'As for Penthesilea, I have not yet been able to warm up to her. She is of so wondrous a race and moves in such an alien region that I shall need time to get accustomed to both.' Also, he added, it pained him to see a young man of intelligence and talent 'waiting for a theatre that has yet to come.' In so many words he said: 'The theatre is alive and well! It's your play that's the problem!'

Goethe, who recognized Kleist's literary skills, put on the young man's play *Der zerbrochene Krug* (*The Broken Jug*). It was a disaster. The play was supposed to be done with no interval. Goethe divided it into three acts with two intervals. After almost four hours, the audience was catatonic. It seemed to Kleist like a deliberate act of destruction, on top of Goethe's failure to recognize the genius of *Penthesilea*. He never forgave him for the double slight.

And yet Kleist was in some ways ahead of him. *Der zerbrochene Krug* became an enduring success and is still done today. And *Penthesilea* foreshadows something that was very much yet to come. Freud, writing a century in the future, might have used the play as a case history. It is like a door into the unconscious, Kleist's and ours.

---

[41] It works better in German, but not much: *Küsse, Bisse, das reimt sich.*

Ours because it is fine raw material for psychological analysis. Love is, after all, a consuming passion. To heighten reality (which he did well in other plays), Kleist makes it literally consuming, and with a very specific target. It is the right breast that Penthesilea lacks, as do all the Amazons on stage, as did their ancestral figure Tanais, who tore off her right breast when founding her nation – or so Kleist has Penthesilea say, though Tanais was a city and a river (the Don), not an Amazonian founder. She goes for Achilles's *left* breast.

A psychoanalyst might continue:

Penthesilea is an incomplete woman and that drives her to seek completion. The desires and conflicts strip her of adult reactions and turn her into a child, who cannot engage with the other. She vacillates, now feeling all-powerful, now utterly worthless, a conflict that reduces her to silence, even unconsciousness. She sees Achilles not as an individual but as an extension of herself – an extension over which she has no control. She expects him to share her feelings even before meeting him, to understand her aggression as courting, so that when he fells her, her sense of rejection and incomprehension inspires wild rage. As one psychoanalytical paper puts it, 'Through the course of the play, she regresses to ever more archaic mental and psychic levels, finally and tragically to a level that is pre-verbal, oral, and so primitive that it no longer knows the distinctions of up and down, bite and kiss, self and other.'[42] If only she can *incorporate* Achilles, she will make herself whole again. When she thinks Achilles will be hers, she becomes rapturous:

---

[42] Ursula Mahlendorf, 'The Wounded Self'. See Bibliography.

> Oh, let this heart
> Dive under, like a sullied child, and bathe
> Two minutes in this stream of limpid joy!
> With every stroke beneath its bounteous waves
> A blemish from my breast is washed away.

Achilles, too, is reduced to childishness by his passion. In one scene, when he thinks he has killed Penthesilea, he is so appalled that he throws off his armour, makes himself vulnerable and so virtually guarantees his own death.

The play also casts a light on Kleist's unconscious. He had a very odd attitude towards women, indeed towards gender generally, his own included. He didn't much like women. Yes, as a product of the Enlightenment he accepted they were supposed to exercise restraint over men by being gentle and submissive, but: 'Their demands for decency and morality destroy the whole nature of the drama.' In a word, he was conflicted, especially about his sister Ulrike, who liked to dress as a man, and whom he thought as coolheaded as a man, while he himself was a prey to intense 'feminine' emotions. He envied her, and disapproved of her at the same time. 'Amphibian,' he asked of her in a new year's wish for 1800, 'you who inhabit two elements always, waiver no longer, choose a definite gender at last.'

He suffered from similar ambiguities, as he made explicit in a letter to his friend Ernst von Pfuel, future Prussian general, war minister and prime minister. The two were old friends from their army days. Pfuel was a good swimmer. In 1802–3, Kleist was living on an island, now named after him, in the River Aare, Switzerland, writing his first plays. Pfuel came to visit and the two went swimming in Lake Thun. Three years later, with Europe convulsed by the Napoleonic Wars, Kleist wrote to him, recalling that happy time:

> Why can I no longer venerate you, whom I still love above all, as my master? How we rushed into one another's arms a year ago in Dresden! What we loved in one another then were the highest qualities of mankind . . . We felt – or at least I did – the delightful enthusiasm of friendship! You brought back the times of ancient Greece to my heart, I could have slept with you, dear boy; thus all my soul embraces you. Often, as you rose before my eyes in the Lake of Thun, I would gaze at your beautiful body with truly girlish feelings . . . Were I an artist, it might perhaps have inspired me with an idea for a god. Your small, curly head set on a sturdy neck, two wide shoulders, a sinewy body: the whole a model of strength, as though you had been designed after the fairest young bull ever sacrificed to Zeus. All the laws of Lycurgus, as well as his concept of the love of youths, have become clear to me through the feelings you awakened in me. Come to me! . . . I will never marry, be a wife, children and grandchildren to me.

Was this a recollection of a gay affair? Many think so. Lycurgus was the legendary founder of Sparta, who not only established the system of young men training together, but also laid down many other laws on which Sparta rose to dominance. Sex seems to be explicit. If it's not, it was surely in Kleist's mind as a possibility, a thought – a wish – a memory that lay behind the conflicts revealed in *Penthesilea*.

Goethe, the poet, knew Kleist was wonderful with language. *Penthesilea* is certainly brilliantly poetic. But as a play? He could not see it. You can have violence and gore, but it 'verges on comedy', he said to a friend, to have a one-breasted heroine on stage assuring the audience that her female feelings are not diminished, because they have all been focused into the other breast. This is really not funny, but he had a point: as theatre, it's very hard to take seriously. Most modern directors, actors and producers agree. It's much studied, but hardly ever put on.

Kleist never heard about Goethe's private opinion. He was dead before it saw the light of day. After the quarrel with Goethe, there followed three years of intense creativity – a collection of short stories and several plays, which made him a reputation and would eventually ensure him a place as one of Germany's finest writers. But Kleist, now aged thirty-three, had convinced himself that death was the only answer to the miseries of his life. He contacted a friend, Henriette Vogel, who had terminal cancer and knew she had not long to live. This is what happened next, as reported by the London *Times*:

Madame Vogel, it is said, had suffered long under an incurable disorder; her physicians had declared her death inevitable; she herself formed a resolution to put a period to her existence. M. Kleist, the poet, and a friend of her family, had also long determined to kill himself. These two unhappy beings having confidentially communicated to each other their horrible resolution, resolved to carry it into effect at the same time. They repaired to the Inn at Wilhelmstadt, between Berlin and Potsdam, on the border of the Sacred Lake [Kleiner Wannsee]. For one night and one day they were preparing themselves for death, by putting up prayers, singing, drinking a number of bottles of wine and rum, and last of all by taking about sixteen cups of coffee. They wrote a letter to M. Vogel [Henriette's father], to announce to him the resolution they had taken, and to beg him to come as speedily as possible, for the purpose of seeing their remains interred. The letter was sent to Berlin by express. This done, they repaired to the banks of the Sacred Lake, where they sat down opposite to each other. M. Kleist took a loaded pistol, and shot Madame Vogel through the heart, who fell back dead; he then re-loaded the pistol, and shot himself through the head.

Today, nearby, in a pretty grove of ivy-covered trees, an austere block of stone is their memorial. You can hire head-phones to hear the story of what happened.

10

THE AMAZONS OF 'BLACK SPARTA'

FROM ALL THE LEGENDARY NONSENSE, A LITTLE SENSE emerges. Yes, there were many individual Amazons, warrior women who fought with their men, and sometimes led them. No, there was never anywhere a *nation* of Amazons. But there was once a regiment of women warriors, some 6,000 of them. For 150 years, they served the king of the West African state of Dahomey, in today's Benin. Locally, they were *ahosi*, the 'king's wives', but when European explorers came across these tough, disciplined, brave and extremely scary fighters in the 1840s, they drew on their own traditions and called them Amazons. The name is spurious, imposed by English and French imperialists, but it stuck. Today, everyone refers to them as Amazons, including the museum in Abomey, Dahomey's former capital.

The regiment is interesting enough. Even more intriguing is the way these Amazons reflected the role of women in Dahomean society. They formed a shadow administration, in which women were doubles of the male officials, looking over their shoulders, checking up on what they were doing, providing solid foundations for a fiercely militaristic kingdom – a 'black Sparta' as it has been called – that would otherwise have been as unstable as most others in an unstable continent. This system, unmatched before or since, vanished in 1892, blown into oblivion by French guns.

The origins of Dahomey's Amazons were in the eighteenth century, in pre-literate times, when every ruler, petty or powerful, rivalled every other in the capture of slaves and their delivery to European coastal forts for the stinking and often fatal voyage to the Americas. Dahomey, the nation-state of the Fon people, rose to power after conquering two lesser kingdoms in the 1720s. Other kingdoms had armed female guards at their courts, but the Dahomean king, Agaja, put together a unique force. Since he would allow no men to sleep within the walls of his palace in the capital, Abomey, he had to rely on women, plus a few eunuchs. In 1772, an English trader, Robert Norris, noted that the palace guard house had forty women armed with muskets and cutlasses. By the end of the century, there were several hundred women bodyguards. Sometimes they fought, especially in disputes over the succession. Norris recorded 285 women killed after the death of a king in 1774. Another visitor, Archibald Dalzel, said 595 of them were killed after the next royal death fifteen years later.

It was Dahomey's ninth king, Gezo (1818–58), who turned his female guards into soldiers. He was eager to resist adjacent states, in particular to fill the vacuum left by the collapse of the rival Oyo empire of the Yoruba people in neighbouring Nigeria. Also he was preparing to oppose the British-led campaign to end the slave trade on which his economy depended. He could do with all the warriors he could get. In 1845, a Scottish explorer, John Duncan, watched the annual display of military might which included (he estimated) 6–8,000 women, who had fought against Mahi, a rival kingdom to the north (the Mahi are still an important group in central Benin). Five years later, a naval officer, Frederick Forbes, said that there were 5,000 women – out of a total force of 12,000 – and that they had fought against Atakpamé, a mini-state to the west (now a city in Togo).

There was never any doubting how formidable these women were. They formed teams of hunters known as *gbeto*, and would eagerly attack elephants and crocodiles (some wore caps with a crocodile logo to prove their success). 'Their appearance is more martial than the generality of the men,' wrote John Duncan. 'If undertaking a campaign, I should prefer the females to the male soldiers.' In the opinion of a naval office, Arthur Wilmott: 'They are far superior to the men in everything – in appearance, in dress, in figure, in activity, in their performance as soldiers, and in bravery.' The men fired their muskets wildly from the hip, and reloaded on average in fifty seconds; the women fired from the shoulder and took thirty seconds to reload.

They could not, however, guarantee victory in warfare. In 1851, 6,000 women, with another 10,000 men, attacked Abeokuta, in today's south-west Nigeria. They lost, disastrously, and this became the defeat that had to be avenged. A story told later in Abeokuta claimed that the use of women warriors helped the defenders, because when they attempted to castrate one of their attackers, they discovered they were fighting women and were so ashamed by the possibility of defeat by women that they redoubled their efforts and won a stunning victory. According to the disputed estimates, Dahomey's Amazons lost 2,000 in that battle.

The most vivid portrait of these warrior women came from that most colourful of Victorian personalities, Richard Burton. Into his forty years he had already crammed lifetimes of adventure, travel and scholarship. A youth spent back and forth in France and Italy, with various tutors, taught him French, Italian, Neapolitan, Latin and also (rumour had it) Romany, the result of a love-affair with a gypsy. A genius at languages, he was an outsider, with broad interests and little respect for convention. At Oxford he studied Arabic, took up fencing and falconry, and got expelled for attending a steeplechase, which was against college rules. Fit for nothing but to be shot at (as he said), he joined the East India Company and was posted to Gujarat, where he learned another six Indian languages – Hindi, Punjabi, Gujarati, Sindhi, Marathi and Persian – seven if you count Saraiki as a language rather than a dialect of Punjabi. Never had any outsider gone quite so native.

Turning his dark, smouldering good looks and bushy, drooping moustache to advantage, Burton took on the persona of a Persian named Mirza Abdullah and was put to undercover work. His research included the brothels of Karachi, which employed boy prostitutes, a subject on which he wrote in rather too much detail for some. Despite this, or perhaps because of it, he was given leave to go on the annual Muslim pilgrimage to Mecca – in disguise, of course, because if discovered he risked death. He prepared by having himself circumcised. Claiming to be a Pashtun to explain his accent, he displayed a convincing knowledge of Islamic traditions, kept meticulous notes and survived to tell the tale, which, when published, made him famous.

Back with the political department of the East India Company and supported by the Royal Geographical Society, he headed into the East African interior – becoming the first European to enter Harar in Ethiopia – an expedition that ended in an attack by Somalis, which left one member dead, the co-leader John Hanning Speke severely wounded and Burton with a spear through his cheek. More books followed. A later expedition with Speke was supposed to check out the possibilities for trade, but a hidden agenda was to find the source of the Nile, which had become one of the greatest issues of the day. Many diseases later, they found Lake Tanganyika. Burton was too ill to continue and Speke, half blind, went on without him, to find Lake Victoria, which is very nearly the Nile's source. Back in London, claim and counter-claim led to a violent quarrel between the two. They were in the midst of arguing the matter in public when Speke walked out. Later that day he went hunting and in a bizarre accident, never properly explained, apparently shot himself while climbing a stile. Later expeditions under Grant, Baker, Livingstone and Stanley would confirm the Nile's real source, ending the second greatest controversy of the century, at least in England (the greatest being the one swirling around Darwin's *Origin of Species*).

Meanwhile, Burton, eager for a post that would allow for his scholarly interests, had been appointed consul in West Africa, based in Port Clarence on the island of Fernando Po. He arrived at a crucial moment. For over 200 years, the West African coast had been both a treasure trove and a malarial death-trap for slavers. In the words of a well-known couplet:

Beware and take heed of the Bight of Benin,
Where few go out and many go in.

Though ships still slipped through to Cuba and Brazil, the trade was virtually over, thanks to the British navy. Coastal forts were closing, the interior opening, turning West Africa, indeed all Africa, into a free-for-all. Europeans and others – French, Dutch, English, Spanish, Brazilians – were beginning what would later be called the Scramble for Africa, carving up tribes and cultures and ecologies with lines on empty maps. No one knew much about the interior, but as quinine brought relief to the scourge of malaria, explorers began to trace the great rivers, traders sought new products and missionaries dreamed of converts by the uncounted million, all of these elements dragging government in their wake. In West Africa, with kings determined to control the coast, returned slaves threatening upheaval and middlemen wanting their cut of exports – in particular of palm oil – European nations, Britain being the main one, sought to impose law and order.

Dahomey, though, was not easily reached. Quite a few had been there – missionaries, naval officers, consuls, traders

– most trying to get King Gezo on side. These efforts had achieved little when Gezo was killed by a Yoruba sniper in 1858. In 1860, with a new king, Glele, in place, events took an uglier turn. From Lagos the consul and the Church Missionary Society reported that Dahomey was about to attack Abeokuta again. That would ruin decades of trade and missionary work. The government considered sending in troops, then reconsidered, and annexed Lagos. The Foreign Office decided on diplomacy. They sent a naval mission to Abomey to persuade King Glele to sign a treaty: slavery should stop, human sacrifices should stop, there should be peace with Abeokuta. To these demands Glele said no, no and no. Foreigners could not just come in and change centuries of tradition; his country had been invaded four times by Oyo. The navy, with better things to do than argue the British case, withdrew.

Over to Burton. He could hardly wait. He had started to study the Fon language and had read everything available about them. He saw, noted and understood more than anyone before him, and many who followed, until modern anthropologists and historians filled the gaps, as best they could for a culture that had vanished.

Carried northwards, slung between the shoulders of five bearers known as 'hammock-men', with six guards and a Dahomean escort of twenty, Burton had been provided with a selection of gifts requested by Glele: a 40-foot silk tent, a silver pipe, two silver belts with 'lion and crane in raised relief', two silver-and-gilt stands, and a coat of mail, with gauntlets. Glele had also asked for a horse-drawn carriage, such as befitted sovereigns like Queen Victoria and himself. Burton was told by the foreign minister, Lord John Russell, to explain that transporting a carriage and horses to the West African coast was tricky, and that 'it would be very doubtful, from the nature of the country and climate, whether they would long survive.' Burton was then supposed to hurry on with a reassurance: if future relations 'should be of a nature to warrant such a proceeding, Her Majesty's Government would not hesitate to endeavour to comply.'

What he found on the plateau between two swampy, wooded rivers was a mini-nation of no more than 200,000. The capital, Abomey, had perhaps 20,000 inhabitants. For 200 years, the kings had ruled by exercising strict control of their many wives and children. They tried to avoid disputes over succession by nominating heirs in good time and favouring women as administrators. There were still altercations, but far fewer than among neighbouring groups; the average reign of the eleven Dahomean kings (1650–1894) was twenty-two years.

Women were favoured in an extraordinary way. The system in which every official had a female counterpart prescribed a 'mother' whose job it was to shadow the official's movements, policies and finances. Even the king had a shadow, based in the countryside, though a male shadow, not a female one. When and why this system evolved no one knows – possibly it went back to rule by twins in the early days of the kingdom – but it imposed checks and balances that would have amazed Jefferson and the other Founding Fathers of American democracy, and might have given some radical ideas to women in England on their slow march for women's rights.

Several Europeans had written of this strange society, but Burton was the first to record many of the details, with scathing comments, some witty, some crudely offensive, occasionally both. On the first day, a few miles short of the capital, there was a reception, including jesters who specialized in making faces and pretending to be deaf and dumb, which in Burton's view made each of them 'as lively as a professionally engaged mourner'. There were march-pasts, toasts, presentations of flags, and gun-salutes. The viceroy of the port of Whydah (today's Ouidah), a former slaving kingdom conquered by Dahomey, introduced himself, doffing his felt hat. 'His appearance revolts,' wrote Burton, who knew him by reputation. 'He is as bad as he looks, and his avarice is only to be equalled by his rapacity.' Singers, drummers and bards followed, and 'a truly barbarous display: eight human crania dished up on small wooden bowls like bread-plates, at the top of very tall poles.'

A slow walk along a pebble road led to the palace compound. Eight gates, with guards under umbrellas of many colours – signs of status – opened on to thatched sheds about 30 metres long, tall at the front, sloping almost to the ground at the back. Rank upon rank of officials are all listed and described. One, 'very old, with a peculiarly baboon-like countenance', wore 'a long coat which makes him look like a magnified bluebottle fly'. Finally came the royal reception: King Glele was 'athletic, upwards of six feet high, lithe, agile, hair of the peppercorn variety', eyebrows scant, hair thin, teeth sound, eyes bleary, which Burton put down to tedious receptions, perpetual smoking of a long-stemmed pipe and 'a somewhat excessive devotion to Venus.' He was on a bench swathed with red and white cloth and cushions. Behind him sat a throng of spouses. 'If perspiration appears upon the royal brow, it is instantly removed with the softest cloth by the gentlest hands.' He rose and shook hands vigorously. Through his prime minister and interpreter, he asked after Queen Victoria's health, and that of her ministers, people and all recent visitors that he could remember. Stools were placed, toasts drunk, guns fired.

Outside again for a pageant, under a canopy, Burton took notes, to the delight of the king. A line of twenty-four scarlet, green, purple and white umbrellas shielded the monarch and his wives. Male warriors were divided from female ones by bamboo palms. In lofty chairs sat a woman known as the Akutu, 'a huge, old porpoise', who was the 'captainess' of the king's bodyguards (Burton feminized nouns whenever possible), and the corresponding 'veteraness' on the prime minister's side, 'also vast in breadth', for 'the warrioresses begin to fatten when their dancing days are done, and some of them are prodigies of obesity.'

'The flower of the host was the mixed company of young Amazons lately raised by the King; this corps (about 200) . . . was evidently composed of the largest and finest women in the service.' Each had a strip of blue or white cloth binding the hair, a sleeveless waistcoat and a skirt of blue, pink and yellow, kept tight around the waist by a sash, a cartridge box, belt or bandolier, a bullet bag on a shoulder strap, a knife and a flintlock in a black monkey skin.

While a selection of Amazons danced and sang, officers grovelled in the dust, 'and shovelled it up by handfuls over their heads and arms, showing that they were of lower rank than the ministers,' an act common to 'all semi-barbarous societies.' Before the king, even the highest officers rolled, crawled or shuffled forward on their knees, to frequent cries of 'King of all kings!'

More songs, more dances followed, this time in the presence of

a dozen razor women, who, defiling past the King . . . took their stations near the throne; they held their weapons upwards in the air like standards, with a menacing air and gesture. The blade is about 18 inches, and shaped exactly like a European razor; it closes into a wooden handle about two feet in length, and though kept in position by strong springs, it must be, I should think, quite as dangerous to the owner as to the enemy. These portable guillotines were invented by a brother of the late king Gezo.

Perhaps because they were both impractical and recently invented, we hear nothing more of them in the fighting that is to come. There were more displays from 'bayoneteeresses' and 'blunderbuss-women', a final song –

We like not to hear that Abeokuta lives;
But soon we shall see it fall.

– then the king wrapped his robe around himself and left, 'every inequality of ground was smoothed, every stick and stone was pointed out, lest it might offend the royal toe', and the reception was over.

As 1863 gave way to the new year, Burton witnessed the annual so-called Customs, celebrations during which executions supplied the previous king 'with fresh attendants in the shadowy world.' In a 30-metre shed, which had a tower 'not unlike that of an English village church', were twenty prisoners in long white shirts, tied to posts, destined for sacrifice.

They were well looked after, and apparently unconcerned. At the entrance to a tent-like shed, which contained the relics of King Gezo, sat the king, surrounded by wives, protected by a mass of coloured parasols, and attended by Amazons squatting 'with their gun-barrels bristling upwards'. A crowd of perhaps 2,500 watched. Burton and his companions were seated under white parasols. The king spoke, sang, danced, wiped his brow with a forefinger and scattered his sweat over the delighted audience. So it went for five days: speeches, pageants, songs, music, dancing, feasting, military displays, parades of fetishes and oaths to defeat Abeokuta. Hunchbacks, of which there were many, cut swathes through the crowds with whips. At one point, the king threw cowrie shells, which were used as currency, into the crowd, starting a free-for-all. 'No notice is taken if a man be killed or maimed in the affair; he has fallen honourably . . . Some lose eyes and noses; the Dahomeans . . . bite like hyenas – I have seen a hand through which teeth met – and scratch like fisherwomen.'

Burton adds a note on human sacrifice. True, when kings died they were followed into the grave by a court of wives, eunuchs, singers and drummers; and it was the custom to execute criminals. But things were not so bad when compared to practices back in England. After all, in that very year 'we hung four murderers upon the same gibbet before 100,000 gaping souls in Liverpool,' and strung up five pirates in front of Newgate prison. In Dahomey, 'The executions are, I believe, performed without cruelty.' That year, about eighty were to be beheaded, half of them 'female victims killed by the Amazons in the palace, and not permitted to be seen by man.' Adding those slain on suspicion of witchcraft, Burton guessed the annual toll to be 500. He reported that twenty-three were killed on the final night of the Customs. 'The practice originates from filial piety, it is sanctioned by long use and custom, and it is strenuously upheld by a powerful and interested priesthood . . . Gelele [Burton's spelling] I am persuaded could not abolish human sacrifice if he would; and he would not if he could.'

Turning to the Amazons, he points out that they still maintained their roles as 'wives' and bodyguards, for 'Gelele causes every girl to be brought to him before marriage, and if she pleases, he retains her in the palace.' But now they were mostly warriors, 'the masculine physique of the women enabling them to compete with men in enduring toil, hardships and privations.' The force, some 2,500 – much reduced after the losses under the walls of Abeokuta – had five specialist units: 'blunderbuss-women', each with an attendant carrying ammunition; elephant hunters, the bravest of the brave; razor women; infantry, the bulk of the force; and archers, not many now that most had muskets, and used mainly as scouts. He saw them on the march. They were not exactly Grecian in their looks: they seemed old, Burton said, ugly, grumpy-looking, with immense buttocks. He might have added that they were determined, fiercely loyal, strong and willing to die for their king and country, just the sort of spirit needed in warfare.

The privates carried packs on cradles, like those of the male soldiery, containing their bed-mats, clothes and food for a week or a fortnight, mostly toasted grains and bean-cake, hot with peppers. Cartridge-pouches of two different shapes were girt around their waists, and slung to their sides were water-gourds, fetish-sacks, bullet-wallets, powder-calabashes, fans, little cutlasses . . . flint, steel and tinder, and Lilliputian stools, with three or four legs.

Supposedly the women were all celibate, since they were all legally the king's wives; not that he had sex with many of them, and those few were exempted from military action. The rest were indeed celibate, at least while they were Amazons, because adultery with a royal wife meant dire punishment, even death. Not much of a deterrent, apparently: Burton reports that 150 Amazons were found to be pregnant and were tried with their lovers, eight of whom were executed, the rest being imprisoned or relegated. Some eyewitnesses suggested that enforced celibacy increased their ferocity. It also had another effect, as Burton claims in a footnote of surprising obscurity, given his interests. The Amazons, he says, prefer 'the peculiarities of the Tenth Muse'. Today, the Tenth Muse is a comic-book heroine who is, somehow, the daughter of Zeus. Back in Burton's day, some of those privileged with a classical education knew about the nine Muses who presided over all the arts, and also knew that Plato and many later writers referred to Sappho as the Tenth Muse[43] – Sappho the poetess of Lesbos, renowned for her 'amorous disposition' towards her female companions, in the coy words of Lamprière's *Classical Dictionary*. Burton meant the Dahomey Amazons were lesbians, a statement for which he provided no evidence at all.

They were undoubtedly very much the king's women. Another eyewitness, a naval officer named Frederick Forbes, was told by one Amazon that the king 'has borne us again,

[43] In an epigram: 'Some say there are nine Muses; but they should stop to think. Look at Sappho of Lesbos; she makes a tenth'.

we are his wives, his daughters, his soldiers, his sandals'. They formed an elite, well supplied with food and slaves, cut off from their families, devoted exclusively to the king and the interests of his nation. They gloried in their power and ferocity, singing:

Let the men remain at home,
Growing corn and palms!
We, the women,
We're going to bring back entrails
With our hoes and our machetes.[44]

At first sight, this looks as if the Amazons were a vanguard for women's rights. Not so, because the women spoke of themselves as transformed into men. 'We were women, we are now men,' one of them told Forbes. Or as an ancient Amazon interviewed in the 1920s said, after she had killed and disembowelled her first enemy she was told, 'You are a man.' For them, the path to self-advancement lay through, rather than out of, subservience.[45]

Ferocity was encouraged. As part of their training, the Amazons made mock assaults over barriers of thorns, 'tearing their flesh as they crossed the prickly impediment,' in the words of a Portuguese traveller in 1830. Others witnessed numerous staged attacks, slave-hunts and battles under the eyes of King Gezo and his successor Glele. All was done with tremendous zest, which often tipped over into brutality. In 1850, at the annual Customs celebrations, two visitors (the

[44] Recorded by A. le Hérissé in 1911. My translation from the French. See Bibliography.
[45] From Robin Law, 'The "Amazons" of Dahomey'. See Bibliography.

British trader and consul John Beecroft and the naval officer Frederick Forbes) watched four trussed and gagged prisoners carried in large baskets through the waiting crowds on to a platform, where four Amazons tilted the baskets and tumbled the prisoners to their deaths at the hands of the bloodthirsty mob. There were many beheadings. In 1889 and 1890, French visitors saw what was apparently an annual ritual, in which Amazons tore an ox apart with knives and their bare hands, smearing themselves with the entrails. Perhaps, they suggested, this was 'insensitivity training', hardening them to bloodshed.

Burton was the opposite of a natural diplomat. He handed over all the gifts immediately, and told Glele what was expected of him in no uncertain terms. He said slave-raiding and slavery had to stop, ignoring the fact that ending it would destroy the relationship with Brazilian slavers, deprive the king of the income to support his army and officials, and generally wreck the economy. Glele was appalled. Peace with neighbours? Impossible. Oyo had invaded four times in the previous century, Glele's predecessor had been shot by a Yoruba. Burton had a strong case, morally, but he was – as a black pastor who was present put it – all 'hot passion and harsh temper'. Glele himself commented afterwards 'that if the Queen send such Commissioners to him it will spoil everything.' In fact, it did. There would be no treaty, no more presents, no more missions from the British. Burton's days in West Africa ended shortly afterwards, in turmoil, because he had authorized payment in a court case that the Foreign Office refused to reimburse.

A month after Burton's departure, Glele set out to take his revenge on Abeokuta, with some 10–12,000 troops, including

3,000 Amazons. They arrived exhausted, after a twenty-two-day march. It was a disaster. The inhabitants were ready for them, behind repaired walls. The Amazons fought with fanatical zeal. Only four warriors managed to climb the earth ramparts, all Amazons, all killed. A popular story told of an Amazon who, to show her scorn of the enemy, sat on a copper cauldron not far from the ramparts, turned her back and began smoking a long pipe, bullets zipping around her, until a sniper shot her dead. The inhabitants sent out a sortie, cut off her head and displayed it around town. It was all over in an hour and a half. Glele escaped, losing his tent, throne, sandals, 1,000 captured and some 2,000 dead, including 700 Amazons. Abeokuta remained an obsession for Dahomey for another twenty-five years. There were later raids, but no victory.

In those years, Glele launched several other campaigns beyond his borders. In 1879, he destroyed a Yoruba town, Meko, seizing 3,000 captives and taking 4,000 heads; Ketu, a town of 20,000 with a 7-kilometre wall and a 5-metre ditch, fell twice, in 1883, when its king was beheaded, and again two years later.

Meanwhile, beyond Glele's reach, greater forces were gathering. The French claimed authority over the ports of Porto-Novo and Cotonou, on the fringe of Glele's territory. Glele agreed, then changed his mind and sent raiding parties into nearby villages. A French delegation went to Abomey to negotiate, but to no effect, for by then King Glele was dying. Jean Bayol, the head of the mission, was shocked when a 'ravishing' sixteen-year-old Amazon recruit named Nansica was called upon to kill for the first time. Her victim was a prisoner tied up and sitting in a big basket. She severed his head with three swings of her sword, cut the last bit of flesh connecting head to trunk, then (according to one witness) swept the blood from the sword with her fingers and licked them clean.

In early 1890, France built up a contingent of 359 Africans under French officers in Cotonou – small, but newly armed with eight-shot Lebel repeating rifles, which could kill at 300 metres with high-velocity bullets. These bullets seem to have been dum-dums (named after an armoury in Calcutta), with soft lead heads that expanded on entry, leaving a fearsome exit wound. Winston Churchill recorded the effects after seeing action on India's North-West Frontier in 1898: 'The Dum-Dum bullet, though not explosive, is expansive . . . On striking a bone this causes the bullet to "set up" or spread out, and it then tears and splinters everything before it, causing wounds which in the body must be generally mortal and in any limb necessitate amputation.' The Lebel far outgunned the attackers' muzzle-loading flintlocks.

The French arrested some Fon officials and set up a log fence in front of their trading post. In the darkness before dawn on 4 March, several thousand Dahomeans, including a 'regiment' of Amazons, attacked the stockade, prising the logs apart to fire inside. Bayol saw a young Amazon behead a white sergeant before being shot down. He recognized her as the 'ravishing' Nansica, who had decapitated the prisoner back in Abomey. French firepower, supported by a gunboat shooting from the shore, forced the Dahomeans back, leaving 120 men and seven women dead, with 'several hundred' others nearby uncounted. A Fon tale relates an incident that has become legendary, in which an Amazon, disarmed by an African-French soldier (or 'French officer', for versions vary), ripped his throat out with her sharpened teeth.

Six weeks later, some 350 French troops and 500 locals

intercepted the Dahomean army at the village of Atchoupa, some 7 kilometres north of Porto-Novo. The Dahomeans, with a huge numerical advantage, routed the African contingent, but the French formed a square. Retreating steadily, they poured withering fire from their Lebel rifles. Over 600 Dahomeans died, including many Amazons, for the loss of eight on the French side. That was the First Franco-Dahomean War.

A treaty ensued, by which Dahomey recognized France's authority over Cotonou and Porto-Novo, but clearly more violence would follow. The new king, Béhanzin, started buying modern weapons from German traders, including lever-action Winchesters (the 1873 version of which is known as the 'gun that won the West').

It was the Second Franco-Dahomean War of 1892 that finally did for the Amazons. War came quickly. In March, Fon warriors raided villages on the Ouémé River claimed by Porto-Novo. The French sent a gunboat to investigate. It was attacked. The French protested. The king rejected the protest. France declared war. The king said, in effect, bring it on: 'If you want war, I am ready.' So were the French, their army pumped up with Foreign Legionnaires, engineers, artillery and cavalry to over 2,000 men, with another 2,600 porters. In early July, gunboats shelled villages on the Ouémé and two months later the French were 80 kilometres upriver, at a village called Dogba on Dahomey's border. On 19 September, some 4-5,000 Fon soldiers attacked.

That was the first of twenty-three engagements over the next seven weeks, in all of which some 2,000 or more Amazons, from a total force of about 10,000, fought with conspicuous bravery. 'Oh, those Amazons!' wrote a French officer later. 'How they excited the soldier's curiosity!' The Fon, said another, fought with 'ferocious rage, spurred into action by their fetishers [priests] and the Amazons.' Their assaults were suicidal, given the effects of the Lebel repeating rifles. Twenty-four kilometres upriver, after several furious charges by the Fon, the French replied with their first use of bayonets, which outreached the Fon swords and machetes. In hand-to-hand fights, Amazons fought to the death. In one incident, one of them bit off a marine's nose; at his scream, a lieutenant turned and cut her down with his sword.

In the penultimate battle, the French suffered forty-two casualties: five Europeans killed, twenty wounded, the rest being African troops. One participant described seeing

> a little Amazon; quite young almost pretty, her big eyes open, glazed by a short agony. A Lebel bullet had fractured her right thigh, turning the limb completely inside out, chewing up the femur and detaching a hundred splinters. A very small hole could be seen on the inside edge of her left breast, while below her shoulder blade on the same side was a gaping wound.

'When the bullet encounters a bone,' said another, 'the latter is pulverized, shredded; the flesh around it is chewed up. It was a heart-rending spectacle.'

Setting out on the final 40 kilometres to Cana, where the king had his residence, another battle on 6 October left 95 bodies, including 16 Amazons, for the loss of 6 dead on the French side. Fon sources suggest far worse: of 434 Amazons fighting, only 17 escaped. As the French made slow progress, hardly more than a kilometre a day, attacks came daily. On 26–27 October, the French fought with bayonets across

California: The Mythical Island of New World Amazons

In the early 16th century, the Spaniards who first explored the west coast of the Americas were entranced by European novels based on the idea that Queen Califia and her Amazon warriors lived in some New World island. They named California after her and guessed that the peninsula of Baja California, now part of Mexico, was her island. The belief lasted for over a century, as this 1676 map shows.

The Amazon: A Legend, a River, an Image

Opposite page, top: Orellana's Challenge 1: 1,200 kilometres inland, the Amazon is still a freshwater sea. Here, its sediment-rich 'white' waters from the Andes meet the nutrient-poor Rio Negro. Orellana, the first to explore the Amazon, came here in June 1542, noted that the waters were 'black as ink' and named the river accordingly.

Right: Orellana's Challenges 2 and 3: the people, the environment. It takes expertise to live in the rainforest. In the 1980s, this Waorani man, Tedikawae, was living in the rainforest south of the Napo. He has killed a nocturnal curassow using a blow-gun and darts tipped with curare, a nerve-poison – tools and skills that evolved over centuries.

Opposite page, bottom: Folklore trumps reality in this 1598 woodcut of 'Amazons in their mating season', in a landscape that owes nothing to the rainforest that was their supposed home.

Below: Over the years, Amazons became stock figures in theatre. This is a 19th-century stage Amazon in 'traditional' costume: loose skirt, cross-gartering, Phrygian cap and bow.

Below: An Amazon as seen on a late 19th-century educational card included in a box of French chocolates.

CHOCOLAT GUÉRIN-BOUTRON

76

LA MYTHOLOGIE

AMAZONES. — Les Amazones faisaient partie d'une peuplade de femmes qui habitaient les bords du Thermodon en Cappadoce. Elles étaient réputées pour leur courage mâle et guerrier.

Women Warriors Yesterday and Today

Right: An 1890 German lithograph shows Dahomey's 'Corps of Amazons'.

Below left: Before take-off in Moscow to fly across Russia in 1938, the three women pilots pose before their long-range bomber, *Rodina* (*Motherland*). Marina Raskova, founder of Russia's all-female air squadrons, is on the right.

Below right: A team of 'Night Witches' in front of their Po-2 biplanes.

DAS
Amazonen-Corps
unter Führung
der Oberkriegerin „**GUMMA**"

Left: Kurdish women fighters in a march-past near Sulaymaniyah, Iraq, July 2014.

Left: Lajos Kassai, the Hungarian who revived and popularized the sport of horseback archery. He has taught many women across Europe and the US, who find the results empowering and inspiring.

Above: Zana Cousins-Greenwood, co-founder of the Centre of Horseback Combat, Hemel Hempstead, west of London.

Left: Pettra Engeländer, who trained with Kassai and now runs her own horseback archery centre about 100 kilometres north-east of Frankfurt, Germany.

An Amazonian Princess Saves the World

The first appearance of Wonder Woman inside *All Star Comics* No. 8 in December 1941 was followed by this cover appearance a month later. Though an Amazonian princess, Diana, she springs up as an all-American heroine to help with the war effort.

trenches, while Amazons mounted counterattacks, 'uttering terrible cries and making their big cutlasses whistle'. A few warriors were found drunk in their fox-holes, apparently having sought Dutch courage in the face of defeat. For a last-ditch stand in early November, the king assembled some 1,500, mostly Amazons, according to one account. After four hours of fighting, the Dahomeans withdrew, leaving the field strewn with dead. On 4 November came the final battle, and one of the most deadly. A last bayonet charge killed or scattered the remnants.

There would be no surrender, despite a few days' grace. The king, having lost some 2–3,000 dead, burned his capital and fled north. The French hoisted the Tricolour over Abomey on 17 November. Their losses: 52 Europeans and 33 Africans dead. Another 200 died of disease, mainly dysentery and malaria.

Though the king tried to rally his surviving troops, there was no more fighting. Two years later, his brother was chosen as king. Béhanzin surrendered and was sent off to Martinique with five wives. In 1900, the French abolished the monarchy and began direct rule.

Many reports of the war followed. Accounts are dotted with words of praise for the Amazons: 'Extreme valour' . . . 'Outstandingly brave' . . . 'Savage tenacity' . . . 'Remarkable for the courage and ferocity' . . . 'Prodigious bravery' . . . 'Really strange to see women so well led, so well disciplined.' 'They bring to battle a veritable fury and a sanguinary ardour,' concluded Major Léonce Grandin in his two-volume account of the war, 'inspiring by their courage and indomitable energy the other troops who follow them.'

There were many survivors, but they didn't adapt well.

Many never married, considering marriage to be servitude, and those who did, in the words of one historian, Auguste le Hérissé, writing almost twenty years later, seemed 'to have reserved from their former condition only a certain bellicose temper . . . directed especially against their husbands.' A friend of another writer described how in 1930 in Cotonou, Benin's largest city, he once saw an old crone leaning on a stick and muttering until she heard a stone being thrown, and took it to be a rifle-shot. She straightened. Her face lit up. She crawled. She pretended to load and fire a rifle. She pounced on an imaginary prey, and then, just as suddenly, stopped, hunched and staggered away. 'She is a former warrior,' an adult explained. 'In the time of our former kings, there were women soldiers. Their battles ended long ago, but she continues the war in her head.'

In 1943, Eva Meyerowitz, a South African sculptor-turned-anthropologist, described how she had seen 'the only Amazon still alive . . . A very old woman, hanging around the courtyards of the former royal palace.'[46] There could have been others. If Nansica, killed at sixteen, had had friends, and if they had survived into their eighties, they could have lived to see her Dahomey meld into a French protectorate, which, almost sixty years later, became independent as today's Benin.

---

[46] In the *Geographical Magazine*, the journal of the Royal Geographical Society. See Bibliography.

11

AMAZONS WITH WINGS:
RUSSIA'S NIGHT WITCHES

THERE'S NO SHORTAGE OF WARRIOR WOMEN. WEBSITES LIST
them by the score. Some fought, some were great leaders, some
visionaries, some (like Joan of Arc) all three, but that's not the
same as being Amazons. The defining trait of the Amazons
was nothing to do with any of their qualities as individuals; the
point was that they were a group. That makes them so out of
the ordinary that, for almost all their history, they existed only
in legend. Even their real prototypes, the Scythian Amazons,
were not a group, regiment or nation: they were an integral part

of their societies – honoured warriors and eminent leaders.

Until a few decades ago, there were many who found it hard to accept the non-existence of Amazons en masse. Quite the opposite: in the late nineteenth century, Amazons enjoyed something of a renaissance. Up until about 1860, conventional wisdom held to the idea, based on the generations as listed in the Bible, that mankind was created by God and that the Earth was only 6,000 years old. There simply wasn't the time for a succession of prehistoric societies, of which the Amazons would have to be one. Not everyone believed Genesis, but few dared deny it, because there was no evidence and no theoretical framework. Then came Darwin, proclaiming slow evolution combined with a geological revolution that rubbished Genesis. Suddenly, here was a timescale that could accommodate any number of prehistoric societies. In the late nineteenth century, social anthropologists became convinced that matriarchy, of which an Amazonian nation would be an extreme example, was a foundation from which patriarchies evolved. A pomposity[47] of male Victorian academics became obsessed with the supposed sexual promiscuity in which these hypothetical prehistoric societies lived. What they were looking for was a pattern of cultural evolution, as the 'survival of the fittest' explained biological evolution. It was all wishful thinking. Cultures may be similar, but similarity does not mean they are connected (as, for instance, Lafitau thought that Hurons and Amazons were connected). A writer on the history of anthropology, Marvin Harris, called this 'one of the most heated and useless discussions in the history

---

[47] A pomposity is a collection of professors, as a murmuration is a collection of starlings.

of the social sciences.'[48] But it did not die easily. Through much of the twentieth century, archaeologists and feminists, picking up the baton dropped by anthropologists, pointed to prehistoric 'fertility' statuettes of women with drooping breasts and distended stomachs to claim that during the thirty centuries of early agricultural society (*c.*6500–3500 BC), Europeans worshipped a Great Mother Goddess, and that the fundamental form of government was a village-based matriarchy. But the evidence fell short. It is not possible to use statuettes from preliterate times to say anything firm about social structures.

Anthropology worldwide has had no better luck. In all the hundreds of societies, proto-states, tribes and clans studied in the field, no true matriarchies have ever been discovered. Yes, there were and are a number of egalitarian societies in which men and women are of equal status. I lived with one of them, the Waorani of Ecuador, who are considered not only egalitarian but also sometimes referred to as one of the few 'simple' societies, with very few artefacts or rituals, and basic social structures. But in none of them were there bands of women warriors. Apparently Amazons as a group existed only in legend – or in Dahomey.

Well, not quite so. There is a recent example of a group of female warriors, a unique product of a large-scale, complex society under intense pressure.

Before we get to them, it's worth asking if there are other examples of groups of women that might have become violent if the circumstances had been just a bit more pressurized.

---

[48] Though in 2017 Choo Waihong published her account of a near-matriarchy, *The Kingdom of Women*, describing the Mosuo people of Yunnan, whose households are run by grandmothers, with the men acting as labourers and mates without parental responsibilities. The history of the matriarchy debate is covered in great depth in Cynthia Eller's *Gentlemen and Amazons*. See Bibliography.

Two come to mind: the Women's Christian Temperance Union, which campaigned vociferously to ban alcohol in the US, and succeeded for thirteen riotous years (1920–33); and the Suffragettes, who fought for votes for women on both sides of the Atlantic. Many in both groups had the warrior spirit, being prepared to destroy property, suffer and in a few notorious cases die for their cause. But neither group espoused assassination, let alone all-out warfare. They were, after all, part of the societies they sought to reform. They wanted change, not conquest or victory through violence.

Nothing creates more intense pressure than war, except plague and famine. In 1937, Russia had been at war for over twenty years, first against Germany in 1914–17, then against itself – in the 1917 Bolshevik Revolution, a terrible civil war, and a class war, all involving a nationwide struggle for industrial advancement. Grim times, made worse by a state sending millions to a variety of battlefronts and Stalin's secret police sending millions more 'enemies of the people' to Siberian prison camps. But for young women not stigmatized by the arbitrary arrest of some family member, there were new socialist freedoms: equality, childcare, education, divorce and work, bringing unheard-of opportunities, in cash, in status, in self-confidence.

For women in the armed forces, the ground work had been laid in 1917, in the last days before the Revolution, when Russia was still fighting Germany. A peasant woman named Maria Bochkareva had suggested countering poor morale among front-line troops by forming a 'Women's Battalion of Death'. She commanded some 300 recruits in one inconclusive action, but then vanished from history after opposing the

Bolsheviks. Aviation promised new opportunities. The Soviet government saw air travel as the best way to tie together their vast nation with commercial planes and to defend it with long-range bombers. By 1941, there were over 100 military flying schools. Despite opposition from conservative commanders, 25–30 per cent of all pilots were women, though they were not registered for military service.

One of these was Marina Raskova, a good-looking, intelligent and strong-willed daughter of the Revolution. She started work in a chemical plant, got married (Raskova was her married name), had a daughter, got divorced, and restarted work at an air-force academy. That inspired in her a new, thrilling, romantic vision. She wanted to fly. So did many other young men and women. There were more pilots than planes, but not enough navigators. That gave her an opening. At twenty-two, Raskova became the Soviet Union's first female navigator, and proved perfect fodder for the Soviet propaganda machine, which was keen to promote the nation's successes by idolizing 'heroes' in many different fields, including air travel. Women as aviators made excellent heroes, promoting both aviation and socialist ideals of achievement and equality. Raskova took part in two record-breaking flights, and then, in September 1938, in a spectacular attempt to fly non-stop the length of Mother Russia, from Moscow to Komsomolsk in the Far East, 6,500 kilometres, one-sixth of the globe, which would be a world record for straight-line flight without refuelling. The venture was a propaganda epic, followed by the nation. Stalin himself took a personal interest. In a long-range bomber[49] named *Rodina*

---

[49] An Ant-37, newly redesigned and redesignated as a DB-2. It was a prototype, never mass-produced.

(*Motherland*), there were two women pilots, with Raskova as navigator in a glass nose-cone with no door to the rest of the aircraft.

It didn't work out as planned. The plane hit bad weather, and lost radio contact after ten hours, sparking a massive search-and-rescue operation that cost the lives of sixteen people, killed in a mid-air collision, of which the public was told nothing. Raskova, with rudimentary maps, was trying to navigate with a sextant and compass over landscapes no one had ever seen from the air. Over the immensities of the Siberian forests, circling above low cloud in search of a gap and some place to land, the plane ran low on fuel. Since a crash-landing would most likely kill Raskova, in her glass nose-module, she bailed out. Landing safely, warmly dressed, but with only half a bar of chocolate, she set off walking in the direction she thought the plane must have crash-landed. For ten days, she survived on berries, mushrooms and one square of chocolate per day. She lost a boot, and became weaker, supporting herself with a stick. On the brink of collapse, she saw rescue planes circling, followed them, and found *Motherland*, which had belly-flopped in a swamp. It had covered 5,947 kilometres in 26 hours, 29 minutes, a world record. The three women, with a collapsible canoe, walked and paddled their way back to civilization. The nation went wild with carefully orchestrated joy. They were taken back to Moscow and driven in an open car to the Kremlin, while adoring crowds threw flowers. Stalin greeted them with kisses and a speech about avenging the oppression of women. All three were made Heroes of the Soviet Union, the first women to receive the honour. Raskova was the favourite, with her astonishing survival story, her good looks and a bestselling book, *Notes of a Navigator*. She had the world at her feet.

Then, suddenly, she didn't. At 0415 on 22 June 1941, German bombers struck sixty-six Soviet aerodromes, opening the invasion codenamed Operation Barbarossa. By noon, over 1,000 Soviet aircraft had been destroyed on the ground, the first of 6,500 lost over the next three months. 'We have only to kick in the door,' Hitler told his chief of staff, General Alfred Jodl, 'and the whole rotten structure will come crashing down.' Not so easy, as it turned out. Stalin turned from brutal oppressor to the saviour of his nation. Factories and people moved eastwards by train and road. By October, the Germans were at the outskirts of Moscow, but General Winter was coming to the rescue, as he had come when Napoleon's army stood at Moscow's gates in 1812.

Meanwhile, many female pilots, mostly members of flying clubs, had written to Raskova saying they wanted to fight and complaining that no one would take them. She decided to form a regiment of women military pilots. With her fame, legendary toughness and status, she had a direct line to the top. This was in early October 1941, with Moscow likely to fall to the Germans in days. The Defence Ministry, perhaps Stalin himself, gave the go-ahead (accounts conflict[50]). So the world's first women's combat aviation unit came into existence not because there was a shortage of pilots – far from it, because so many planes had been destroyed on the ground

[50] Pilot Evgeniia Zhigulenko said, 'Marina Raskova . . . went to Stalin about this. And strange as it may seem this monster told her "You understand, future generations will not forgive us for sacrificing young girls." It was she herself who told us this, this fascinating woman.' (Quoted originally in Helene Kayssar and Vladimir Pozner, *Remembering War: A U.S.–Soviet Dialogue* (OUP, 1990); requoted by Reina Pennington. See Bibliography.

– nor for propaganda (of which there was remarkably little), but almost entirely because one formidable woman cajoled and argued until she got her way.

There were to be three regiments: fighters, heavy bombers and night bombers, all staffed by women – pilots, navigators, mechanics, armourers, support personnel. Raskova gathered a few dozen of the volunteers and got uniforms issued – male ones, with massive overcoats and oversized boots. On 15 October Stalin ordered the evacuation of government departments and armament factories from Moscow. Over the next two weeks, 200 trains and 80,000 trucks headed east with the contents of 500 factories. Two days after Stalin's order, Aviation Group 122, as Raskova's 300–400 young women were called, marched in their ill-fitting uniforms past immobile trams and closed-up shops to Kazansky Station, and piled into goods wagons for the journey to the town of Engels, on the Volga, 800 kilometres to the south-east. It took eight days to get there. Hours were spent in sidings as troop trains lumbered westwards, while others headed east to the lands beyond the Volga with the wounded, government staff and heavy machinery. There were no toilets, and the food was grey bread, herring and water. Raskova went from car to car, keeping up morale. No one complained. Many of the women, scarcely more than girls – average age twenty – had been raised in harsher circumstances. All dreamed of serving Stalin, the Motherland and Marina Raskova.

Engels, chosen because it was a safe distance from the front and had a flying school, was a grim little place of houses made from clay mixed with straw and brushwood, and just four stone buildings – three Party houses and a cinema. The women lived in barracks in one large room, each with a plank bed, with a straw mattress and a blanket. For training pilots it was perfect. To the west ran the Volga, 2 kilometres across, but in every other direction lay steppe, flat and treeless to the horizon, in effect one vast runway.

There were hard decisions to be made, because everyone wanted to fly. The class system was supposedly consigned to the dustbin of history, but some were still more equal than others. Armourers and mechanics wanted to be navigators, navigators wanted to be pilots, pilots wanted to be *fighter* pilots. The three units got names: 586th Fighter Regiment, 587th Heavy Bomber Regiment and 588th Night Bomber Regiment. Top pilots with competition experience in aerobatics became fighters; those who had flown in civil aviation or had been flying instructors would fly heavy bombers; and those with the least experience would be night bombers. But character sometimes trumped experience in Raskova's eyes, and she spent much time cajoling, reassuring and explaining her decisions to the many who objected to them.

So began a harsh military life, under male instructors – months of drills, parade-ground humiliation, early-morning roll-calls, indoctrination by Party officials, flights in training aircraft, navigation, firearms, equipment maintenance, and a total convent-like ban on long hair, make-up, fancy clothes and socializing with men (not that the ban always worked). There was no toothpaste, toilet paper or shampoo. No one thought of issuing them with anything but men's clothing – no bras or women's underwear, not even the basic designs produced for the general public. Occasionally, they sewed underwear from torn parachutes, much in demand because they were made of silk. For twenty-year-olds, it was tough, un-relieved by the fact that there was no real action. December

1941 gave way to a bitter new year. They had no aircraft, and anyway the advancing Germans were over 400 kilometres away, too far to reach by plane. They had little idea of the defeats and the deaths by the hundred thousand along the 2,000-plus kilometres between besieged Leningrad and the Caucasus.

Through all this Raskova proved a true leader. Since she supervised the training of all three regiments she was on duty twenty-four hours a day. 'We did not notice any outward signs of fatigue,' wrote one of her pilots. 'To all of us it seemed that this woman possessed unprecedented energy.' When one of her team tried to get her to rest, she replied, 'We'll rest when the war's over.' She could fall asleep instantly and wake up instantly. She was firm, yet always soft-spoken. One of her subordinates, Ekaterina Migunova, said in a 1976 interview, 'I don't remember a single case when she yelled or even raised her voice, or rudely interrupted a subordinate . . . She never punished anyone in a fit of temper.' In pursuit of her aims, however, Raskova was a force of nature. As a friend of the director of the factory that was making good the disastrous loss of planes, she demanded priority in receiving the superb new Yak-1s for her women, and she got them. Her one form of relaxation was to play the piano, which she did extremely well. No wonder the women adored her.

The first fighter planes – the Russian equivalent of the Spitfire, the Yak-1, named after its designer, Alexander Yakovlev – arrived in January, and 20 Pe-2 dive-bombers (designed by Vladimir Petlyakov) in the summer,[51] all with

---

[51] They had started with outdated two-seater Su-2 light bombers, but upgraded to Pe-2s in June, with three seats: pilot, navigator and gunner/radio operator.

radios, thanks to Raskova's perseverance. These two regiments employed some men as mechanics and administrators, so our focus is mainly on the most Amazonian of the the women's regiments, the Night Bombers, a female contingent from top to bottom for the whole war, and always with the same commander, Yevdokiya Bershanskaya.

Their task was to fly over enemy lines at night to bomb fuel dumps, trenches and supply depots. They flew flimsy biplanes designed principally for flight training fifteen years previously. Each plane had two open cockpits, one for the student or pilot, the other for the instructor or navigator. It was made of plywood covered with densely woven cotton known as percale, in effect sturdy bedsheets, which made it a flying tinderbox. Driven by a clattering little 100-horsepower engine, its top speed was 120 kilometres per hour. No radio, no brakes. It was about as basic as a plane could be: a small, cheap, lightweight, manoeuvrable and low-speed workhorse, rather like the plane in Hitchcock's *North by Northwest*, in the scene when Cary Grant is driven into and then out of a cornfield by a crop-duster. It was the brainchild of a great designer, Nikolai Polikarpov, who was able to focus on his work rather more intensely than he would have liked because he spent much of his life in prison under interrogation by the secret police. Designated the U-2, it is not to be confused with the later U-2, the 1950s American spy plane which was pretty much the complete opposite of Polikarpov's. This U-2 (re-designated as Po-2 in 1943) was ideal for transporting the wounded and dropping supplies, slowly and at very low altitudes. It could take off from a forest clearing and land on a road. Thirty thousand of them were produced over thirty years, up until 1958. When war broke out, air clubs had U-2s by the hundred, all quickly requisitioned for front-line work.

It was Polikarpov himself who suggested that his U-2 could be used for night bombing, gliding in over enemy territory and releasing either two or four bombs tucked under the wings. But action would start in a Russian winter, in an open cockpit, in brutal cold that froze exposed flesh in minutes. If a bare hand touched metal, the skin froze to it and got stripped away. Snow could blot out the horizon, and induce delusions about what was up and what was down. And the women would be flying at night, when they couldn't see the ground and had to rely on rudimentary instruments, when a single light below might be mistaken for a star and guide a disorientated pilot to her death. There was, of course, no parachute. Chief of staff Irina Rakobolskaya explained in an interview with Reina Pennington for her book on the women fliers: 'The frame of mind was such that if you caught fire over enemy territory, it would be better to die than with the help of a parachute to be taken prisoner. And if you were damaged over your own territory, then you would be able to land the aircraft somehow.'

All this to inflict minor damage with four 50-kilogram bombs, a tenth of what a heavy bomber could carry. Was it really worthwhile? Yes, as the official agenda of the Night Bombers said, it was vital 'to harass the enemy, to deprive him of sleep and rest, to wear him down, destroy his aircraft on his own airfields, his fuel depots, his munitions and food supplies, disrupting transport movements, hindering the work of his headquarters.' And the women had no doubts. 'We were all sportswomen, with good coordination,' said one of them, Galina Brok-Beltsova, at that time just seventeen, interviewed for Italian TV in 2016 at the age of ninety-one. 'We were fit, in control of our bodies. But most of all we had the will to win, and we were a community.'

But this was a dangerous life, even before real action started. On 10 March, training flights ran into wind-whipped snow, which obscured the horizon and the runway lights. Two U-2s crashed, two of the women died. After their bodies were recovered, Raskova organized the funeral, placing flowers on the coffins. Nina Ivakina, administrator for Komsomol (the youth organization), wrote in her diary, 'We tenderly put the coffins with our friends, who only yesterday had been so full of fun and laughter, on the truck and to the strains of the Funeral March slowly accompanied our dear young falcons on their last journey, to the graveyard.' Raskova spoke the oration: 'Sleep, dear friends; we shall fulfill your dreams.'

In May, before the German advance on Stalingrad, the Night Bombers were put into action. Raskova led them in a flight from Engels to a village near Morozovskaya, some 230 kilometres from the front line, where they would form part of the Night Bomber division of Fourth Air Army on the Southern Front between Stalingrad and the Black Sea. On arrival they were inspected by the divisional commander, Dmitrii Popov. 'I've received 112 little princesses,' he complained to Fourth Army's boss, General Konstantin Vershinin. 'Just what am I supposed to do with them?' 'They're not little princesses, Dmitrii Dmitrievich,' Vershinin replied. 'They're fully fledged pilots.'

Raskova, called to Moscow for new orders, left them with uplifting words: they had to show that women could fight as well as men, 'and then in our country too women will be welcomed into the army.' It was the last the Night Bombers saw of her. By June, after a month of further training, they were ready for action, flying out of their new base near Krasnodon, only 30 kilometres from the front, and part of the effort to stop the German advance on Rostov and Stalingrad, the lynchpin of the Russian south.

But there was no stopping the enemy. Rostov went up in flames, driving endless lines of refugees eastwards through unharvested grain fields. The Night Bombers retreated with the Soviet army, flying out of base after base, learning to navigate first on the endless, featureless steppe, using the stars or a church or railway station to find their way, then in the mists of the North Caucasus mountains. They trained by day and flew at night on successive one-hour missions, because that was how long the fuel lasted; over 100 missions per night – five or more, sometimes ten, for each pilot – even in high summer.

The stress was constant: finding their way in darkness without instruments, blinded by searchlights, deafened by anti-aircraft shells, coughing to get rid of the gunpowder smoke, focusing to drop their bombs, then finding their way home to an unfamiliar field, guided in by kerosene lanterns or car headlights. They were constantly, desperately short of sleep. They slept where they could, an hour here, an hour there, in the cockpit, under a wing, in abandoned peasant huts. How did they endure it? Partly because they were all there by choice, all volunteers, able to leave if they wished. No one did. Partly pride: they were eager to prove they could do anything the men could, and more. They kept careful notes: Polina Gelman recorded that she flew 860 combat flights. Partly, they were all in a tight-knit community, as efficient as a pit-stop in a car race. Mechanics could refuel and re-arm a plane in five minutes – faster, they noted, than any of the men's regiments. Also there were remarkably few losses. So morale remained rock solid. 'It's really difficult to shoot a plane down,' wrote Zhenya Rudneva reassuringly to her parents. 'If anything happens, though, what of it? You will be proud that your daughter was an airwoman! Being up in the air is really such a joy!' Later, after the war, they were amazed at themselves. 'Even I find it difficult to believe sometimes that we, young girls, could endure such incredible stress in our combat work,' recalled Raisa Aronova. 'Apparently, our moral strength was immeasurable.' The chief of staff, Irina Rakobolskaya, put it down to group solidarity: 'Women fight more effectively in a separate unit than men. The friendship is stronger, things are simpler, there is greater responsibility.'

The Germans hated the U-2s. They drifted in low like ghosts – at scarcely more than the speed of an owl, 80 kilometres per hour – too low to be held by a searchlight, the air flowing over the wing-struts making a soft whooshing noise, then in seconds they were gone again, leaving an ammunition dump ablaze, a bridge destroyed or a slit-trench blown apart. It was over before there was time to mount an effective defence. When the Germans learned from Russian broadcasts that their tormentors were women, they started to refer to them as the *Nachthexen*, the Night Witches. The Russian women pilots loved that – *Nochnye Vedmi*, Night Witches: that's what they have been ever since.

In August 1942, German forces clogged the roads to Stalingrad. The city, a symbol of victory for both sides, seemed about to fall. Hitler said it would, ordering a massive air assault on 23 August that set the city ablaze. Stalin said it would not, must not fall – 'Not one step back!' had been his famous order in July 1942. The city would be held, at least enough of it for long enough for armies to build up around the besieging Germans. Then the Germans would become the besieged. The Night Witches played their part, flying from Salsk to bomb the Germans as they crossed the Don, then moving eastwards ahead of them.

What might have been their greatest moment came in September 1942, in the Caucasus, when they were ordered to destroy the headquarters of General Paul von Kleist. As part of Operation Edelweiss, he was leading 1,000 tanks through the Caucasus towards Baku, the source of 80 per cent of the Soviet Union's oil, and had set up his HQ on the Terek River in Georgia. While the German forces were crossing the river, the Night Witches attacked, killing 130 Germans, but failing to kill Kleist himself. Their attack remained a footnote in Russia's desperate resistance to a vast operation, which would anyway grind to a halt, mainly because of German losses on other fronts and a consequent lack of supplies to this one.

To the north, Stalingrad was in dire peril. The eight women in Raskova's 1st Fighter Squadron were re-allocated to the two vastly outnumbered air regiments defending Stalingrad. The women lived inside a bubble of ignorance and bravado. Without any idea of the catastrophe unfolding in the city, they were thrilled at the thought of combat on equal terms with men, fighting in their Yak-1s, which they could all control as Amazons had once controlled their horses. But these were brief, disappointing assignments: the commander of one regiment kept the women clear of all danger, and the second regiment was disbanded after two weeks. The girls flew only two missions, losing sixteen aircrew and twenty-five aircraft in that short time.

Back in their base in Saratov, 300 kilometres up the Volga from Stalingrad, Raskova's 2nd Squadron had a remarkable success. On the night of 24 September, a searchlight picked out a twin-engine Junkers Ju-88 bomber. Valeriya Khomyakova in her Yak-1 attacked, machine gun blazing, and apparently killed the pilot, for the huge plane banked right, went into a dive and exploded on the ground. She checked the crash site later – the four crew members had bailed out, but too close to the ground for their parachutes to open, and their bodies lay around the plane's shattered hulk. It was the first kill by Raskova's fighters and the first enemy bomber shot down at night by a woman. The next morning there was vodka and watermelon for breakfast, plus 2,000 roubles in cash for the regiment from Comrade Stalin, followed by a trip to Moscow for Raskova to receive a medal, the Military Order of the Red Banner, from the hands of the eminent revolutionary and head of state Mikhail Kalinin. This success was followed, two weeks later, by a sudden reversal. Valeriya Khomyakova, who had been dozing in a dug-out and had no time for her eyes to adapt to the darkness, crashed on take-off and was killed. Commanders were blamed, fired and replaced by men. That was the end of 586th Regiment as the only group of all-female fighter pilots.

The Night Witches, meanwhile, were still divided between Stalingrad and the front further south in the Caucasus. In Stalingrad, searchlights presented a big problem. The Germans arranged flak guns and searchlights in concentric circles around probable targets. Planes flying in pairs in a straight line across the perimeter risked being ripped to shreds by flak. So the Night Witches developed a way of dealing with the problem. They flew in groups of three. Two would go in and deliberately attract the attention of the Germans. When several searchlights were pointed at them, and just before they judged the guns would open fire, the two pilots suddenly separated, flying in opposite directions and manoeuvring wildly to shake off the searchlights. The third pilot would fly in through the dark path cleared by her two teammates and hit the target virtually unopposed. She would then get out, rejoin the other two, and they would switch places until all three had delivered their payloads. It took nerves of steel to risk attracting enemy fire, but it worked well.

In the Caucasus, they were raiding the German front line, which crossed what is now a clutter of little republics on Georgia's northern border with Russia. Their successes, with no casualties, were rewarded with praise and medals – more of them were Heroes of the Soviet Union than in any other bomber regiment (twenty-four by the end of the war). In November, their commander, Yevdokiya Bershanskaya, received a letter from Konstantin Vershinin, commander of Fourth Army: 'Comrade Bershanskaya and all your fearless eagles, glorious daughters of our Motherland, intrepid pilots, mechanics, armourers and political workers!' Her boss had something more in mind than praise and medals. He was sending 'certain necessary but non-standard accessories', namely women's underwear.

Why now, after all this time? Because of an incident referred to by Vershinin. Two women gunners had taken the parachute from an aerial flare bomb and sewed themselves panties and bras. Someone had denounced them for undermining the war effort. A military tribunal sentenced them to ten years' imprisonment. But Vershinin saw that Mother Russia could not afford such a waste. 'As regards the two girls who were guilty of error, give them the opportunity to carry on working in peace, and at some later date file an appeal to strike out their criminal records.' A supply of underwear would save careers and lives.

Now it was not the Soviet army but the German Sixth Army that was trapped in Stalingrad. Soviet forces had held small pockets of land inside the city, down by the Volga, with building-to-building fighting around them and a fearful aerial war in the skies above, until the Volga froze and trucks could bring supplies across. On 19 November 1942, a vast build-up of guns, tanks and infantry began the counter-attack. By mid-December, 250,000 German troops were surrounded. Bombs, bullets, frostbite, disease and starvation took a terrible toll.

The 587th Women's Heavy Bomber Regiment, still commanded by Raskova but operating from several different airfields, was ordered to Stalingrad. On 4 January 1943, Raskova was due to join them from her base in Arzamas, 750 kilometres north of Stalingrad. The weather was bad: dense fog. She knew that the instruments in her Pe-2 dive-bomber would not be good enough to cope with the fog, but she was keen to join the regiment, as were the three others with her – a navigator, gunner-and-radio-operator and the squadron's chief mechanic – so she planned to land halfway, in Petrovsk, and wait for the fog to clear. She was leading two other planes, piloted by Lyuba Gubina and Galya Limanova. Over Petrovsk, it seemed clearer. On Raskova went, heading south, losing touch with the two other planes. In ever denser fog, with night approaching, they managed to crash-land, injured but alive. Of Raskova there was no news. Two days later, when the fog cleared, a search party found her plane.

Apparently she had tried to get under the fog, and dived straight into the steep right bank of the Volga. She and her navigator had been killed instantly. The tail had broken off, leaving the other two hurt but alive. A blood-soaked towel showed they had tried to staunch each other's wounds, before they froze to death.

Their bodies were picked up by a U-2 and flown to Saratov, where the director received orders to bury three of the dead locally, and to prepare Raskova's body for an overnight journey to Moscow. Her shattered head was stitched together, but not well enough to be seen in public. The news spread nationwide. Hundreds filed past her closed coffin before it was put in a special carriage for the train journey to Moscow. All her women pilots, navigators, gunners and technicians in their scattered units gathered in tearful shock. One of the Night Witches took a little comfort from the thought that, though the other two regiments were no longer exclusively female, hers, the 588th, had remained true to Raskova's ideals.

The whole nation mourned. *Pravda*'s front page described this, the first state funeral of the war: the funeral hall, the strips of black crêpe cascading from the ceiling either side of the funeral urn with Raskova's ashes, the gathering of the top politicians, the guard of honour, the slow march with the urn to the walls of the Kremlin, the threefold volley of shots, and the fly-past, all proclaiming 'that Marina Raskova, hero of the Soviet Union, great Russian aviatrix, has concluded her glorious career.'

A new commander, Raskova's No. 2, Zhenya Timofeyeva, led the Women's Heavy Bombers into combat against Germany's besieged Sixth Army, trapped in the charred, snow-covered ruins of Stalingrad. Several raids were shared with planes flown by men, until 30 January, when the women were allowed to go in on their own, preparing the ground for assaults by tanks and infantry. The next day, Hitler, who had ordered General Friedrich Paulus never to surrender, made him a field marshal, on the grounds that no field marshal in German history had ever surrendered. But Paulus had no choice. On 1 February, a German soldier crawled out of the basement of the Sixth Army's HQ, the Central Department Store, waving a white flag. Two days later, the news reached the final, isolated pocket of Germans, and it was all over. Russian deaths in the siege were over 100,000, while the Germans lost 160,000 dead, with a further 90,000 shuffling off into captivity and to almost certain death. On the Eastern Front, the tide of war had turned. Russian forces began to advance westwards, the Women's Heavy Bombers with them.

In the Caucasus, the Night Witches started to move north-wards and westwards, into devastated lands. It was the first time they had seen war close up, as if the women lived in a world of their own, sowing damage and death, never seeing the results first hand, until now. Moving forward yet again, in Rasshevatka, 400 kilometres north of their old front-line base on the Terek River, navigator Natasha Meklin and her pilot Irina Sebrova saw dead Germans for the first time. The place had just been liberated. The village was on fire, bodies of men and horses lay scattered about. The first German she saw was young, Meklin recorded, 'pale and waxen, the head thrown back . . . straight fair hair frozen to the snow.' She felt a flow of emotions: depression, revulsion, pity, and a sudden insight into the effects of what she was doing. Not that she was deterred. 'Tomorrow, I shall be bombing again, and the day after that, and the day after that, until the war is over, or I am killed myself.'

Spring came, turning the steppe to mud, bogging down planes and fuel trucks, curbing operations. The pilots of 296th Regiment, which had absorbed Raskova's women fighters, had to share the fifteen surviving planes, which was OK by fighter pilot Lilya Litvyak, because the man she was sharing with was about as small as she was, so there was no need to adjust the pedals. Life for her was fine, because she was in love with another pilot, Alexei Salomatin. They had official permission to marry. He was a bit reckless and she notoriously sharp-tongued, but they were a popular couple, so the others did their best to give them time together as the regiment moved forward, even if it was only in one abandoned peasant hut after another.

Litvyak, still just twenty, was a star, thanks to the Soviet propaganda machine. In February she had claimed a Stuka (a Junkers Ju-87 dive-bomber), in March another Stuka and a Ju-88 fighter-bomber, an encounter that left her with a bullet in the thigh and in a damaged plane, which she managed to land safely. 'The Girl Avenger', as she was called in a magazine article, was the perfect heroine, '20 years old, a lovely springtime in the life of a maiden! A fragile figure with golden hair as delicate as her very name – Lilya,' a fragility that contrasted with her fighting spirit: 'When I see a plane with those crosses and the swastika on its fin tail, I experience just one feeling – hatred. That emotion seems to make my grip firmer on the firing buttons.' She left hospital after a few days, still limping, but happy, and eager for some

R & R with family in Moscow. Her brother recorded that she had with her a dress made of German parachute silk, trimmed with little green bits made from viscose that had once held gunpowder in German anti-aircraft shells. She fought well, and sewed well too.

In May, Litvyak was back on duty in Pavlovka, almost on the Ukrainian border, sitting in her cockpit waiting for action. Her lover, Alexei Salomatin, was in the early-summer skies above, flying his Yak, training a new pilot. Two women mechanics were sitting on Litvyak's wings, chatting to her. Suddenly they heard the noise of a plane engine, rising to a roar. It cut off with a boom at the far end of the runway. Someone else had seen a Yak come out of the clouds doing rolls, far too close to the ground. The three women ran to the crash site. It was Salomatin, killed by his youthful reckless-ness, or as the official report put it, because of 'undue self-confidence, self-regard and lack of discipline'.

Lilya Litvyak faced death many times in the next two months. Two immense Russian counterattacks were under way: to the north, the greatest ever tank battle around Kursk, and to the south, along the Mius River, where Soviet forces were trying to break the line formed by reinvigorated German armies. She had a string of successes and narrow escapes: in June, she and her wing-mate, Sasha Yevdokimov, set on fire two German observation balloons; on 16 June, she was leading a new arrival into the air when she veered off course, causing the pilot following her to crash to his death; that same afternoon, she and Yevdokimov were chased by four Messerschmitts, returning to base with several bullet holes in their machines; five days later, her Yak was hit by a Messerschmitt, but she crash-landed safely.

On 1 August, having moved further west to Krasnyi Luch in Ukraine's coal-rich Donbass, Litvyak flew three sorties in support of Ilyushins attacking German ground troops. When she was climbing into her Yak for her fourth sortie – leather boots, khaki tunic, dark-blue flying breeches, blue beret tucked into her map case – her mechanic, Nikolai Menkov, tried to talk her out of it. He recalled the scene vividly later; it was etched into his memory by what happened next.

'It's very punishing for one person to fly so many missions in this heat,' he said. 'Do you really need to do so much flying? There are other pilots.'

She replied, 'The Germans have started using weaklings! They're wet behind the ears and I feel like blasting one more of them!'

She said goodbye, bright and cheerful as usual, closed the canopy and took off. She and five other Yaks were escorting eight Ilyushins. Approaching the front line, they shot down two Messerschmitts then, as they turned for home, another Messerschmitt emerged from clouds, fired at Litvyak's Yak, and vanished again. Two of the other pilots saw her plane falling out of control, and guessed that she had been shot and was either dead or seriously injured. She did not bail out, and no one saw an explosion on the ground. Back at the base, everyone waited and hoped, until hope died. A day later, as the Soviet troops advanced, Yevdokimov and the mechanic Menkov searched the villages and gulleys where they thought she had crashed, but found nothing. Then two weeks later, Yevdokimov was killed, and no one went looking for Lilya any more. 'Lost without trace,' said the official letter to her mother.

But the loss of a heroine often inspires legends, especially if she's a slender, feisty, good-looking blonde of twenty-one. A returning prisoner said he had seen Lilya in captivity. Rumours spread that a plane had landed in a village in German territory, that a girl had been driven off by Germans. Or perhaps the Germans had buried her with full military honours. Political officers asked questions. Could she have gone over to the other side? Another returning prisoner claimed she had. But these were strange times, with prisoners being re-imprisoned by their own people, and forced 'confessions' made and retracted, and cancerous jealousies in the regiment of Lilya's looks and skills and popularity. There was never any evidence, only hints to the contrary: in the 1970s, village boys pulling out a grass-snake from its hole found fragments of a helmet and underwear made of parachute silk. But the discoveries were buried and, despite continuing research and much controversy, Lilya remained lost without trace, and remains so today.

Her memorial is the record of what she achieved in her two years of service: the first woman pilot to shoot down an enemy plane, 66 sorties, 11 or 12 solo victories and 4 shared (though these figures too are disputed, like so much in her life and death), giving her the greatest number of kills by a woman pilot.

The day before Lilya Litvyak vanished, some 400 kilometres to the south, the Night Witches, now honoured as the 46th Guards Night Bomber Aviation Regiment, suffered their worst night. The Russians had driven the Germans back along the Taman Peninsula, which divides the Black Sea from the Sea of Azov. The Germans needed it as a base for regaining all the ground they had just lost. Fifteen Russian U-2s took off that night, as searchlights sliced through the

46TH GUARDS NIGHT BOMBER AVIATION REGIMENT

← Rebasing movements

darkness ahead. Strangely, the anti-aircraft guns fell silent. The pilots soon learned why. The Germans had for the first time deployed a night-fighter,[52] who had perfect targets in the spotlit, slow-moving U-2s, each as 'clear as a silvery moth caught in a spider's web', as one of the returning Night Witches put it.

Serafima Amosova, one of the surviving pilots, recorded what happened:

The searchlights came on, the anti-aircraft guns were firing, and then a green rocket was fired from the ground. The anti-aircraft guns stopped, and a German fighter plane came and

---

[52] His name was Oberfeldwebel (Staff Sergeant) Josef Kociok, a flying ace who had determined to deal with the troublesome Night Witches. He became a *Nachtjäger*, 'night hunter', one of a small specialist unit against which the Night Witches had no defence. He died in September 1943 when his plane hit a crashing Russian Ilyushin DB-3 bomber and his parachute failed to open.

shot down four of our aircraft as each one came over the target. Our planes were burning like candles. We all witnessed this scene. When we landed and reported that we were being attacked by German fighters, they would not let us fly again that night. We lived in a school building with folding wooden beds. You can imagine our feelings when we returned to our quarters and saw eight beds folded, and we knew they were the beds of our friends who perished a few hours ago.

Success in the Taman campaign brought more fame and more honour to the Night Witches, redesignated as the 46th 'Taman' Guards. They fought on to the end of the war, moving westwards with the land army – to Belorussia, Crimea, East Prussia, Poland, and in May 1945 to Berlin and victory. They were disbanded in October 1945, because women were being reintegrated into society. Motherhood and factory work took over from fighting as Soviet ideals.

Postscript: A few statistics[53]

The 588th/46th Guards Night Bomber Aviation Regiment served for three years, June 1942–May 1945. How many achieved what? Many figures are quoted, few of them well sourced. Twenty-four thousand-plus sorties? That's easily possible – forty planes (maximum) with two- or three-person crews flying several sorties per night for three years. The tonnage of bombs dropped? Perhaps 3,000 (23,000 is one figure given online, which must be nonsense, because U-2s/Po-2s could carry only 300 kilograms, maximum).

[53] Mainly from Reina Pennington's *Wings, Women, and War*.

Twenty-four pilots made Heroes of the Soviet Union, out of thirty-three awarded to women in the whole war. Twenty-six dead in combat, out of a total of 124 Night Witches (pilots and navigators), backed up by ninety-nine mechanics, armourers and engineers.

12

WONDER WOMAN: THE SECRET ORIGINS OF AN AMAZON PRINCESS

'BEFORE SHE WAS WONDER WOMAN, SHE WAS DIANA, PRINCESS of the Amazons.' So begins the storyline of the 2017 blockbuster movie. As always with superheroes, the plot involves saving the world, which suggests that the film is nothing but fun, at best, and utterly lacking in significance. Not at all. Wonder Woman is a lot more important than you might think. How an Amazon from several centuries BC became today's superhero (or superheroine; usage varies) is not the point of the movie, but it's a story in its own right, leading back almost 100 years into an America of dominant men, a few rebellious women, and one man who was, amazingly, a feminist in one respect – he dreamed up Wonder Woman as an icon of female power and independence. 'Feminism made Wonder Woman,' as the Harvard history professor Jill Lepore puts it in her superb account,[54] 'and then Wonder Woman remade feminism.'

The starting point is the mix of radical themes, events and people forming the campaign for women's rights before, during and after the First World War, many of which – the ones I focus on here – played into the themes, events and people forming the context for the creation of the original Wonder Woman and her Amazonian origins. In what follows, watch out for themes now familiar to us, including: Greeks; a women's homeland of infinite happiness; sexual equality; a rejection of marriage; obsessions about secrecy, lies and truth; patriotism; bondage; and an obscure item of jewellery. The story is an intriguing mixture of very public exposure and a veil of secrets.

Take first the extraordinary Charlotte Perkins Gilman, a feminist sociologist who wrote *Women and Economics* (1898) and several other very serious books arguing for women's rights. Luckily for her cause and her readers, she also had a sense of humour. Born in Hartford, Connecticut, she lived out her ideals, leaving her husband, Charles Stetson, and taking their daughter Katherine to California. After the divorce, she and her ex agreed that Katherine should live with

[54] *The Secret History of Wonder Woman*, on which this chapter is largely based. See Bibliography and Acknowledgements.

Charles. He married one of Charlotte's best friends. Everyone got on well. She remarried (George Gilman, a first cousin) and moved back to New York, where she continued lecturing and writing: half a dozen non-fiction books and three novels by 1915, winning wide respect for both her feminism and her socialism. She worked ferociously hard, writing every word of her own magazine, the *Forerunner* (1909–16), in which she serialized her three utopian novels, expressing her anti-traditionalist views: that women were as courageous, creative, generous and virtuous as men; that male dominance was not a given; that culture can trump biology; that revolution should happen; and that it should come as the result of non-violent action by women.

Herland, written in 1915 and one of those novels serialized in the *Forerunner*, is the story of three male adventurers who stumble on 'an undiscovered country of a strictly Amazonian nature' (the only mention of 'Amazon' in the book). It is the homeland of a society of women who live without men, in which virgin birth produces only girl children and in which community is all. The women are anti-Amazons, driven to cooperate, not to fight and conquer. There are no family homes, which Gilman thought created inequality and inhumanity. All the women look after all the children. Explaining their ways to the three aghast intruders, they were used by Gilman to spotlight the oddities of American society. Why, one of the women wonders innocently, do those Americans with the fewest children have the most servants? Terry, the most macho of the three men, complains that even young and beautiful women are unsexy because they lack deference and fragility. In fact, the women have had sexual desire bred out of them, and they are the better for it. If the men want to marry them, they can only do so on the basis of equality.

In later life, after her husband's death, Gilman moved back to California, where she was joined by her first husband's wife, herself a widow. In 1932, she was diagnosed with terminal breast cancer. Three years later, having finished her autobiography, she used chloroform to kill herself.

Gilman was writing at a time when women's rights were a major issue. Women were now going to college in ever-increasing numbers,[55] and among them were 'suffragists' demanding the vote – 'New Women' who were often referred to as Amazons. In 1908, Mary Woolley, president of the first women's college, Mount Holyoke, helped found the National College Equal Suffrage League. She was also a feminist, aiming to establish gender equality in all things, leading an American equivalent of Emmeline Pankhurst's campaign in Britain. Included in this was birth control, spearheaded by Margaret Sanger in the magazine *Woman Rebel*, with its challenging subhead: 'No Gods, No Masters'. She campaigned to break the bonds of prejudice and prudery wherever she saw them. In the US, as in England, there were arrests for distributing information about contraception, with frequent trials, imprisonments and hunger strikes. Margaret Sanger's sister, Ethel Byrne, was the first woman prisoner in the US to be force-fed. Sanger got her released by guaranteeing that she would not break the law again, something for which Byrne never forgave her. Sanger pursued her agenda in the teeth of official opposition. Just after the 19th Amendment

---

[55] Many to the 'Seven Sisters': Mount Holyoke (the first, founded in 1837), Barnard, Bryn Mawr, Radcliffe, Smith, Vassar and Wellesley.

gave women the vote in August 1920, she published *Woman and the New Race*, arguing for even greater equality and for birth control – 'the revolt of women against sex servitude', as she called it – a cause for which she travelled internationally, including to England, where she, being an advocate of free love and needing money for her work and family, married the oil millionaire J. Noah Slee, then started a long-lasting friendship and occasional love-affair with H. G. Wells.

One of the New Women at Mount Holyoke was Elizabeth (then known as Sadie) Holloway, whose boyfriend William Moulton Marston was at Harvard. Marston was doing research in experimental psychology and also dabbling in 'photoplays', as screenplays for silent movies were known. He was clever, handsome, restless, ambitious, and not at all the bulky figure he would become. He had had an idea: that telling a lie raised blood pressure, and that if this could be measured during an interrogation it would be possible to see if someone was telling the truth or lying. He and Holloway did an experiment. Using crime stories written by Holloway, Marston asked questions about the fictional crimes, identifying liars by their rising blood pressure and then comparing his results with judgments made by mock-juries. There were 107 tests. He was right 103 times – 96 per cent. The jury was right about 50 per cent. That's how the lie detector was invented. His paper, based on these and later experiments, remained fundamental to future research into lie detection[56] (it would ultimately prove rather less reliable, and was never accepted in court). Marston and Holloway married in 1915,

---

[56] Marston, 'Systolic Blood Pressure Symptoms of Deception', 2 *J. Exper. Psychol.*, 117 (1917).

and both went to law school, he in Cambridge (Harvard), she in Boston (Radcliffe).

In 1918, Marston was sent to Camp Upton, New York, for six months to treat shell-shock victims. The librarian there was a certain Marjorie Huntley (née Wilkes), a deeply committed suffragette. They started an affair, which ceased when Marston returned to Harvard, where he got his PhD in 1921. Both he and Holloway read Margaret Sanger's *Woman and the New Race*. She was keen on Greek, and had a special love of Sappho, poetess and Lesbian, literally and perhaps sexually. All this had interesting consequences for the creation of Wonder Woman, as we shall see.

There is a fourth to be added to the list of characters: Olive Byrne, Ethel Byrne's daughter and Margaret Sanger's niece. She did medicine at Tufts, her tuition being paid for by her aunt's new millionaire husband, J. Noah Slee. She was radical, witty and popular. She wore on her wrists heavy silver bracelets, one African and the other Mexican. She had a fat friend who loved candy and helped her with her maths (bear with me: it's relevant). She cut her hair like a boy, dressed like one as well, and was a vital source of contraceptives for her female friends.

In 1925, Tufts acquired William Marston as a new assistant professor of psychology. Aged thirty-two, he was now vastly overweight – 'Not fat,' as Olive Byrne described him later, 'just enormous all over'; and also, she said, 'the most genuine human being I've ever met.' He was equally taken with her. She received As in Experimental Psychology and was soon acting as his assistant, principally with his work on what he called 'captivation', what we would call 'bondage', because bondage and submission were part of the college induction rituals that the participants seemed to enjoy. Marston was very interested in submission and dominance, which, along with compliance and inducement, were (according to his theory) the four primary emotions. Soon after, Olive Byrne moved in with Marston and Holloway.

This story is drifting in a rather strange direction. Marston has a wife, has had a mistress and now has a third woman, much younger, living in the family home. It should be a recipe for disaster. But these were interesting times, full of novelty and experiment, psychological, social and sexual. Every week, the four of them – husband, wife, mistress (when she was around), acolyte and second mistress – used to meet in Boston at the apartment of Marston's aunt, Carolyn Keatley, along with five others. Keatley was a nursing supervisor who believed that this was the beginning of a New Age, the Age of Aquarius, the age of peace and love.[57] Notes of what happened suggest that this was a sort of sexual training clinic to explore an interplay of dominance and submission. Marston was particularly interested in what he called 'love binding', the importance of inducing submission by tying and shackling. Females,

in their relation to males, expose their bodies and use various legitimate methods of the love sphere to create in males

[57] These twelve 'ages' follow each other as the Earth's axis of spin rotates, or precesses, like a child's spinning top. All twelve signs of the zodiac appear in sequence behind the Sun at dawn at the autumnal equinox, or would do if you could see them. The whole cycle takes about 26,000 years. Astrologers read meaning into this. A new age starts when one constellation gives way to another, every 2,500 years or so. There is no agreement on the borders, so astrologers argue about whether we are in the new age or not. But they generally agree that Aquarius is better than its warlike predecessor, Pisces. It presages, among other things, peace, idealism and nonconformity.

submission to them, the women mistresses or Love leaders, in order that they, the Mistresses, may submit in passion to the males . . . During the act of intercourse between the male and his Mistress, the male's love organ stimulates the inner love organs of the Mistress, and not the external love organs . . . If anyone wishes to develop the consciousness of submission, he or she must keep the sexual orgasm in check.

They were a threesome, and occasional foursome. What they all seemed to be after was independence. How to achieve this, given the difficulty of dealing with male dominance, marriage, children and careers? The question was not just theirs. It was asked in countless magazine articles, with no good answers. Holloway had a particular problem: she got pregnant, but had no intention of leaving her job as an editor for the *Encyclopedia Britannica*. Between the four of them, there was a solution. Marston could keep his mistress, Holloway would have the baby, and Olive Byrne would give up her PhD to look after it. It would be fine as long as the arrangements were kept secret, which was something at which everyone in this little group had considerable talent.

Secrecy was vital, for professional reasons. All four collaborated in a way that would have been scandalous, indeed ruinous, if revealed, not only because of their domestic arrangements but also because they scratched each others' backs to the point of professional corruption. Marston's latest book, *Emotions of Normal People*, largely ignored by the press and academics, received a great review in the *Journal of Abnormal and Social Psychology*. It was written by Olive Byrne, who had collaborated with Marston on the book. He himself had never quite made it in academia. Now his lectureship (at Columbia) was not renewed, ostensibly because the post vanished, more likely because his interests were just too eccentric. Holloway helped by commissioning him to write an article for the *Britannica*, 'Emotions, Analysis of'. Other than that, he was out of work and about to become a father. In his turn, Marston was happy to acknowledge his debt to his women.

He returned to the movies, and the network grew. At Columbia, one of his friends was Walter B. Pitkin, psychologist, journalist, American editor of the *Britannica* and thus Holloway's boss. He and Marston used to go to movies together, and discuss the whys and wherefores of their psychological and emotional impact. In January 1928, in a publicity stunt, Marston and Byrne set up an experiment in a New York theatre, measuring the excitement – that is, blood pressure – in six pretty girls watching Greta Garbo in the silent movie *Flesh and the Devil*. The experiment with the 'love meter' was widely reported. By chance, Carl Laemmle, head of Universal Studios in Hollywood, was looking for a psychologist who would help with the coming age of talking movies and also find ways of pre-empting the strict rules of censorship. Laemmle read about the 'love meter' experiment and invited Marston to Hollywood as director of PR. He, Holloway, Byrne and the new baby, Pete, spent almost three years there, with Marston working on films that included *Show Boat* and *Dr. Jekyll and Mr. Hyde*. Marston got Pitkin hired as a story editor, and the two wrote a book together, *The Art of the Sound Picture*, offering advice on how to write a script with universal appeal, which meant giving it a flavouring of 'erotic passion'.

While in Hollywood, the group took another step into

deception and nonconformity. Olive Byrne married someone claiming to be William Richard, who was in fact William Marston. There would be two children, both named after their non-existent 'father', who (she told them) had died as a result of being gassed in the First World War. The three children could now be looked after by Byrne, while Holloway earned the money to support them, working from home, until Universal decided that what they really needed was a way to measure audience reactions, and opted for a rival lie detector, the polygraph.

Back the Marston entourage went to New York, to an apartment on Riverside Drive, where they were joined occasionally by Marjorie Huntley. Soon Holloway bore another child, a girl, and kept on working, while the others spent time in family places in Cliftonville, Massachusetts, and Cape Cod, with all four adults and the four children – not so much a family, more a commune – moving to Rye, New York state, in 1935. Holloway commuted daily to support everyone. They all did their bit. Everyone loved the children. Marston and Holloway formally adopted Olive Byrne's two sons, who thereafter had two mothers. It all worked surprisingly well, this odd mix of feminism and love and commitment and secrecy swirling round a massive male weighing 21 stone 6 pounds (136 kilograms).

Olive Byrne landed a job as staff writer on an up-and-coming weekly called *Family Circle*. Writing under the name Olive Richard, her first article was a profile of Marston, whom she pretended never to have met, describing her own children as though seeing them for the first time – truth peppered with lies, as her whole life was. Fittingly, the article was called 'Lie Detector'. There were to be many others with the same formula. Marston was doing odd writing jobs, yet still – after science, the law, films, advertising, writing and a good deal of self-promotion – had not found a proper outlet for his talents.

All this while, Margaret Sanger had been fighting to legalize birth control. In 1937, she arranged to have a crate of Japanese diaphragms mailed to her. They were seized as obscene and destroyed by US Customs. On appeal, the court ruled they were not obscene if prescribed by a doctor. Soon afterwards, the American Medical Association endorsed birth control.

On 10 November 1937, Marston seized a window of opportunity to promote his latest book, a collection of self-help essays called *Try Living*. He called a press conference in the Harvard Club of New York and announced, 'Women have twice the emotional development, the ability for love, than man . . . They will clearly come to rule businesses and the nation and the world . . . The next 100 years will see the beginning of an American matriarchy – a nation of Amazons in a psychological rather than a physical sense.' The press loved it: 'NEGLECTED AMAZONS TO RULE MEN IN 100 YEARS, SAYS PSYCHOLOGIST' (*Washington Post*); 'FEMININE RULE DECLARED FACT' (*Los Angeles Times*).

The same year saw the birth of a phenomenon: comic books. They had started as cheap magazines made up of strips of newspaper cartoons, or 'funnies'. For several years they were used to promote sales for half a dozen retailers: buy the comic for 5 cents, get a 5-cent reduction on what-ever else you were buying. The business was dominated by Maxwell Charles Gaines, who realized that if there was a good market, he could commission his own comics, sell direct and keep the profits. Suddenly, here was a new art form, a crossover between books and movies. He founded All-American Publications to exploit this novel idea. Others followed, in a publishing explosion. Many websites track the titles, companies, editors, writers and artists who worked in a fury of creativity that would turn the 1940s into a Golden Age of comic books. In 1938, *Action Comics* introduced Superman (in Issue 8, an original copy of which has sold for over $3 million). By summer of 1939, Superman had graduated to a comic book of his own. He soon had dozens of rivals, one of them being Batman in *Detective Comics* (Issue 27, for which collectors today would pay over $1 million). At 10 cents a copy, comic books sold by the million to kids who would never have bought a book, and also to book readers like the Marston children.

The comic-book boom coincided with the outbreak of the Second World War. Superman suddenly seemed less of a fighter for justice, more like a Nazi Stormtrooper. Besides, some educationalists deplored comics. There was a great deal of violence in them. Some asked, were comics Fascist? A despicable campaign to undermine children's minds?

It was Olive Byrne who gave Marston his opening into comic books. In a *Family Circle* article, she profiled him as the one man who could tell American mothers about the dangers and benefits of comics. Her formula was the same: she was a naïve reporter who had no connection with Marston, he the great psychologist. She quoted him as saying that Superman was an excellent model, developing 'national might' to protect 'innocent peace-loving people'. Comics were fine, he said, as long as they didn't show torture.

Max Gaines, or Charlie as he was to some, wanted to counteract the criticisms levelled at comics. He decided that an editorial advisory board would do the job, one member of which would have to be a psychologist. He happened to read Olive Byrne's *Family Circle* article and saw a solution to his problem. He offered Marston the position of consultant psychologist on the advisory board of what had just become DC Comics (DC stands for Detective Comics).

Marston wondered about developing a different sort of superhero, one who conquered not through violence but through love. To which, according to one source,[58] Elizabeth Holloway said, 'Fine. But make her a woman.' True or not, Marston was in a good position to follow up his Harvard Club announcement three years previously that women would – should – will – rule the world. What was needed, he told Gaines, was a female superhero, a latter-day Amazon.

He wrote up his experiences and arguments in an article published in the *American Scholar* a couple of years later, 'Why 100,000,000 Americans Read Comics'. First, he pointed out the astonishing size of the potential readership: 1.5 *billion* comic strips in the 2,300 dailies, 2.5 billion in the comic sections of the Sunday papers. 'They have become a seven-day, morning-afternoon-and-evening mental diet for a vast majority of Americans.' Critics say comics are for only 'the most moronic of minds'. No, because comics appeal to something fundamentally human: 'They rouse the most primitive, but also the most powerful, reverberations in the noisy cranial-box of consciousness . . . Pictures tell any story more effectively than words.' They always have. With modern printing, comics have evolved way beyond anything comical,

[58] Marguerite Lamb, 'Who was Wonder Woman?', *Bostonia* magazine, Fall 2001.

and beyond being just adventure strips: 'Their emotional appeal is wish-fulfillment.' That's the appeal of Superman. But there's a problem with Superman: there is no real drama because he is invincible. Sure, he does good, but might it not be possible to give kids a more constructive model?

It seemed to me, from a psychological angle, that the comics' worst offense was their blood-curdling masculinity. A male hero, at best, lacks the qualities of maternal love and tenderness which are as essential to a normal child as the breath of life. Suppose your child's ideal becomes a super*man* who uses his extraordinary powers to help the weak. The most important ingredient in the human happiness recipe still is missing – *love*. It's smart to be strong. It's big to be generous. But it's sissified, according to exclusively masculine rules, to be tender, loving, affectionate, and alluring. 'Aw, that's girl's stuff!' snorts our young comic reader. 'Who wants to be a *girl*?' And that's the point; not even girls want to be girls so long as our feminine archetype lacks force, strength, power. Not wanting to be girls, they don't want to be tender, submissive, peace-loving as good women are. Women's strong qualities have become despised because of their weak ones. The obvious remedy is to create a feminine character with all the strength of a Superman plus all the allure of a good and beautiful woman.

Max Gaines was sceptical. There had been heroines in comics, and they hadn't worked.

Ah, countered Marston, 'but they weren't *superwomen* – they weren't superior to men in strength as well as feminine attraction and love-inspiring qualities.'

'Well,' said Gaines, 'if a woman hero were stronger than a man, she would be even less appealing.'

'No,' replied Marston, 'men actually submit to women now. Give them an alluring woman stronger than themselves to submit to and they'll be *proud* to become her willing slaves!'

Gaines reluctantly agreed to give it a go. 'Well, Doc, I picked Superman after every syndicate in America turned it down. I'll take a chance on your Wonder Woman. But you'll have to write the strip yourself. After six months' publication, we'll submit your woman hero to a vote of our comic readers.'

Wonder Woman made her debut in *All Star Comics* Issue 8, in December 1941, with Marston credited as consulting psychologist and writer (under a partial pseudonym, Charles Moulton). 'Introducing Wonder Woman' opens with a sprinting figure dressed in a sporty, star-spangled skirt, as if made from an American flag. She has bracelets on her wrists and a tiara holding her dark, curly hair. The opening text, in easy-to-read capitals (and many exclamation marks!), joins past and present, hinting at her links with Greek gods, ignoring the fact that in Greek legends the Amazons were not Greeks or Greek allies, but enemies:

AT LAST, IN A WORLD TORN BY THE HATREDS AND WARS OF MEN, APPEARS A *WOMAN* TO WHOM THE PROBLEMS AND FEATS OF MEN ARE MERE CHILD'S PLAY ... WITH A HUNDRED TIMES THE AGILITY AND STRENGTH OF OUR BEST MALE ATHLETES AND STRONGEST WRESTLERS, SHE APPEARS AS THOUGH FROM NOWHERE ... AS LOVELY AS APHRODITE – AS WISE AS ATHENA – WITH THE SPEED OF MERCURY AND THE STRENGTH OF HERCULES, SHE IS KNOWN ONLY AS WONDER WOMAN.

She lives on uncharted Paradise Island, peopled only by women. A plane crashes. A princess and her friend pick up the injured pilot and take him to hospital. The queen, Hippolyte (spelled in the Greek style), arrives to ask what's going on. Papers on the man identify him as Steven Trevor, US Intelligence. The princess tends him and falls in love with him. The queen tells her why this is wrong, AND THIS IS THE STARTLING STORY UNFOLDED BY HIPPOLYTE, QUEEN OF THE AMAZONS, TO THE PRINCESS, HER DAUGHTER! The text continues in regular format, because there's a lot to cram in.

'In the days of Ancient Greece, many centuries ago, we Amazons were the foremost nation on earth. In Amazonia, women ruled and all was well,' until Hercules arrived. Hippolyte challenged him, knowing that she could not lose, because she had a magic girdle given her by Aphrodite, goddess of love. She won, but Hercules tricked the girdle from her and enslaved the Amazons, chaining them in manacles. Aphrodite helped Hippolyte regain the girdle. The Amazons freed themselves and left by ship to find a new home. But they all had to wear bracelets to recall the man-forged manacles, remind them 'always to keep aloof from men' and act as shields that can deflect bullets. They found Paradise Island, where there is 'no want, no illness, no hatreds, no wars.' The girdle gives them all eternal life.

Because of the deal with Aphrodite, the American must go home. A Magic Sphere reveals his world, for 'we are not only stronger and wiser than men – but our weapons are better – our flying machines are more advanced!' With it, the princess, as yet unnamed, has been taught 'all the arts and sciences and languages of modern as well as ancient times'. What Hippolyte sees in the Magic Sphere is that Steve Trevor was the victim of a German plot, managed by the evil von Storm, whose accomplice praises his boss with the classic line: 'The malignance of your ideas is refreshing, mein Herr.' What to do? Hippolyte consults Aphrodite and Athena. They tell her the world is in a mess and that 'American liberty and freedom must be preserved'. Steve Trevor must be sent back, and with him 'your strongest and wisest Amazon – the finest of your Wonder Women!' Races and competitions reveal the princess as the one. Hippolyte sends her off in – of all ridiculous things – an invisible plane, with a suitable American-style costume and a name at last: 'Let yourself be known as Diana, after your godmother, the goddess of the Moon!'

AND SO DIANA, THE WONDER WOMAN, GIVING UP HER HERITAGE AND HER RIGHT TO ETERNAL LIFE, LEAVES PARADISE ISLAND TO TAKE THE MAN SHE LOVES BACK TO AMERICA – THE LAND SHE LEARNS TO LOVE AND PROTECT, AND ADOPTS AS HER OWN!

For a mass-market comic, that's quite a back-story (though since then revamps, relaunches and re-boots, all recorded in mind-numbing detail by comic-book historians, have added many other elements, one of which was to rename Paradise Island Themiscyra, as the Amazon homeland was known in Greek legend). It is a mish-mash of much of Marston's whole life, and there would be more of it in the adventures to come. The Greek connection has its origins in Huntley's love of Greek language and literature, in particular Sappho. The Eden-like bliss of Paradise Island recalls the perfections of female-only society in Gilman's *Herland*. Most crucial of all is the influence of those feminists, particularly Margaret Sanger, fighting for equality, birth control and sexual liberation – not that Marston could make much of that explicit.

It was enough to create a rule that, as an Amazon, Wonder Woman cannot marry. Marston had seen that it was hard for Holloway to earn a living and raise a child, so hard that he organized Olive Byrne to do it for her. That would not have been possible in a traditional marriage. Marriage enslaves, he thought, as Hercules enslaved the Amazons. Diana's bracelets, an idea he got from Olive Byrne's habit of wearing similar ones, play several roles: they symbolize a memory of male oppression, they protect her, and they represent weakness, because if they are chained together – yet more bondage, please note – she loses her strength. The bracelets are one of her attributes, for Greek characters, whether divine or human, usually had features that acted as character traits, like Cupid's bow, Athena's owl (for wisdom) or Aphrodite's dove (for peace). Another attribute is her Golden Lasso, or Lasso of Truth, which has the magical ability to force those whom she catches with it to submit to her and tell the truth. It was in effect a lie detector, rather more effective than the one Marston spent much of his life developing, and a form of bondage, in which he maintained his obsessive interest.

Traditionally, damsels in comics were constantly being made into damsels in distress by evil characters tying them up; this damsel does the tying and induces submission with her Lasso of Truth. Truth, or rather its absence, was a major factor in the lives of Marston and his women. He was happy to distort the truth to promote himself; the four of them lived a secret life to hide their unconventional ways, and Byrne's work on *Family Circle* was possible only because she hid the fact that she was the mother of Marston's children. Wonder Woman, too, has a secret life: as Olive Byrne became Olive Richard by 'marrying' the spurious William Richard, so

Wonder Woman must hide her identity. Her aim is to look after Steve Trevor in hospital, so she buys credentials from a nurse and works under the nurse's name as Diana Prince.

Many details come from the lives of Marston and his women. Elizabeth Holloway told DC Comics that a suitable exclamation for a woman from an island of women was 'Suffering Sappho!' Like Olive Byrne, Diana Prince/Wonder Woman has a fat friend called Candy, who loves candies.

The themes and details were probably simply the result of a writer grabbing what he could from his memory and his unconscious to make a story. But there was also an undercover agenda. Marston wanted Wonder Woman to be 'psychological propaganda for the new type of woman who should, I believe, rule the world.' First, of course, there were bonds to be broken, an aim made explicit by an opening cartoon for his article, harking back to the days of Woolley and Sanger:

Wonder Woman was a hit. After five months, Gaines did indeed ask his readers for their opinion, comparing her against seven male characters. She came out ahead 40 to 1 over her nearest rival, taking 80 per cent of all votes. As Marston wrote, 'They were saying with their votes, "We love a girl who is stronger than men, who uses her strength to help others, and who allures us with the love appeal of a true woman!"' In January 1942, she became the lead character, and thus became the third superhero, along with Superman and Batman, to have their own series. She's never been out of print since.[59]

To see her influence, fast-forward twenty years. Forget the 1950s, a bit of a wilderness for women's rights, and for Wonder Woman, who spent much of that time as the sub-wonderful Diana Prince. But in the 1960s, feminists came out fighting. A powerful sisterhood of thinkers and activists – Shulamith Firestone, Betty Friedan, Gloria Steinem, Bella Abzug, Shirley Chisholm – demanded equality, liberation, abortion rights, nothing less than a political and social revolution. The Equal Rights Amendment, first introduced to Congress forty years previously (drafted by Alice Paul, a hunger-striker back in 1917, still going strong in her eighties), finally passed into law in June 1972. Wonder Woman played her part. In July, with Shirley Chisholm (the first black woman in Congress) still in hopeful-but-hopeless contention for the Democratic presidential nomination, Wonder Woman

[59] William Marston developed polio, and died in 1947. Marjorie Huntley died in 1986. Olive Byrne and Elizabeth Holloway lived together for the rest of their lives. Byrne died in 1990, Holloway in 1993. The secret of their lives together, and of their roles in Wonder Woman's creation, remained veiled until revealed by Jill Lepore's research in 2014.

was on the cover of *Ms* magazine, on the march down Main Street under the slogan 'WONDER WOMAN FOR PRESIDENT'. Inside was a pull-out reprint of the original 'Introducing Wonder Woman' comic book. It was a heady moment, but a moment only. Conservatives fought back, feminists fought each other. Even as women's history boomed in academia, feminism stalled. Radicals accused moderates of conspiring to sabotage the cause. Embedded in the rage, as Jill Lepore points out, there was a point about Wonder Woman: 'Who needs consciousness raising and equal pay when you're an Amazon with an invisible plane?'

Yet she endured. A TV series in the 1970s made Lynda Carter a star. Several attempts to resurrect her for TV series and feature films failed, but she was still enough of an icon to be named by the UN as an honorary ambassador for the Empowerment of Women and Girls in 2016, the seventy-fifth anniversary of her first appearance; and enough of a symbol of a man-made, large-breasted, scantily clad Stars-and-Stripes pin-up to inspire protests. But Wonder Woman is bigger than any appointment or protest. Lynda Carter herself spoke up for her ever-youthful alter-ego, calling her a non-predatory symbol of 'the beauty and the strength and the loving kindness and the wisdom of women' – as much of a role model now as she was when she first arrived from Themiscyra and her Amazonian past. That same year she made it on to the big screen, with a brief appearance in *Batman v. Superman*, a warm-up for her starring role in the 2017 blockbuster bearing her name. As I write, her future seems secure, and so do her pseudo-Greek origins as Diana, princess of Amazons.

Epilogue

HALFWAY TO AMAZONIA

I WONDERED IF THERE ARE STILL AMAZONS TODAY. A QUICK online search suggested there are – Kurdish women warriors fighting Islamic State in Syria and Iraq. The media interest in these young women seemed a little sensationalist, but maybe it was worth learning more. Luckily, near where I live in London there is a Kurdish Community Centre. In a large hall, where bearded men in work-clothes play billiards, two charming young Kurds, Arzu and Aladdin, offered help in making contact. After discussing how to arrange a phone call to the bitter battlegrounds of Kurdistan, we realized that Skype would serve our purpose.

By then, I knew it would be worth it, because Aladdin had said, 'Why don't you just go? We can arrange for someone to meet you.'

'Well,' I hesitated, 'time is short, and besides, it's winter.'

'For Kurdish women fighters,' he said, 'there is no winter.'

That was good enough for me. These women, as individuals and as a group, seemed to combine the toughness of the Scythian mounted archers with the solidarity of Penthesilea's legendary band. It sounded as if they were as close to modern Amazons as I could hope to find.

Of course, in one sense there are countless millions of 'Amazons'. To call a woman an 'Amazon' has become a cliché, usually a male one, usually pejorative, suggesting power, commitment, ruthlessness and inappropriate success. To her detractors, Margaret Thatcher was an 'Amazon' armed with big hair and a handbag. In this sense it's a cartoon term, too far removed from its origins to carry weight. And in another sense there are hundreds of thousands of 'Amazons', for almost all nations now include women in their armed forces, increasingly as front-line troops. Libya's strongman Gaddafi employed forty female bodyguards on the assumption that Arab assassins would never gun down women. Known as 'the Amazonian Guard', they were well trained in martial arts and firearms, and also had to take an oath of chastity, which explained their alternative title, 'the Revolutionary Nuns'. Most women soldiers, though, are integrated, not in separate battle contingents.

The Kurdish women fighters are the best modern example of a regiment of women warriors. Fighting for Kurdish autonomy in the borderlands of Turkey, Syria, Iraq and Iran, they are increasingly independent from male domination. That is a surprise, given that they have emerged in a society that is intensely patriarchal. A patriarchy might inspire women to *want* liberation; but you would not expect them to *get* it. Why was it not suppressed?

The reason is that, for both sexes, Kurdish patriarchy is trumped by Kurdish nationalism, especially in its modern manifestation.

The Kurds were demanding independence before the present nation-states came into existence. The term 'Kurdistan' dates back to the twelfth century. A century ago, when the victors of the First World War were drawing new borders across the ruins of the Ottoman empire, a delegation of Kurds came to Europe to plead for recognition. They made no impact on those drawing the borders. Like the Basques, with whom they have a lot in common, they ended up with a strong sense of nationhood but no state, sharing their homeland with four recognized nation-states and an interfusion of Turks, Arabs, Syrians and several other ethnic groups. They are linked by religion – mostly a mild form of Sunni Islam; by language (in five dialects); by almost universal fluency in at least two languages; and by their sense of identity. Lacking a state, and divided politically, they, like the Basques, have to wrestle with ways to handle oppression and division: to fight, assert, cooperate or submit? They have tried all four. There are no easy answers, especially in a region now torn apart by war, civil war, terrorism and the peculiar horrors unleashed by the sect known in the West as Islamic State, locally as Daesh and several other variants.

Kurdish women fighters have a history of their own. They look to two different sources: a tradition of female militancy, and a radical ideology of Kurdish nationalism that is remarkably feminist. They remember Adela Khanem, who before and during the First World War ruled the Halabja region with such skill that the Kurds nicknamed her 'the Queen Without a Crown'. They remember 'Kara' (Black) Fatma, who commanded a unit of 700 men and 43 women in the Turkish army during the First World War; and Leyla Qasim, aged twenty-two, arrested in Iraq in 1974 for trying to assassinate Saddam Hussein, then tortured and hanged. In the late 1980s, Kurdish women began to organize. Gatherings, groups and congresses led to their involvement in both politics and in the Kurdish armed forces (some 2,000 women fighters by 1994). Usually action is inspired by ideology. Not in this case. Here, action came first and the ideology followed.

It came mainly from a man, surprisingly: Abdullah Öcalan, a burly figure with a bushy moustache now in his seventies. He is a contradictory mix of radical, nationalist, feminist, freedom-fighter and peace-lover. Raised in a dirt-poor village in Turkey by a downtrodden father and tough mother, he saw as a child the consequences of violence, female strength and oppressive traditions. 'Once when Öcalan was beaten badly by some other boys and he ran crying home to his mother, she threw him out of the house, warning him not to return until he had exacted revenge.'[60] His sister, Havva, was sold for a few sacks of wheat and a handful of cash into a loveless marriage. 'If I was a revolutionary,' he thought at the time, 'I would not let this happen.'

The child became the father to the man. As a student in Ankara in the 1960s, he absorbed both long-established

[60] Aliza Marcus. See Bibliography.

socialism and evolving Kurdish nationalism. Different Kurdish groups in the four neighbouring states rose, argued and occasionally attacked their dominant cultures, achieving little except repression. In 1972, Öcalan was arrested and spent seven months in jail, where conversations with his cell-mates confirmed his commitment to left-wing politics and violent revolution. In 1978, he founded the PKK, the Kurdistan Workers' Party, and in 1984 declared war on the Turkish state. Based in Turkey's enemy Syria for security reasons, he was forced out in 1998, tracked by various intelligence agencies, and captured in Kenya, an event that inspired Kurds to riot in many European cities. He was taken to Turkey, tried and condemned to death – briefly, as it happened, because Turkey abolished the death penalty, including Öcalan's, in preparation for joining the EU. By then, in a move that astonished his fellow nationalists, Öcalan had abandoned the armed struggle for an independent state, claiming he would work with Turkey for peace within established national borders. Some Kurds accused him of cowardice, self-service and egomania, but he remains the Kurds' leader in the evolution of what they call 'democratic confederalism', which is basically democracy without a state. Since his capture, he has been held in the prison-island of Imrali in the Sea of Marmara, between the Mediterranean and the Black Sea. He was the sole inmate for ten years, before being joined by a few other prisoners in 2009. He has had more than enough time to think, to propose political solutions to the Kurdish question – which to date has no answers – and write (forty books so far).

His top priority is the liberation of women, which he believes is the key to liberation for the Kurds, the Middle

East, and indeed the world. *Liberating Life: Women's Revolution*, published in 2013, is a manifesto that combines history, feminism, ecology and anti-capitalism, all expressed in sweeping generalizations. There is little directly about Islam, but much implied criticism. Here's a quick guide to his views and style:

> In Neolithic times, society was egalitarian, communal and matriarchal. The 5000-year-old history of civilisation is essentially the history of the enslavement of woman by the dominant male. Woman's biological difference is used as justification for her enslavement. All the work she does is taken for granted or denigrated. Her presence in the public sphere is prohibited by religion, progressively excluding her from social life. Treating women as inferior became the sacred command of god. Thus woman, once the creator, became the created. This sexual rupture resulted in the most significant change in social life ever. In Middle Eastern culture, woman is wrapped in veils, and becomes a captive within a harem, which is but a private brothel. This explains why Middle Eastern society fell behind Western society. There is a need to radically review family and marriage and develop common guidelines aimed at attaining gender equality and democracy. Without gender equality, no demand for freedom and equality can be meaningful. From the liberation of woman will come a general liberation, enlightenment and justice.

It's heady stuff, especially if you happen to be a Kurdish woman oppressed by any one of four states and by the men in your life. Kurdish women had their share of honour killings, dependence, domestic violence and exclusion, and many still do. For those ready and able to listen, Öcalan was and is a political prophet, who summons them to cast off the chains of religion and tradition, and stand up for themselves, working – and fighting – towards a glorious, new, free, democratic world. Surrounded by civil war and collapse, it is no surprise that so many of them believe they have nothing to lose but their chains, and a world to gain.

As individuals and encouraged by gatherings, groups and congresses, women became directly involved in politics and in the Kurdish armed forces. With 2,000 women fighters in the early 1990s, their ranks grew over the next twenty years to more than 7,000, fighting in the PKK's mixed-sex military wing, the Syrian-based YPG. In 2004, a riot in the Syrian town of Qamishli drove thousands of Kurds into Iraq, and spurred many women to join up. In 2012, the women got their own contingents, the Women's Defence Units (YPJ), based in the Kurdish part of Syria, Rojava. Numbers climbed again, to about 20,000, and they became famous for their role in fighting Islamic State in both Syria and Iraq. In 2014, IS turned on the Syrian Yazidis (also spelled Ezidis), a Kurdish sub-group with their own pre-Islamic religious traditions, killing 5,000 of them in their main city, Sinjar, and forcing another 200,000 to flee. Some 50,000 took to the bare flanks of nearby Mount Sinjar, where they faced imminent extermination. In response to widespread media coverage, President Obama ordered US intervention. US bombers, the YPJ and their male counterparts drove off the IS fighters and saved the Yazidis.

In this chequerboard of interlinked wars, civil wars and sectarian strife, the Kurdish women fighters have been a steady focal point at the heart of a unique experiment in democracy. Like many partisans down the centuries, they believe they have a worthy cause: fighting for their homeland, their political rights, their freedom. Sharia law holds no sway in most of Kurdistan. There are fewer hijabs and niqabs in Kurdish cities these days, and very few indeed in Rojava, the heartland of the revolution.

Advised by a woman acting as a roving ambassador for the Kurds, Aladdin got a Skype call through to Nujin, a burly and soft-spoken YPJ fighter wearing, as you would expect, camouflage fatigues. She talked long and eloquently about the political foundations of the YPJ, then explained why she had joined up.

My journey started with the uprising in Qamishli against Assad's regime. There was a football match between Arabs and Kurds, and Arabs held up pictures of Saddam Hussein [deposed by the US invasion, captured the previous year]. We were angry, because Saddam Hussein had killed over 100,000 Kurds in 1988.[61] In Syria, we remembered how Syria had sent Arabs into Kurdistan to divide us from our compatriots in Iraq and Turkey. In response the Kurds held up the Kurdish flag. People started to throw stones. Violence spilled out on to the streets, and the Syrian security forces replied with tanks and helicopters. About 70 died. In addition, the system was against women, so I was ready to get my revenge. People in the community were not used to a woman taking up a gun and fighting next to a man, so it was hard when we

[61] The so-called al-Anfal campaign. According to Human Rights Watch, this was attempted genocide by Saddam Hussein's cousin, Ali Hassan al-Majid (known as 'Chemical Ali'). An estimated 182,000 died.

started. The religious system, the community, our families, the state – we had to oppose all of them. In 2011, during the 'Arab Spring', a few young people of both sexes started to come together, discussing what we could do, and I said 'This is really the time,' so without questioning I joined the group, even before the YPJ was founded the next year. The first time I went to Aleppo, that was where I fought first. On the first day of fighting, with my first bullet, I felt something like [words seemed to fail her at this point] . . . I couldn't believe what I was doing. But I also saw the cost. Someone called Dayika ['Mother'] Gulé was working hard to organize the movement, and she was one of the first women martyrs in that circle. That affected me a lot.

Outside Rojava, in a fast-changing imbalance of states, armies, sects and militias, there are no conclusions. Towns are taken, sieges started, sieges ended, towns retaken, and retaken again. Borders open and close. Aid flows, and ceases. Bosses in Moscow and Istanbul and Damascus act as puppet-masters. Where it will end, God or Allah only knows; though there's no reason to think he does.

But in Rojava itself, city after city – Kobani, Derik, Afrin – has been liberated by Kurds, mostly peacefully. There has been a lot of media interest in the YPJ. On social media, a good-looking young Kurdish woman holds up her hand in a V for Victory sign; in a much-repeated quote, IS fighters supposedly fear the YPJ because they believe 'they will not go to Heaven if killed by a woman.' Women's magazines like *Elle* and *Marie Claire* ran long articles on the YPJ. In Australia, the *60 Minutes* TV programme carried a documentary about them, 'Female State'.

Behind the news stories, the women organize and fight, alongside their male colleagues. As Asya Abdullah, co-chair of the Democratic Union Party, says: 'How can a society be free when its women aren't free?'[62] It is, in traditional terms, a limited kind of freedom. As the Kurdish academic Nazand Begikhani – human-rights advocate, specialist in gender-based violence, French-educated, now at Bristol University – told me, these women fighters are forbidden any expression of sexuality: 'Falling in love is not allowed!' Yet, she says, 'they tell me that they feel liberated, unconstrained by family, house and children'.

The result in Rojava is a remarkably avant-garde political structure. It has de facto independence, prepared to defend itself but not take part in the civil war. Women ready to die for their cause play important roles organizing a bottom-up democracy based on local councils. If they are not headed by women, commissions, councils and courts have a joint male–female leadership. Women run research units, academies, schools, health centres, even their own radio station and press association. In the YPJ, women seek out new ways to assert themselves, developing what Öcalan calls *Jineologi*, 'woman's science', to give them access to knowledge that was once controlled by men. Not all men are happy, but few dare dissent.

The women warriors of the YPJ form more of a female community than the Scythian warrior women, and less than the Amazonian state imagined by the Greeks. They seem to be building something between the two – a core of committed,

---

[62] Quoted in Knapp, Flach and Ayboga, *Revolution in Rojava*. See Bibliography.

well-informed, independent women fighters working with their male partners and civilian colleagues to create a safe haven in a chaotic world.

BIBLIOGRAPHY

Adams, Maeve E., 'The Amazon Warrior Woman and the De/
construction of Gendered Imperial Authority in Nineteenth-
Century Colonial Literature', *Nineteenth-Century Gender
Studies*, Vol. 6, No. 1, 2010

Ascherson, Neal, *Black Sea*, Vintage, London, 1996

Baumer, Christoph, *The History of Central Asia: The Age of the
Steppe Warriors*, I. B. Tauris, London, 2012

Baynham, Elizabeth, 'Alexander and the Amazons', *The
Classical Quarterly*, Vol. 51, No. 1, 2001

Benbow, Heather Merle, '"Weil ich der raschen Lippe Herr nicht
bin": Oral Transgression as Enlightenment Disavowal in
Kleist's *Penthesilea*', *Women in German Yearbook*, Vol. 22,
2006

Burton, Sir Richard, *A Mission to Gelele, King of Dahome*, ed.
and intro. by C. W. Newbury, Routledge and Kegan Paul,
London, and Frederick A. Praeger, New York, 1966

Carvajal, *see* Medina

Choo Waihong, *The Kingdom of Women: Life, Love and Death in China's Hidden Mountains*, I. B. Tauris, London, 2017

Condamine, Charles Marie de la, *Relation abrégée d'un voyage fait dans l'intérieur de l'Amérique méridionale*, Paris, 1759

Čugunov, Konstantin V., Hermann Parzinger and Anatoli Nagler, *Der skythenzeitliche Fürstenkurgan Aržan 2 in Tuva*, Verlag Philipp von Zabern, Mainz, 2010

Dalzel, Archibald, *The History of Dahomy: An Inland Kingdom of Africa*, 1793; reprinted with intro. by J. D. Fage, Frank Cass & Co., 1967

Davis-Kimball, Jeannine, *Warrior Women: An Archaeologist's Search for History's Hidden Heroines*, Warner Books, New York, 2002

Davis-Kimball, Jeannine, and C. Scott Littleton, 'Warrior Women of the Eurasia Steppes', *Archaeology*, Vol. 50, No. 1, 1997

Eller, Cynthia, *Gentlemen and Amazons: The Myth of Matriarchal Prehistory, 1861–1900*, University of California Press, Berkeley, 2011

Everett, Dan, *Don't Sleep, There Are Snakes: Life and Language in the Amazonian Jungle*, Pantheon Books, New York, 2008

Franklin, Margaret, 'Boccaccio's Amazons and Their Legacy in Renaissance Art: Confronting the Threat of Powerful Women', *Woman's Art Journal*, Vol. 31, No. 1, 2010

Franklin, Margaret, 'Imagining and Reimagining Gender: Boccaccio's *Teseida delle nozze d'Emilia* and Its Renaissance Visual Legacy', *Humanities*, Vol. 5, No. 6, 2016

Gilman, Charlotte Perkins, *Herland*, Pantheon Books, New York, 1979

González-Ruiz, Mercedes, et al., 'Tracing the Origin of the East-West Population Admixture in the Altai Region (Central Asia)', *PLOS ONE*, Vol. 7, Issue 11, 2012

Griffiths, Elystan, 'Gender, Laughter and the Desecration of Enlightenment: Kleist's Penthesilea as "Hundekomödie"', *Modern Language Review*, Vol. 104, No. 2, 2009

Guliaev, Valeri I., 'Amazons in the Scythia: New Finds at the Middle Don, Southern Russia', *World Archaeology*, Vol. 35, No. 1, 2003

Hardwick, Lorna, 'Ancient Amazons – Heroes, Outsiders, or Women?', *Greece & Rome*, Vol. 37, No. 1, 1990

Hérissé, A. le, *L'Ancien Royaume du Dahomey: Moeurs, Religon*, Histoire, Paris, 1911

Herodotus, *The Histories*, trans. Aubrey de Sélincourt, Penguin Books, London, 1994

Jordana, Xavier, et al., 'The Warriors of the Steppes: Osteological Evidence of Warfare and Violence from Pazyryk Tumuli in the Mongolian Altai', *Journal of Archaeological Science*, Vol. 36, No. 7, 2009

Kleinbaum, Abby Wettan, *The War Against the Amazons*, McGraw-Hill, New York, 1983

Kleist, Heinrich von, *Penthesilea: A Tragic Drama*, trans. and intro. Joel Agee, HarperCollins, London, 1998

Kleist, Heinrich von, *Penthesilea: Ein Trauerspiel*, Hamburger Lesehefte Verlag, Husum/Nordsee, 2009

Knapp, Michael, Anja Flach and Ercan Ayboga, *Revolution in Rojava: Democratic Autonomy and Women's Liberation in Syrian Kurdistan*, Pluto Press, London, 2016

Law, Robin, 'The "Amazons" of Dahomey', *Paideuma: Mitteilungen zur Kulturkunde*, Vol. 39, 1993

Lefkowitz, Mary R., *Women in Greek Myth*, Johns Hopkins University Press, Baltimore, 2007

Lefkowitz, Mary R., 'Wonder Women of the Ancient World', *The Women's Review of Books*, Vol. 1, No. 4, 1984

Lepore, Jill, *The Secret History of Wonder Woman*, Scribe Publications, London, and Vintage Books, New York, 2015

Mahlendorf, Ursula, 'The Wounded Self: Kleist's *Penthesilea*', *German Quarterly*, Vol. 52, No. 2, 1979

Marcus, Aliza, *Blood and Belief: The PKK and the Kurdish Fight for Independence*, New York University Press, New York, 2007

Markham, Sir Clements R. (trans. and ed.), *Expeditions into the Valley of the Amazons, 1539, 1540, 1639*, Hakluyt Society, London, 1859

Marston, William Moulton, 'Why 100,000,000 Americans Read Comics', *The American Scholar*, Vol. 13, No. 1, 1943–4

Mayor, Adrienne, *The Amazons: Lives and Legends of Warrior Women Across the Ancient World*, Princeton University Press, Princeton, 2014

Medina, José Toribio, *The Discovery of the Amazon, According to the Account of Friar Gaspar de Carvajal and Other Documents*, trans. Bertram T. Lee, American Geographical Society, New York, 1934

Meyerowitz, Eva L. R., '"Our Mothers": The Amazons of Dahomey', *Geographical Magazine*, Vol. 15, 1943

Montalvo, Garci Rodriguez de, also credited to João de Lobeira, *The fifth book of the most pleasant and delectable history of Amadis de Gaule*, London, 1664, trans. Uncredited; digital edition by Early English Books Online

Montalvo, Garci Rodriguez de, *Le Cinquièsme Livre d'Amadis de Gaule*, Paris, 1550, trans. Nicolas de Herberay; reprinted Facsimile Publisher, Delhi, 2016

Murphy, Eileen, 'Herodotus and the Amazons Meet the Cyclops: Philology, Osteoarchaeology and the Eurasian Iron Age', in *Breaking Down Boundaries: The Archaeology*

– *Ancient History Divided*, Taylor and Francis, 2004

Murphy, Eileen, *Iron Age Archaeology and Trauma from Aymyrlrg South Siberia*, Bar Publishing, Oxford, 2003

Murphy, Eileen, et al., 'Prehistoric Old World Scalping: New Cases from the Cemetery of Aymyrlyg, South Siberia', *American Journal of Archaeology*, Vol. 106, 2002

Pennington, Reina, *Wings, Women, and War: Soviet Airwomen in World War II Combat*, University Press of Kansas, Lawrence, 2001

Place, Edwin B., 'Fictional Evolution: The Old French Romances and the Primitive Amadís Reworked by Montalvo', *PMLA*, Vol. 71, No. 3, 1956

Plutarch, *Lives*, 'Theseus'

Poeschel, Sabine, 'Rubens' "Battle of the Amazons" as a War-Picture: The Modernisation of a Myth', *Artibus et Historiae*, Vol. 22, No. 4, 2001

Quintus of Smyrna, *The Trojan Epic Posthomerica*, trans. and ed. Alan James, Johns Hopkins University Press, Baltimore, 2004

Rolle, Renate, *The World of the Scythians*, trans. F. G. Walls, University of California Press, Berkeley, 1989

Rudenko, Sergei I., *Frozen Tombs of Siberia: The Pazyryk Burials of Iron Age Horsemen*, trans. M. W. Thompson, J. M. Dent & Sons, London, 1970

Schmidt, Ricarda, 'Sparagmos, Weiblichkeit und Staat: Gewalt als Produkt von Erziehung in *Penthesilea* and *Die Hermannschlacht*', in *Heinrich von Kleist: Konstruktive und destruktive Funktionen von Gewalt*, Königshausen & Neumann, Würzburg, 2012

Sporleder, Rolf F., 'The Bassae-Frieze: 200 Years of Guesswork', in Christoph Klose et al. (eds), *Fresh Perspectives on Graeco-Roman Visual Culture*, Humboldt-Universität, Berlin, 2015

Stone, Brad, *The Everything Store: Jeff Bezos and the Age of Amazon*, Transworld, London, 2013

Strabo, *Geography*, XI, 5, 1–5

Tarbell, Frank, 'Centauromachy and Amazonomachy in Greek Art: The Reasons for Their Popularity', *American Journal of Archaeology*, Vol. 24, No. 3, 1920

Thevet, André, *Les Singularitez de la France antarctique, autrement nommée Amérique*, 1555

Vinogradova, Lyuba, *Defending the Motherland: The Soviet Women Who Fought Hitler's Aces*, MacLehose Press, London, 2015

Wilde, Lyn Webster, *On the Trail of the Women Warriors*, Constable, London, 1999

Woollett, Anne T., and Ariane van Suchtelen, *Rubens and Brueghel: A Working Friendship*, J. Paul Getty Museum, Los Angeles, 2006

Wright, Celeste Turner, 'The Amazons in Elizabethan Literature', *Studies in Philology*, Vol. 37, No. 3, 1940

ACKNOWLEDGEMENTS

With thanks to: Karl Baipakov, Almaty; Nazand Begikhani, University of Bristol; Zana Cousins-Greenwood, Centre of Horseback Combat, Hemel Hempstead; Nujin Derik, Kurdistan, Syria; Pettra Engeländer, Independent European Horseback Archery School, Hofbieber, Germany; Xavier Jordana, GROB, Barcelona; Isabel Käser, SOAS, London; Lajos Kassai, Kaposmérö, Kaposvár, Hungary; Eileen Murphy, Queen's University, Belfast; Hermann Parzinger, Stiftung Preussischer Kulturbesitz, Berlin; Arzu Pesmen, London; Ricarda Schmidt, Exeter University; Sinam Sherkany, Kurdistan, Syria; Aladdin Sinayic, London; Katie Stearns, Flying Duchess Ranch, Seattle, USA; Henry Vines, Transworld, London, and Brenda Updegraff, Hampshire, for superb editing; and all at Felicity Bryan Agency, Oxford.

PICTURE ACKNOWLEDGEMENTS

All photos courtesy of the author unless otherwise stated.

First section

Page 1: Battling Amazons © De Agostini Picture Library/A. Dagli Orti/Bridgeman Images; Amphora © Ashmolean Museum, University of Oxford, UK/Bridgeman Images; Parthian shot © CM Dixon/Print Collector/Getty Images; Urfa mosaic © Mick Palarczyk.
Page 2: Temple of Apollo © Bettmann/Getty Images; Bassae Frieze © Martin Beddall/Alamy Stock Photo.
Page 3: Achilles battles Penthesilia © De Agostini Picture Library/G. Dagli Orti/Bridgeman Images; the Greeks battle the Amazons © PHAS/Universal Images Group via Getty Images.
Page 4: Pazyryk tomb © Alexander Demyanov/Shutterstock.com; Pazyryk excavations © Sisse Brimberg/Getty Images; the royal couple of Arzhan 2 © V. Efimov.
Page 5: Tattoos on the skin of the Ukok Princess © Sputnik/Science Photo Library; reconstruction © Elena Shumakova, Institute of Archeology and Ethnography, Siberian Branch of the Russian Academy of Sciences; skull with a sword wound © Eileen Murphy.

Page 6: Comb © AKG Images; stag © Heritage-Images/CM Dixon/ AKG images; saddle decorations © De Agostini Picture Library/A. Dagli Orti/Bridgeman Images.

Page 7: stag © AKG Images/De Agostini Picture Library/A. Dagli Orti; gold earrings © De Agostini Picture Library/A. Dagli Orti/ Bridgeman Images; hunter pursuing a hare © Heritage-Images/CM Dixon/AKG Images; sword and scabbard © Pictures from History/ Bridgeman Images; plaque © AKG Images/De Agostini Picture Library/A. Dagli Orti.

Page 8: Gold Man © Franka Bruns/AP/Rex/Shutterstock.

Second section

Page 1: 1676 map of California © Historic Map Works LLC and Osher Map Library/Getty Images.

Page 2: Love feast of the Amazons © Granger/Bridgeman Images.

Page 3: Waorani © John Wright; theatrical costume © Florilegius/ SSPL/Getty Images; French educational card © Look and Learn/ Bridgeman Images.

Page 4/5: *Battle of the Amazons* by Peter Paul Rubens © PHAS/ Universal Images Group via Getty Images.

Page 6: Dahomey lithograph © AKG Images; Russia's Night Witches © AKG Images/Universal Images Group/Sovfoto; Kurdish soldiers © Vianney Le Caer/Pacific Press/LightRocket via Getty Images.

Page 7: Lajos Kassai © Kassai Horsearchery School; Zana Cousins-Greenwood © Rosie Hallam/Barcroft Media; Pettra Engeländer © Pettra Engeländer/Independent European Horseback Archery School.

Page 8: Sensation Comics cover © DC Comics/Image Courtesy of The Advertising Archive.

INDEX

INDEX

INDEX

INDEX

Saladin

John Man

Saladin remains one of the most iconic figures of his age. As the man who united the Arabs and saved Islam from Christian crusaders in the twelfth century, he is the Islamic world's preeminent hero. Ruthless in defence of his faith, brilliant in leadership, he also possessed qualities that won admiration from his Christian foes. He knew the limits of violence, showing such tolerance and generosity that many Europeans saw him as the exemplar of their own knightly ideals.

But Saladin is far more than a historical hero; he is a man for all times, and a symbol of hope for an Arab world once again divided. Centuries after his death, in cities from Damascus to Cairo and beyond, Saladin continues to be an immensely potent symbol of religious and military resistance to the West. He is central to Arab memories, sensibilities and the ideal of a unified Islamic state.

In this authoritative biography, historian John Man brings Saladin and his world to life in vivid detail. Charting his rise to power, his struggle to unify the warring factions of his faith, and his battles to retake Jerusalem and expel Christian influence from Arab lands, *Saladin* explores the life and the enduring legacy of this champion of Islam, and examines his significance for the world today.

'Fast-paced . . . thrilling'
THE TIMES

The Terracotta Army

John Man

In 1974 local farmers digging a well near present-day Xian unearthed parts of clay figures, opening the way to one of the greatest archaeological discoveries of all time. The Terracotta Army was a total surprise – some 8,000 life-size clay warriors and horses buried in 210 BC as a 'spirit army' to guard the tomb of the First Emperor. They had been lying forgotten in their three pits for over 2,000 years.

The First Emperor, the brilliant and ruthless ruler who united China and built the first Great Wall, was beset by paranoia and a desire to dominate in the afterlife, as he had in this one. Around his giant tomb-mound, as yet unopened, other pits concealed a whole spirit world of officials, entertainers, armour, and bronze chariots.

1,000 of the warriors now stand with many other finds in a site that attracts some two million visitors a year. As work continues, there are surely more surprises to come. As John Man suggests, there could even be more warriors still to be discovered. One day, perhaps, the tomb-mound itself will be opened and its legendary treasures revealed.

Weaving together history and first-hand experience from his travels in China, John Man tells the story of how and why these astonishing artefacts were created. In doing so, he sketches vivid portraits of the 'spirit army' and the man who formed the roots of China today.

'One couldn't wish for a better storyteller
or analyst than John Man'
SIMON SEBAG MONTEFIORE

The Mongol Empire

John Man

The Mongol Empire forever changed the course of history. Driven by an inspiring vision for peaceful world rule, Genghis Khan – mass-murdering barbarian to his enemies; genius and demi-god to his people – united warring clans and forged an empire that spanned Asia, bringing people, cultures and religions together and opening intercontinental trade.

Later his grandson, Kublai Khan, fuelled by the belief that Heaven had given the world to the Mongols, doubled the empire's size until, in the late thirteenth century, he and his family controlled one sixth of the world's land area. Along the way, he conquered China, made Beijing his capital and gave the nation the borders it has today, establishing the roots of the twenty-first-century superpower.

Charting the rise and eventual fall of Genghis's 'Golden Family', John Man's authoritative account brings the empire vividly to life, providing essential reading for anyone with an interest in history, geopolitics, and the complex and volatile world of today.

'A narrative of wonderful dramatic energy'
GERARD DeGROOT, *THE TIMES*

Samurai

John Man

The samurai – with their elaborate armour and weapons, fierce sense of honour and brilliant swordsmanship – are the ultimate warriors. Novels, videos, martial artists by the million and films, from *The Seven Samurai* to *Kill Bill*, have made them legendary. But the truth is as astonishing as any legend.

John Man portrays these warriors through the life of the real 'last samurai', Saigo Takamori. Saigo lived when samurai ways were under threat. In the mid-nineteenth century, the arrival of American ships had forced Japan into frantic modernization, after 250 years of isolation. Dedicated to *bushido*, 'the way of the warrior' – death-defying bravado and loyalty to the Emperor – Saigo led several thousand samurai in a desperate rebellion. His extraordinary life and dramatic death would make him one of Japan's greatest heroes.

John Man tracked him on his heroic last stand for honour and tradition, and reveals how he has shaped the Japan we know today. Through his example we discover what it really means to be a samurai.

'John Man has scholarly gifts as well as acute intelligence and a winning way with words'
INDEPENDENT

Xanadu

John Man

Marco Polo's journey from Venice to China in the late thirteenth century was one of the most audacious ever. He uncovered an unknown world of vast wealth and exotic cities, including Xanadu, where the emperor Kublai Khan – the most powerful monarch in the 13th-century world – spent his summers.

Xanadu, famous for its 'stately pleasure dome', as Coleridge called it, was – and is – a reality, with a real 'dome' of gilded bamboo. For the first time, this book reveals what it may have looked like.

On his return, Marco – adventurous, curious, charming, and ambitious – became the first and best-known of travel writers. But he was also infuriatingly unreliable.

John Man travelled in Marco's footsteps in search of the truth. He follows Marco to Xanadu, then to Beijing and through modern China. He tells the intriguing story behind Marco's book and its enduring impact, and paints a vivid picture of the man behind the myth.

'An in-the-footsteps-of-Marco-Polo journey through Europe to China which really makes you feel you are wearing Polo's threadbare, sweat-stained slippers as you go'
THE SCOTSMAN